DATE DUE

| Brodart Co. | Cat. # 55 137 001 | Printed in USA |

St Antony's Series
General Editor: **Jan Zielonka** (2004–), Fellow of St Antony's College, Oxford

Recent titles include:

Richard Clogg (*editor*)
BEARING GIFTS TO GREEKS
Humanitarian Aid to Greece in the 1940s

Stefania Bernini
FAMILY LIFE AND INDIVIDUAL WELFARE IN POSTWAR EUROPE
Britain and Italy Compared

Tomila V. Lankina, Anneke Hudalla and Helmut Wollman
LOCAL GOVERNANCE IN CENTRAL AND EASTERN EUROPE
Comparing Performance in the Czech Republic, Hungary, Poland and Russia

Cathy Gormley-Heenan
POLITICAL LEADERSHIP AND THE NORTHERN IRELAND PEACE PROCESS
Role, Capacity and Effect

Lori Plotkin Boghardt
KUWAIT AMID WAR, PEACE AND REVOLUTION

Paul Chaisty
LEGISLATIVE POLITICS AND ECONOMIC POWER IN RUSSIA

Valpy FitzGerald, Frances Stewart and Rajesh Venugopal (*editors*)
GLOBALIZATION, VIOLENT CONFLICT AND SELF-DETERMINATION

Miwao Matsumoto
TECHNOLOGY GATEKEEPERS FOR WAR AND PEACE
The British Ship Revolution and Japanese Industrialization

Håkan Thörn
ANTI-APARTHEID AND THE EMERGENCE OF A GLOBAL CIVIL SOCIETY

Lotte Hughes
MOVING THE MAASAI
A Colonial Misadventure

St Antony's Series
Series Standing Order ISBN 0-333-71109-2
(*outside North America only*)

You can receive future titles in this series as they are published by placing a standing order. Please contact your bookseller or, in case of difficulty, write to us at the address below with your name and address, the title of the series and the ISBN quoted above.

Customer Services Department, Macmillan Distribution Ltd, Houndmills, Basingstoke, Hampshire RG21 6XS, England

Physical Processing

Order Type: **NTAS**

Sel ID/Seq No:

Cust/Add: 158330000/04

Cust PO No. **4612**

POKC-N   **OKANAGAN COLLEGE LIBRARY**

148978

/30

BBS Order No: **E1289177**   Ln: **4**   Del: **1**

Cust Ord Date: **09-Apr-2008**

0230500358-31081785

BBS Ord Date: **10-Apr-2008**

(9780230500358)

Sales Qty: **1**   #Vols: **001**

Bearing gifts to Greeks

Subtitle: **humanitarian aid to Greece in the 1940s**   Stmt of Resp: **edited by Richard Clogg.**

HARDBACK   Pub Year: **2008**   Vol No.: _____   Edition:

Clogg, Richard.

Ser. Title:

Acc Mat:

Profiled   **Barcode Label Applicati Spine Label Protector U:**

Tech   **Base Charge Processing   Spine Label BBS US**

Services: **Property Stamp US**

          Security Device US

Fund: **HSP**

Location: **Kelowna Circulating**

Stock Category:

Department:

Class #:   Cutter: Collection:

Order Line Notes:

Notes to Vendor:

371101

Blackwell Book Services

Bearing Gifts to Greeks

Humanitarian Aid to Greece in the 1940s

Edited by

Richard Clogg
Emeritus Fellow
St Antony's College

in association with
St Antony's College, Oxford

First published 2008 by
PALGRAVE MACMILLAN
Houndmills, Basingstoke, Hampshire RG21 6XS and
175 Fifth Avenue, New York, N.Y. 10010
Companies and representatives throughout the world

PALGRAVE MACMILLAN is the global academic imprint of the Palgrave
Macmillan division of St. Martin's Press, LLC and of Palgrave Macmillan Ltd.
Macmillan® is a registered trademark in the United States, United Kingdom
and other countries. Palgrave is a registered trademark in the European
Union and other countries.

ISBN-13: 978-0-230-50035-8   hardback
ISBN-10: 0-230-50035-8   hardback

This book is printed on paper suitable for recycling and made from fully
managed and sustained forest sources. Logging, pulping and manufacturing
processes are expected to conform to the environmental regulations of the
country of origin.

A catalogue record for this book is available from the British Library.

A catalog record for this book is available from the Library of Congress.

10   9   8   7   6   5   4   3   2   1
17   16   15   14   13   12   11   10   09   08

Printed and bound in Great Britain by
CPI Antony Rowe, Chippenham and Eastbourne

Contents

List of Photographs

List of Figures and Tables

Figures

Tables

Notes on Contributors

Mary Jo Clogg was formerly Librarian of Woodbrooke Quaker Studies Centre, Birmingham, UK and, with Richard Clogg, compiled the volume on Greece in the Clio Press World Bibliographical Series (vol. 127) (Oxford, 1981).

Richard Clogg is an Emeritus Fellow of St Antony's College, Oxford, UK. He has also taught at the universities of Edinburgh and London. His publications include *Politics and the Academy: Arnold Toynbee and the Koraes Chair* (1986); *Anatolica: Studies in the Greek East in the Eighteenth and Nineteenth Centuries* (1996); and *Anglo-Greek Attitudes: Studies in History* (2000). His *Concise History of Greece* (2nd edn, 2002) has been translated into a number of languages, including Chinese and Japanese. He is currently working on a large-scale history of the Greek people in modern times which will seek to integrate the history of the Greek East and of the Greek diaspora with that of the Greek state.

Violetta Hionidou is a Lecturer in Modern History at the University of Newcastle upon Tyne, UK. She has also taught at the universities of Southampton and Crete. She has published extensively on the demographic and social history of Greece in modern times, receiving research funding from the European Union and the Wellcome Trust. Her most recent publication is *Famine and Death in Occupied Greece, 1941–44* (2006). She is currently working on the role of hospitals during the famine years in occupied Greece.

Rolandos Katsiaounis obtained his PhD from King's College, London. Since 1991 he has worked as a researcher at the Cyprus Research Centre and at the Political Affairs Division of the Foreign Ministry. He completed his post-doctoral work at the Centre of International Studies, Cambridge (Gonville and Caius College); was a Visiting Fellow at Oxford (St Cross College); and lectures at the University of Cyprus (Department of Turkish Studies and Department of Social and Political Science). He has published on the politics and history of nationalism, the labour movement and the role of Great Powers in Greece and Cyprus. His books include *I Diaskeptiki 1946–1948*, focusing on Britain's effort to solve the Cyprus problem by constitutional means, and a study of United Nations Security Council and General Assembly Resolutions on

Cyprus 1960–2002. He is currently working on a history of the Republic of Cyprus and on a study of the Communist Party of Cyprus – AKEL.

George Kazamias is an Assistant Professor in the Department of History and Archaeology of the University of Cyprus. He previously taught at the University of Bradford. He has published on Greece in the 1940s, Greco-Bulgarian relations from the 1880s to the 1940s, and on Cyprus in the 1940s and the 1960s. He has also edited the diary of a Greek soldier who fought in the Hellenic Forces contingent in the Korean War, *To Imerologio enos Ellina Stratioti ston Polemo tis Koreas* (Athens 2004). He is currently working on the Turkish invasion of Cyprus in 1974, using both archival material and oral history sources.

Alexandros K. Kyrou is an Associate Professor of History and the Director of the Program in East European and Russian Studies at Salem State College in Salem, Massachusetts, USA, where he teaches on the Balkans, the Ottoman Empire, and Byzantium. He received his PhD in East European History at Indiana University and completed his postdoctoral work as a Visiting Research Fellow in the Program in Hellenic Studies at Princeton University. He is also a former Senior Research Fellow of the Kokkalis Program on Southeastern and East-Central Europe at Harvard University, as well as a past Research Scholar at the Institute on Religion and World Affairs at Boston University. The author of numerous publications on Balkan diaspora history and US foreign policy in Southeastern Europe, Professor Kyrou is the Associate Editor of the *Journal of Modern Hellenism*.

Elçin Macar is an Assistant Professor in the Department of Political Science and International Relations of Yıldız Technical University, Istanbul, Turkey. His research interests include modern Turkish and Greek history, minorities in both countries and, especially, the history of the Ecumenical Patriarchate. He has published two books on the history of the Patriarchate, *Fener Patrikhanesi* (1996), with Yorgo Benlisoy, and *Cumhuriyet Döneminde İstanbul Rum Patrikhanesi* (2003). He has also written on two now vanished communities in Istanbul, the Greek and Bulgarian Uniates, *İstanbul'un Yokolmuş İki Cemaati: Doğu Ritli Katolik Rumlar ve Bulgarlar* (2002).

Vasilios N. Makrides is Professor of Religious Studies (with reference to Orthodox Christianity) in the Faculty of Philosophy of the University of Erfurt, Germany. He is currently working on a diachronic history of Greek religious cultures from ancient to modern times.

Marie Mauzy is a Swedish photographer and researcher living in Athens. For many years she was the curator of the Photographic Archives of the American School of Classical Studies at Athens. Her photographs of Greek antiquities have illustrated numerous publications in Europe and the USA. She is the author of *Early Photographic Panoramas of Greece* (with Evi Antonatou, 2002); *The Photographs of Alison Frantz: Revealing Antiquity through the Lens* (with Amy Papalexandrou, 2003); and *The Photographic Journeys of Ioannis Maillis* (with Evi Antonatou, 2004).

Milan Ristović is Professor of Contemporary History in the Faculty of Philosophy, University of Belgrade. He is also the head of the Society for Social History and managing editor of the *Annual of Social History*. His fields of research include the history of South Eastern Europe in the twentieth century and the social history of Serbia in the nineteenth and twentieth centuries. His principal publications are a study of the German 'New Order' in Southeastern Europe during the Second World War, *Nemacki 'novi poredak' i Jugoistocna Evrope 1940/41–1944/45. Planovi o buducnosti i praksa* (Belgrade, 1991); on the flight of Yugoslav Jews from the Holocaust, *U potrazi za utocistem. Jugoslovenski Jevreji u bekstvu od holokausta 1941–1945* (Belgrade, 1998); and *Long Journey Home. Greek Refugee Children in Yugoslavia 1948–1960* (Thessaloniki, 2000) (also in Serbian, 1988). His most recent book focuses on the experience of Greek communists in Yugoslavia during the civil war, *To Peirama Buljkes: 'I Elliniki Dimokratia' sti Giougkoslavia 1945–1949* (Athens, 2006).

Flora Tsilaga completed a PhD thesis at King's College, London, on 'The UNRRA Mission to Greece: the Politics of International Relief, April 1944–June 1947'. She is currently a postdoctoral fellow at York University, Toronto, under the auspices of the Hellenic Heritage Foundation Chair in Modern Greek History.

Alexandros P. Zannas studied sociology in France. He has taught in secondary education and is an archivist in the Historical Archives Department of the Benaki Museum in Athens, Greece. His publications include an edition of the three volumes of the Penelope S. Delta memoirs (*Anamniseis*), and a *Reader* on her work. He also published the *Imerologio Phylakis*, the prison diaries of P.A. Zannas covering the years 1968–1971 (Athens 2000).

1
Introduction: 'Bearing Gifts to Greeks'

Richard Clogg

I say that I would rather be able to send 100 tons of grain to Greece than write an immortal work . . . What does even the Symposium matter compared to the death by hunger of 200 Greeks a day?

Harold Nicolson, 2 January 1942

I suppose an affection for Greece seems to most of us now something we are born with; it is the one country which would appear to possess an unalterable natural affinity for us.

Cyril Connolly[1]

In 2005, the Greek Foreign Ministry published a hefty and lavishly illustrated brochure entitled *Ellada: Pankosmia Dynami Anthropias/Greece: a
Global Humanitarian Power*. This gives details of the many humanitarian
programmes launched by the Ministry's International Development
Cooperation Department (*Ypiresia Diethnous Anaptyxiakis Synergasias*), also
known as Hellenic Aid. These were numerous and embraced a wide geographical area. Almost fifty countries were the recipients of humanitarian
assistance. This took a number of forms. It included the dispatch of a
hospital ship, the *Ocean Monarch* which sailed, with the blessing of
Archbishop Khristodoulos of Athens, to Trincomalee in Sri Lanka to bring
medical assistance to the victims of the 2004 tsunami; the building of
eleven schools, each named after a city in Greece, in the Côte d'Ivoire;
the establishment of an informatics department at the University of Korçë
in Albania; and aid to the victims of catastrophic flooding in Bangladesh
and of the massive explosion near Ryongchon in North Korea. Of particular interest was the provision of a maternity unit and a cultural centre
to the Kalash tribe in north-west Pakistan, the purported descendants of

the armies of Alexander the Great, and still, we are told, speaking an ancient Greek dialect and demonstrating a physical resemblance to their Greek ancestors. On reading this impressive and stylishly produced brochure it is easy to forget that little more than half a century ago Greece was a desperately impoverished country and itself the recipient of massive amounts of humanitarian aid.

Joice Loch, who for many years was engaged in relief work in Greece, graphically described the civil war that wracked Greece between 1946 and 1949 as a conflict 'of the poor against the deadly poor'.[2] The writer, George Mikes, recalling in 1965 a trip to Greece some fifteen years earlier, observed that you would not recognise the place: 'gone are the innumerable beggars, gone are the young mothers who used to gape through the restaurant windows, infant on arm, and look right into your mouth as you ate your steak . . . The miserable, hungry, depressed town [Athens] which had just emerged from the war, to be plunged into an equally terrible civil war, has vanished and has been transformed into a prosperous, busy, bustling and affluent city . . .'[3] Some ten years before Mikes' first post-war visit to Greece, the country was in the grip of a famine of horrific proportions, one of the worst to afflict a European country in modern times. This famine was a consequence of the tripartite Italian, German and Bulgarian occupation that followed the Italian attack on Greece in October 1940 and the subsequent German invasion in April 1941. Some twenty years earlier, Greece had been the recipient of much humanitarian aid following the catastrophic denouement to the Greek occupation of western Anatolia between 1919 and 1922. This resulted in the influx of over a million refugees, many of them destitute and constituting approximately a fifth of the population of Greece itself. In alleviating this particular crisis, the American Red Cross and Near East Relief were heavily involved.[4] Thus during the first half of the twentieth century Greece was the recipient of very large amounts of humanitarian aid. The fact that Greece is now not the recipient but the source of such aid is but one of the indicators of the extraordinary rate of economic growth of the country during the second half of the twentieth century.

There is a very substantial literature on the political and military aspects of the occupation period and of the ensuing civil war.[5] The chapters in this volume focus on a dimension of the occupation of Greece and of the civil war that has been relatively little studied. These are the various humanitarian initiatives undertaken during the decade of the 1940s by outside agencies and by Greeks themselves to relieve the suffering of the population as the country experienced a short-lived war with Italy and Germany, followed by a brutal occupation between 1941–44 in which the Axis powers were joined by Bulgaria and, lastly, a devastating civil war between 1946 and 1949. The papers were originally delivered at a workshop held at St Antony's College, Oxford in March 2005 under the auspices of the Centre of Contemporary Greek Studies.

The appalling famine of the winter 1941–42 was the catalyst of much of this humanitarian activity but famine was by no means the only catastrophe visited on Greece during the 1940s. The German policy of collective punishment meant that any resistance to the occupation met with savage reprisals inflicted on individuals and communities that, for the most part, had had no involvement in resistance activity. These reprisals included the burning of entire villages and the murder of their inhabitants. Moreover, in the space of a few weeks in March 1943, the Jewish population of Thessaloniki was deported to Auschwitz there to meet a horrific death. The once flourishing Sephardi community of the city, which in the early 1940s amounted to a fifth of its population, was virtually wiped out. Most of the Jews of Athens and other cities subsequently met with a similar fate. Famine; German, Italian and Bulgarian atrocities; and the destruction of Greek Jewry took place against the background of one of the worst inflations in recorded history.[6]

Not all aspects of humanitarian relief are covered. For example, the role of the Swiss Red Cross, which worked alongside the Swedish Red Cross, is not treated. Violetta Hionidou in Chapter 2 examines the famine itself, particularly as it manifested itself in the islands, while George Kazamias in Chapter 3 examines the complex negotiations that led to a partial lifting of the British blockade of occupied Greece to allow the import of food.[7] A major factor in the lifting of the blockade was pressure exerted by the US administration, which in turn reflected the effective campaign of the Greek-American community to mobilise public opinion. This campaign signified the coming of age of Greek-Americans as an organised lobby and is discussed by Alexandros K. Kyrou in Chapter 4. The first systematic, albeit small-scale, effort to alleviate the famine was launched from Turkey and is described by Elçin Macar in Chapter 5. Once agreement was reached to partially lift the blockade more substantial and coordinated international efforts to alleviate famine and food shortages in Greece were made. In these the Swedish and Swiss Red Cross played a major part. The role of the Swedish Red Cross in Greece is discussed by Marie Mauzy in Chapter 6. In Greece itself, Greeks were doing what they could to alleviate suffering. Alexandros P. Zannas in Chapter 7 discusses the role of a senior official of the Greek Red Cross, Alexandros D. Zannas, in the crisis and, in particular, the efforts that were made to smuggle horrifying photographs of the victims of the famine out of Greece. This affords an early indication of the power of the visual image in swaying public opinion.

Rolandos Katsiaounis in Chapter 8 examines the role of *Ethniki Allilengyi* or National Solidarity, the welfare arm of the *Ethniko Apeleftherotiko Metopo* or National Liberation Front, much the largest resistance group in occupied Greece, in organising welfare, particularly for political prisoners and their families and for the dependants of resistance fighters. The parallel involvement of the Orthodox Church authorities in humanitarian activities are discussed by Vasilios Makrides in Chapter 9. Quakers played a significant role in the foundation of the Oxford Committee for Famine Relief, an organisation with a particular concern for famine relief in Greece and the precursor of Oxfam. In Chapter 10 Mary Jo Clogg describes the activities of Quakers in relief work among Greeks during the occupation and subsequently. The devastation caused by the occupation presented major problems once Greece was liberated in October 1944 and Flora Tsilaga in Chapter 11 discusses the difficulties that arose in coordinating the relief efforts of the United Nations Relief and Rehabilitation Administration (UNRRA) in Greece at the war's end. During the civil war (1946–49) that followed the occupation, the communist-led Democratic Army was heavily reliant on the Eastern bloc not only for military supplies but also for medical and other assistance. Milan Ristović in Chapter 12 describes the humanitarian assistance afforded to the Greek left by the Yugoslav authorities during the civil war.

Greece's astonishing achievement in repulsing the attempted Italian invasion of October 1941 gave rise to much enthusiastic comment in the British press and helped create a climate in which the plight of the Greek people under occupation captured the public imagination.[8] It contributed significantly to raising morale in the winter of 1940–41, the darkest period of the war from the British perspective when Greece was Britain's only active ally in Europe and it was by no means a foregone conclusion that the United States would enter the war against the Axis. Greece's military successes on the Albanian front moved Winston Churchill famously to declare 'today we say that Greeks fight like heroes, from now on we will say that heroes fight like Greeks'.

The wave of sympathy and enthusiasm for the embattled Greeks gave rise to a significant number of books of philhellenic content which helped to focus continuing attention on the dire circumstances of the Greek people under occupation. These played their part in sustaining a climate of opinion which contributed to the British government's eventual decision to agree to a partial lifting of the blockade of Greece on humanitarian grounds. As the quotations which open this introduction indicate, leaders of public opinion, including politicians, academics and churchmen, many of whom in the 1940s had been nurtured at school and university on the classics, had a strong emotional attachment to Greece. The print runs for some of these Greece-related publications appear to have been large. Indeed, until a few years ago, on entering a second-hand bookshop in Britain, one could be reasonably confident of finding copies of books such as Dilys Powell's *Remember Greece*, published by Hodder and Stoughton as early as July 1941, Compton Mackenzie's *Wind of Freedom: the History of the Invasion of Greece by the Axis Powers 1940–1941*, published by Chatto and Windus in 1943, and, above all, Stanley Casson's, *Greece and Britain*, published by Collins, probably in 1941, and a particularly elegantly produced book given wartime stringency. Casson, an archaeologist and classical scholar in civilian life,[9] was also the author of *Greece against the Axis* (Hamish Hamilton, 1941) and a small pamphlet entitled *Greece*, published in 1942 by Oxford University Press in its Oxford Pamphlets on World Affairs series.

Other books in the genre included 'Symmachos', *Greece Fights On* (n.d., probably 1943), published by Lindsay Drummond in the 'Europe under the Nazis' series. The pseudonymous author was presumably Greek, but not all of its readers would have grasped that 'Symmachos' translates as 'ally'. The book was clearly well-informed and based in part on the information on conditions in occupied Greece available to the Greek government-in-exile, whose Minister of Information, Andreas Mikhalopoulos, contributed a short introduction. The book contained a chapter on the famine, and included a number of harrowing photographs of the starving population of Athens, together with a picture of a Swedish Red Cross vessel, the SS *Stureborg*, loading flour and medical supplies in Haifa in the summer of 1942 for shipment to Greece. *Inter alia*, 'Symmachos' quoted a dispatch written by a correspondent of the Turkish newspaper *Vatan,* who had accompanied the *Kurtuluş*, the ageing vessel first dispatched by the Turkish Red Crescent to Athens in October 1941. The correspondent reported that:

> What I saw in Greece exceeds a hundred times anything that has been written about her plight. It seemed to me as if I had entered Hell . . . When the ship's crew went ashore they were surrounded by hundreds of people who cried out: 'Give us at least a crumb of bread, we are dying of hunger'. German guards dispersed the crowd. Walking through the town we were overcome with horror. The people looked like skeletons.

'Symmachos' also printed a lengthy extract from an article that appeared in another Turkish newspaper *Cumhuriyet* in May 1942. It is worth reprinting much of this as it gives one of the most graphic eye-witness descriptions available of the extremely distressing realities of food distribution in occupied Greece:

> I was present a few days ago at a distribution in the popular soup-kitchen which Mme. Papastrato [a member of the Papastratos family, prominent benefactors whose wealth derived from tobacco] runs in Piraeus for the benefit of the most distressed children. Some 1,200 children, from 3 to 18 years of age, are fed there every day, their sole recommendation the famished look on their faces. They come in from the streets, nearly always alone, very rarely accompanied by their mothers; the only formality consists in stamping their identity cards. It is a vast hall, with plenty of light, equipped with long rows of tables and benches. On one side is the oven with huge soup-pans. The only decoration is on the wall at the far end, an immense fresco in vivid colours, a standing figure of Christ, opening His arms.
>
> The children begin to gather at 11 o'clock in the morning in the courtyard; they are brought in in four batches, each one of some 250 children. In silence they take their places; there is no hurrying or pushing, not a word is uttered. Most of them are in rags, barefooted; some have the remains of torn socks or pieces of material round their feet, not one is wearing shoes. In their trembling hands they carry chipped and cracked plates, iron receptacles of every kind or old jam tins in which to receive the soup. It is an eerie procession, tattered and soundless. Some quite small children carry in their arms still smaller ones whose legs will no longer carry them. Some are as thin as skeletons, others – those who have suffered the most – have swollen cheeks and limbs. The doctor in charge gives me this explanation: 'It is the beginning of the end – one of the most grievous symptoms of the decomposition of the human system through under-nourishment'.
>
> All the children, without exception, have an air of seriousness which baffles description; their emaciated little faces wear an expression of precocious and remote wisdom, one might almost say the prefiguring of another world. Weak and undeveloped bodies carry the heads of old men; a beard is already growing on the sunken yellow cheeks of a boy barely fourteen years of age . . . They go to their places but remain standing. Their eyes are not turned towards the boiling soup, but seem to be straying into vacancy. A short prayer is said . . . and then one by one they advance towards the soup-pans. Not a word is spoken, there is no wrangling among them and yet they are only children.

On that day the distribution consisted of macaroni soup . . . each child had its plate or receptacle well filled, and then from another pan a spoonful of oil was poured over it . . . At the end of the meal, each licks its plate until there is not the slightest trace of oil remaining on it. They then rise from their places and, after a prayer has been said, file out in silence, to make way for the second batch. A young child, pale and weakly, about four years of age, remains huddled in a corner. They ask him whether he isn't going home. He seems to me to be too young and too weak to understand that his turn is finished and that he should now leave. But he replies without sign of nervousness, with an impressive air of seriousness, that he lives too far away and has nowhere to go; he will stay here for the evening distribution of soup. Thereupon he withdraws to his corner with an expression of mingled apathy and fatalism . . .

'Symmachos' also cited an article of May 1942 by the Athens correspondent of the *Stockholms-Tidningen*, Gunnar Cederschiöld, who is mentioned by Marie Mauzy in Chapter 6 as a key figure in prompting the Swedish authorities to become involved in the provision of relief to Greece:

I have never seen anything so ghastly as what I saw recently in Athens, children starving to death without how or why. I saw starvelings everywhere . . . The real famine started in April when 50 babies died in the Foundling Institution in Piraeus Street which normally records practically no deaths. In the waiting-rooms of the Athens clinics I saw undernourished women holding pale emaciated children who were too weak to cry. Many children had a rash caused by inadequate food, most of them suffered from gastric trouble which turned whatever food their mothers could given them into poison. Many had itching rashes and their hands were tied to stop them from scratching off their skin. But this was only a purgatory compared with the hell to be seen at the Foundling Institution. The children cry so long as they have some strength to do so. But most of them lie dumb and exhausted.[10]

Stelio Chourmouzios, in a short pamphlet entitled *Starvation in Greece* (London 1943) published some of the harrowing photographs of the child victims of the famine reproduced by Alexandros Zannas in Chapter 7. He gave a succinct account of the causes of the famine:

it is not surprising, therefore, that the war has upset [the] Greek economy completely. Food was scarce even during the Albanian campaign; but after the occupation of Greece, when the most fertile territories in the North were seized by the Bulgarians, when communications collapsed, when production shrank to infinitesimal proportions owing to the lack of seed, farm-animals and man-power, and when the balance of distribution was upset by the abnormal movement of refugees, Greece found herself before complete chaos, and famine conditions soon became prevalent throughout the country.[11]

Other publications whose purpose was to give readers some idea of the modern history of Greece and, in particular, of its contribution to the Allied war effort include Kathleen Gibberd's small book *Greece*, one of the British Survey Handbooks, published on behalf of the British Society for International Understanding by Cambridge University Press in 1944. Two other similar publications were *The Modern Greeks* (Thomas Nelson, 1944) by A.R. Burn, an archaeologist and classicist in peacetime, who had worked for the British Council in Athens in 1940–41, and *Greece* by A.W. Gomme, another classicist with a close acquaintance with Greece going back to the years before the First World War. This was published by Oxford University Press in The World To-day series in 1945. In 1942, three chapters from *No Other Road to Freedom* (first published in New York in 1941) by an American journalist, Leland Stowe, who had covered the Greek campaign of 1940–41, were published as *A Lesson from the Greeks*. Betty Wason (born in Delphi, Indiana), who had been a pioneering woman war correspondent for the Columbia Broadcasting System in the winter of 1940–41, gave her anti-Axis enthusiasm and imagination free rein in her *The Miracle in Hellas: the Greeks Fight On*, published by the Museum Press in London in 1943. Less obviously morale boosting in intent, although clearly prompted by the political situation, was Edward Forster's *A Short History of Modern Greece*. This was completed in March 1941 and published by Methuen in September of that year. Forster was Professor of Ancient Greek in the University of Sheffield and had an acquaintance with Greece going back to the early years of the twentieth century. He, like Casson, had served in Macedonia during the First World War.

Another genre comprised books published in English by Greek authors. These included two books by Demetrius Caclamanos, a prominent Greek diplomat who had been the Greek minister in London between 1918 and 1935. The first was *Greece – a Panorama*, published in 1942, with a preface by Ernest Barker, by Macdonald & Co. in the Cross-Roads series, intended to provide information on the 'History, Aims and Hopes of the [Allied] Warring Nations'. The second was *Greece in Peace and War*, published, with a preface by Wickham Steed, a prominent British journalist, in 1942 by Lund Humphries. The following year Michael Joseph published *Greek Fire* by André (Andreas) Mikhalopoulos, who was Minister of Information in the government-in-exile between 1941 and 1943. This had a preface by Compton Mackenzie. There were also official publications of the Greek government-in-exile. These included *The Greek White Book: Diplomatic Documents relating to Italy's Aggression against Greece*, published by Hutchinson in 1942, with a preface by Emmanouil Tsouderos, the prime minister of the government-in-exile, on behalf of the Greek Ministry for Foreign Affairs. Another such publication was *Victors in Chains. Greek Resistance 1942–3*. Written by 'Amyntor' (the ancient Greek word for 'avenger'), this was published, probably in 1943, by Hutchinson on behalf of the Greek Ministry of Information. All these books were manifestly intended to evoke sympathy for the Greeks under occupation and to strengthen the traditional close ties between Britain and Greece.

Similar publications appeared in the United States, among them the pamphlet edited by Homer Davis, *Greece Fights On: the People behind the Front*, which was published in 1942 by the American Friends of Greece, a group founded in 1923. Davis, the President of the American-run private school, Athens College, in his contribution (the text of a speech delivered at an American Hellenic Educational Progressive Association (AHEPA) convention in Cincinnati in August 1941) gives an account of the work of the Greek War Relief Association (GWRA) in Greece before and, briefly, following the establishment of the tripartite German, Italian and Bulgarian occupation. Davis had been the treasurer in Greece of the GWRA. In memoirs which were published some fifty years later he gave a graphic insight into the chaotic conditions surrounding relief efforts in the days immediately before the German army reached Athens. He had received instructions from the United States to change two million dollars into drachmas and hand part of this sum over to the Cretan committee of the GWRA (at this stage it was vainly hoped that Crete could still be defended from German invasion) and part to the American Legation to be used for relief purposes. On 26 April 1941, the day before the Germans arrived in the capital, as air-raid sirens sounded, he went with his wife to the Bank of Greece to collect the money. As he had been forewarned that this would be in small denominations he arrived at the bank with a steamer trunk and two large suitcases and accompanied by three helpers. He was then told that the bank did not have enough drachmas to exchange for such a large sum, as the Greek government had taken all the available currency when it had departed for Crete three

days earlier. Davis waited while the Governing Council of the bank discussed whether to validate obsolete notes that had been perforated but
which were still held in the vaults. Eventually the decision was made to
validate them but Davis found that the trunk and suitcases were not
enough to carry the notes away and his party had to bundle up the rest
of the money in their raincoats. Eventually, after further adventures the
money reached the US Legation.[12]

At the war's end, an exhibition was organised at the Royal Academy in
London, partly to draw attention to Greece's plight, but mainly to pay
tribute to the 'men of Greece, Britain and the Dominions who fought
and died for the cause of Liberty in Greece and the Greek Seas'. This was
sponsored by the National Association of Hellenes in Great Britain,
whose president was the diplomat Dimitrios Caclamanos. The Honorary
Committee included a number of prominent figures, among them Ellen
Wilkinson, the Minister of Education, the High Commissioners for
Australia and New Zealand and Sir Kenneth Clark. The exhibition contained artefacts, many from British private collections, from prehistoric
to modern times. No fewer than six El Grecos were included, as were the
set of paintings of scenes from the War of Independence by Panayiotis
Zographos commissioned by General Makryiannis and presented to
Queen Victoria. Paintings by Nikos Chatzikyriakos-Ghika and Photis
Kontoglou were included in the exhibition and were actually for sale. The
most interesting of these modern paintings for the historian of modern
Greece is Valia Semertzidis' painting of what was described as a 'Council
of Self-Administration' established by EAM, the communist-controlled
resistance organisation.[13] The fact that an exhibition on such a scale could
be organised at such a prestigious location under such patronage offers a
demonstration of the hold of Greece on educated opinion in Britain.

A further indication of the way in which the suffering of the Greeks in
the 1940s caught the public's imagination and fired its charitable impulses
is that by the end of the 1946–49 civil war, in Britain alone there were
no fewer than fifteen separate organisations involved in bringing aid to
a Greece devastated by war, occupation, famine and civil war. These were
coordinated by the 'Help to Greece Consultative Committee'. These bodies
were the Anglican and Eastern Churches Association; the Anglo-Hellenic
League; the Refugee Department of the British Council of Churches; the
British Friendship to Greece Society; the Chelsea Committee for European
Relief; the Friends' Service Council (Quakers); International Help for
Children; International Student Service; the National Council of Women
of Great Britain; the Oxford Committee for Famine Relief (subsequently
Oxfam); the Queen's Institute for District Nursing; the Royal College of

Midwives; the Save the Children Fund; the Salonika Reunion Association (veterans of the Macedonian front during World War I); and the Greek Villages Rehabilitation Committee (Edinburgh Fund).

Even after the passage of more than sixty years the humanitarian initiatives that are the subject of this volume, and the people who worked so hard to implement them, in distressing circumstances and sometimes at the risk of their lives, are not forgotten. Every year, in February, there is a commemorative service in the cathedral on the island of Chios and subsequently at a memorial on the harbour front. These mark the bombing, which resulted in many casualties both Greek and Swedish, of the Swedish Red Cross ship, the *Wiril*, on 5 February 1944 by the British Royal Air Force, which mistakenly believed that it was carrying military supplies.

Notes

1. Nigel Nicolson (ed.), *Harold Nicolson: the War Years 1939–1945: Diaries and Letters*, II (New York, 1967), p. 205; Cyril Connolly, review of Terence Spencer's *Fair Greece, Sad Relic* (London, 1954).
2. *A Fringe of Blue: an Autobiography* (London, 1968), p. 210.
3. *Eureka! Rummaging in Greece* (London, 1965), p. 7.
4. Louis Cassimatis, *American Influence in Greece 1917–1929* (Kent, Ohio), pp. 107–49.
5. For this extensive literature on the military/political aspects of occupied Greece, see the bibliographies by Hagen Fleischer and Steven Bowman in John Iatrides (ed.), *Greece in the 1940s. A Bibliographic Companion* (Hanover, NH, 1981) and by Richard Clogg in *Greece 1940–1949: Occupation, Resistance, Civil War. A Documentary History* (London, 2002).
6. An accounting of the massive physical destruction of the occupation years is given by Konstantinos Doxiadis, *Thysies tis Ellados: Aitimata kai Epanorthoseis ston B' Pankosmio Polemo* (Athens, 1947) and the same author's *Such was the War in Greece* (Athens, 1947). For the hyperinflation that afflicted Greece in the first half of the 1940s, see Michael Palairet, *The Four Ends of the Greek Hyperinflation of 1941–1946* (Copenhagen 2000).
7. In connection with these negotiations it is noteworthy that even the British Special Operations Executive (SOE), which was established in July 1940 at the time of the Dunkirk evacuation and charged by Winston Churchill with 'setting Europe ablaze' through the encouragement of resistance movements in the occupied countries, had a peripheral role in seeking to relieve starvation in Greece. Although its remit was essentially military, SOE's Greek operatives were clearly concerned to do what they could to mitigate the effects of the famine. Reference is made to some of the efforts made to secure food aid in the papers of Miltos Spyromilios, one of SOE's key operatives in the early years. In February 1942, one of the Greeks with whom SOE was in touch, P. Mavromikhalis,

a former minister of foreign affairs, met in Ankara with Franz von Papen, the German ambassador to Turkey, in an attempt to secure an undertaking that the Germans would not seize any food allowed through the blockade by the Allies. Von Papen apparently gave his personal support to this proposal and agreed to telegraph this request to Berlin. There was a feeling among SOE's Greek contacts that the Greek ambassador in Ankara was an obstacle to their efforts to secure food aid. An approach to the Romanian government resulted in the offer of limited quantities of food, much of it intended for the Romanian schools established in Macedonia under the terms of the Treaty of Bucharest of 1913. Nothing seems to have come of this offer. In connection with the Turkish relief efforts, there was some vague talk within the SOE that the dispatch of Turkish relief vessels might afford an opportunity to smuggle explosives into Greece for the resistance although nothing came of the idea. Nor were the hands of SOE's US counterpart, the Office of Strategic Services (OSS), entirely clean in this respect. In April 1944, Rodney Young, who was in charge of Greek intelligence-gathering for OSS Cairo, reported to Jack Caskey, OSS's man in Izmir, that 'Uncle' George Skouras, the brother of Spyros Skouras, the Hollywood mogul and national president of the Greek War Relief Association, was willing to offer GWRA cover to those collecting intelligence on behalf of the OSS. (US National Archives and Records Administration, OSS Records RG 226. Unnumbered Box Izmir Mission.)

8. For contemporary accounts see Costas Hadjipateras and Maria Fafalios, *Greece Eyewitnessed 1940–41* (Athens 1995). See also *Martyries 1940–41* (Athens 1982) by the same authors.

9. Casson lost his life in an air crash while working on Greek affairs in the Special Operations Executive. During the First World War he had served with the so-called 'Gardeners of Salonica' on the Macedonian front, about which he wrote a memoir, *Steady Drummer* published in 1935.

10. 'Symmachos', *Greece Fights On* (London, ?1943), pp. 70–4. Mary Henderson (Cawadias) was one of those who ran a Red Cross soup-kitchen for children in Athens, organized by Princess Alice, the mother of the Prince Philip, the Duke of Edinburgh, and the founder of her own somewhat eccentric religious order. Mary Henderson records that, if there was ever any food left over, they would open the doors to the 'famished, emaciated parents' who had been locked outside while their children were fed. These would surge forward 'falling over each other, pushing and screaming like wild animals as they battled to scoop up the last dregs', Mary Henderson, *Xenia – a Memoir: Greece 1919–1949* (London, 1988), p. 48. See also, Hugo Vickers, *Alice, Princess Andrew of Greece* (London, 2000), pp. 292ff.

11. *Starvation in Greece* (London, 1943), p. 6.

12. Homer Davis, *The Story of Athens College: the First Thirty-five Years* (Athens, 1992), p. 254. One of the contributors to *Greece Fights On* was Margaret MacVeagh, the wife of the American minister in Athens at the time of the German invasion, Lincoln MacVeagh. She recorded the activities of the American Bandage Circle in Athens, which made bandages for soldiers wounded on the Albanian front, initially in the Legation and subsequently at the American School of Classical Studies. Lady Palairet, the wife of the British minister, Sir Michael Palairet, was similarly engaged with other Legation wives in knitting comforts for the soldiers. An irreverent wag in the Legation

was apparently in the habit of referring to this group as 'The Four Horsewomen of the Acropolis'. Alison Frantz and Lucy Talcott published an album of photographs of Greece taken by members of the American School of Classical Studies. Called *This is Greece*, the album was published by Hastings House in 1941. Royalties from the book were devoted to civilian relief in Greece.

13. The catalogue was reprinted with photographs of many of the exhibits in Jacqueline Chittenden and Charles Seltman, *Greek Art: a Commemorative Catalogue of an Exhibition held in 1946 at the Royal Academy, Burlington House, London* (London, 1947).

2
Famine in Occupied Greece: Causes and Consequences

Violetta Hionidou

This chapter aims to examine the causes of the outbreak of the famine in occupied Greece and its short-term effects on mortality levels.[1] Before doing so, I should define what I understand by famine since there is no universally accepted use of the term in English. I should also clarify what I mean by 'occupied Greece'. In seeking the causes of the famine I will place emphasis on the extent of requisitions by the occupying powers and on the levels of agricultural production in the years of occupation since both of these are generally blamed for the famine. The increase in mortality during the famine will be outlined before summarising the findings.

Defining famine

There is no universally accepted definition of what constitutes a famine. Here, famine is taken to be 'an epidemic of acute hunger' associated with increases in mortality. According to this definition many contemporary African 'famines' would not be called 'famines'. Alex De Waal's work makes this clear when he distinguishes between 'famines that kill' and famines that do not. Famines that 'do not kill', I believe, should be simply termed subsistence crises/food crises that do not escalate to famine situations either as a result of efficient management by the population itself or by some government agency, or for some other reason.[2]

Here I will also mention the Greek terms *limos* and *loimos*. *Limos* refers to a famine through starvation; *loimos* to increased mortality as a result of disease. The Greek case in the 1940s was almost exclusively a *limos*, while many of the recent African famines have been of the latter type.[3]

14

Defining occupied Greece

With the occupation, the country was divided into three zones, each governed by one of the occupying powers. Bulgaria occupied the northern part of Greece on the borders of the two countries, that is, Eastern Macedonia and Western Thrace. Germany occupied three of the Aegean islands, most of Crete, the rest of Macedonia, the border area with Turkey and the greater Athens area. Italy occupied the rest of the country, including the Cyclades.[4] We know relatively little of what happened in the Bulgarian occupied territories but it seems that the Bulgarian occupation zone was not affected by a serious food crisis if only because this was a food producing area. The Dodecanese islands were at that time not part of Greece. They had been under Italian rule since 1912. We know that these islands suffered a food crisis towards the end of the occupation period. The Ionian islands were also placed under Italian administration immediately after occupation, thus severing links with Athens and, presumably, receiving foodstuffs from Italy. What seems to have happened there is that no major increases in mortality occurred on the islands while under Italian occupation, but such increases did occur while these islands were occupied by the Germans following the Italian surrender in September 1943. While the Ionian islands were occupied by the Italians no relief was permitted to be sent there by the Joint Relief Commission. In this chapter, therefore, references to 'occupied Greece' do not include either the Bulgarian occupied territories, the Ionian islands or the Dodecanese.

Case study populations and sources

Studies of the Greek famine have been severely restricted by the availability of data, and of such studies few provide numerical estimates of the effect of the famine. The lack of published data concerning the country as a whole has thus determined the focus of this work on three specific populations for which data are available. Thus, for the three chosen populations, Mykonos, Syros, and the towns of Chios and Vrontados on the island of Chios continuous data are available and the registration of deaths was not adversely affected by the occupation. Moreover, these records have survived to the present day, which was not the case with similar records in mainland Greece. Many were destroyed during warfare either between the occupying forces and the resistance or during the post-occupation civil war. In examining demographic aspects of the famine, civil registration records, that is, birth and death records, are used. Overall, these data are continuously available and of good quality considering that registration occurred amidst a famine. While some deaths may have not been registered, these omissions were very few in the islands under examination. A total of 12,602 birth and 13,969 death records were transcribed for all three island populations.

While civil registration data constitute the main source of quantitative data, in-depth interviews with survivors of the famine constitute a significant part of the qualitative basis of the evidence. Interviews between 1994 and 2000 in all three islands were conducted by the author. Twenty-two interviews were conducted on Chios, an equal number on Syros and twenty-eight on Mykonos. Informants came from all social classes, rural and urban environments, Orthodox and Catholics, men and women. Naturally, a claim to representativeness cannot be made, if only because the study is not only limited to those who survived the famine but also to those who survived until they were interviewed. In this study, the oral evidence is used to complement the quantitative and archival material rather than as a substitute for it. Significantly, oral evidence has been described as giving 'a voice to people ignored in the written record'.[5] This is certainly true in the case of the occupation years in Greece. Although the last two decades have seen the publication of a significant number of diaries and accounts of these years, most were written by middle-class men.[6] Very significantly, the evidence from the interviews was at times in clear contradiction with that of the written sources, something that led to a more in-depth examination of the written sources. Such was the case concerning the levels of agricultural production in occupied Greece. The oral evidence from time to time touched upon issues that are hardly mentioned in the written sources. For example, the lives and survival of those who escaped from the islands to the Turkish coast during the occupation.

Oral history has rarely been utilised in Greece.[7] Importantly, the complete absence of references to the food crisis of the occupation years in the collective memory of the Greek people is stark. There is a curious lack of a collective or even an official memory of the famine, let alone a collective trauma such as that associated with the Irish famine, for example.[8] Instead, a collective trauma certainly exists in relation to the civil war that started in Greece in the later years of the occupation and continued intermittently until the end of the 1940s. It seems that the trauma of the famine was absorbed by that of the civil war, which, despite the ugliness of the famine, was more far-reaching in its effects, lasted longer and occurred later. This lack of a collective version of the history of the famine enhances the value of the interviews since the informants are providing a personal rather than a collective memory. Still, the absence of collective memory at the national level does not preclude the existence of collective memory at the local level.

Causes of the famine

In economic terms, Greece before the Second World War was predominantly rural, with more than 60 per cent of the population engaged in agricultural occupations which generated 35 per cent of the national income. Nonetheless, the country was heavily dependent on the import of foodstuffs for subsistence. In the period 1935–37, 45 per cent of the required wheat was imported, although this was reduced to 20.5 per cent by 1939.[9] High figures for imported foodstuffs emphasise, if anything, the concentration on the production of cash crops such as tobacco and currants, which were mostly exported.[10] Still, it has been recently argued by Sokratis Petmezas that national production itself was enough to provide adequate calories per capita for the population if the production of the cash crop of currants were to be exported and an equal amount, in terms of calories, of wheat was to be imported.[11] The primary centres of cereal production in Greece were the northern parts of the mainland, whereas the Peloponnese constituted the main producer of olive oil and currants. The islands in general – despite wide variations at the individual level – were usually producers of a cash crop, if any, and also depended either on migrant or seamen's remittances and/or cash earned through seasonal/circular migration.

In the early stages of the Second World War while Greece was still neutral, that is up to October 1940, the effects of extensive pre-war trade between Greece and Germany became apparent: imports of raw material were substantially reduced and unemployment increased.[12] Prices increased and transportation difficulties were serious enough for urban populations to experience difficulties in receiving agricultural supplies from rural areas.[13] During the war against Italy in the winter of 1940–41 the situation worsened markedly. Trade with Germany ceased, economic activity declined, the cost of living increased and a black market emerged.[14]

The invasion of Greece by the German forces was remarkably rapid. It began on 6 April 1941 and by the 27th of the same month Athens was occupied. The Italians occupied the Cycladic islands during the following fortnight.[15] The island of Chios was occupied on 5 May 1941.[16] Many soldiers deserted their military units as soon as they realised that the Greek army was about to surrender.[17] On 16 April, the Greek Minister of War had effectively dissolved the army.[18] The soldiers were now free to return to their home towns or villages. And so they did, on foot and without any provision for their return. They survived on charity and hand-outs from the populace but also by offering their services to peasant households.[19] Those from islands mostly headed for Athens where, after being provided with permits by the Italians and civilian clothing by charities or acquaintances, they aimed to board a caique in order to reach their place of origin.[20] This was an expensive and dangerous undertaking and many did not manage to achieve it. These individuals were stranded in Athens and were among the first victims of the famine.

According to the existing literature, within the first month of the occupation the Germans seized or bought at low prices – paying with 'occupation marks' – all available stocks of olive oil, olives, raisins, figs, tobacco, cotton, leather and pack-animals.[21] The appropriation of all means of transport, including bicycles on Chios, and fuel by the occupation authorities, essentially prevented any transfer of supplies or population after the invasion.[22] Fishing was strictly prohibited, at least during the early stages of occupation, though the situation seems to have varied significantly from place to place and from time to time.[23] The country was further subdivided into 13 zones between which the circulation of food or population was forbidden.[24] Thus, the harvest of 1941 could not have been distributed to the most needy areas – even if the will to do so was there – because of the restrictions imposed.[25] This resulted in differences in the acuteness of the famine in various parts of the country according to the local economy of each area, with urban areas and barren islands being most affected by food scarcity during the early stages of the occupation. The situation was further exacerbated by the naval blockade that was imposed on Greece by Britain as soon as the country was occupied (see Chapter 3). By May the scarcity of food was apparent in Athens and, by June, on Chios and Syros.[26] By mid-May, the situation on Chios was a cause for alarm to the German forces and obliged them to release to the civilian population all supplies of foodstuffs that were 'secured from civilian stores'.[27] A request was also made to the field regiment for supplies for the civilian population since 'there are difficulties [shortages]'.[28] The German plenipotentiary in Greece, Günther Altenburg, warned on 7 May 1941 that if action was not taken in Greece the situation would lead to widespread famine, but his warning was ignored by his superiors, including Hitler.[29] Both Italy and Germany sent some grain to Greece in the period 15 August to 30 September 1941, before the German authorities handed to Italy the entire responsibility for providing Greece with food 'since Greece lies in Italy's sphere of influence'.[30] By June 1941, the occupying forces had offered guarantees to the collaborationist

Greek government that any food sent for the Greek population would not be requisitioned. In November of the same year the above guarantees were repeated to the International Red Cross.[31]

In July 1941, the US minister in Greece, Lincoln MacVeagh, on arrival in New York described the situation in Greece as 'a progression towards famine'.[32] In August 1941, the correspondent of the London *Times* reported people fainting in the streets of Athens due to starvation, and the Greeks appealed to the British and American governments for the shipment of food for the starving children.[33] The British government was from the outset very well informed of the existing situation. Information was supplied, at least initially, by foreign citizens leaving Greece as well as by British soldiers escaping from occupied Greece. Later on, information came from Greek escapees. Responding to these appeals, the Minister of Economic Warfare, Hugh Dalton, authorised assistance from Turkey since Turkey was within the blockade area (see Chapters 3 and 5). Officially, it was the Turkish Red Crescent that initially handled the food shipments, but behind the scenes the whole relief operation was closely supervised and directed by the British. The supplies that arrived in Greece from Turkey between October 1941 and February 1942 were minimal and did not include any wheat, the commodity that was most urgently needed.[34] By December 1941, the famine had reached its peak with reports of hundreds of people dying in the streets of Athens.[35]

On 12 January 1942, the British government allowed a one-off shipment of 8000 tons of wheat through the blockade. The blockade was eventually lifted in February 1942, and on 21 March 1942 the first of a series of shipments of food approved by the British government arrived at the port of Piraeus.[36] Irregular shipments of wheat and flour continued to arrive until August 1942 when an agreement between all involved parties was reached and a monthly shipment of 15,000 tons of grain was secured. Regular shipments of foodstuffs – managed and distributed by the Joint Relief Commission and under the auspices of the International Red Cross Committee – started arriving in November 1942.[37]

Requisitions

From the local studies it seems that food requisitioning by the German occupation authorities was concentrated on local cash crops such as oranges and lemons on Chios, olive oil on Lesvos and olive oil and raisins on Crete.[38] These requisitions were not extensive enough to create a vacuum of food supplies locally, considering that these were cash crops, but at the national level their export did create a vacuum, especially of olive oil.

For the citrus fruits of Chios, considering the abundance of the product and the extreme restrictions on transport it would have been impossible to store them for future use. Similarly, according to the Joint Relief Commission delegate, 'there has been (despite export) a comparatively good supply of dried raisins' in Crete.[39] Moreover, orders were given to return to the population any food supplies that had been requisitioned from civilian sources and to a degree these orders were followed. No evidence of direct requisitioning was found in the Italian occupation zone, possibly because Syros itself did not produce a cash crop. The 'purchase' at a fixed price of tobacco on Samos and the Cyclades occurred, as did purchases of olive oil on Crete.[40] The Germans requisitioned the latter product. According to Gabriella Etmektsoglou-Koehn, by November 1941, 41,458 tons of foodstuffs, most of it cash crops, had been requisitioned by the Italian Army.[41] Again, the purchase of tobacco could not have affected the availability of food. In relation to Cretan olive oil, the Joint Relief Commission delegate who reviewed the situation reported that 'the occupying authorities have exploited for their own ends only a comparatively small part of last year's total production in Crete' while, according to the report, much of this was hoarded and used by the local population.[42]

No further evidence of direct requisitions has been found and it is certain that, from the moment of the arrival of the Joint Relief Commission, no further requisitions occurred.[43] Instead, an exchange scheme was in operation whereby every Greek product taken by the occupation forces would be 'paid for' in foodstuffs of equal calorific value, the whole process being closely supervised by the Joint Relief Commission delegates, who in turn would inform the British government. In late 1942, the first report by the Swedish delegation sent to the Greek government-in-exile, at that time based in London, stressed that 'requisitioning and checking up by the occupation authorities does not mean that the products are consumed. The reports concerning requisitioning at Attica seem inaccurate or in any case very exaggerated.'[44] The British government itself, following an erroneous broadcast by the BBC, admitted that 'wholesale Axis requisitioning of vegetables, fruit etc. undoubtedly took place prior to the arrival of food ships in August [1942] but not we believe since that date'.[45] On the local level, some cases were easily inspected with satisfying results: 'according to Monsieur Arno's information, German imports of wheat into Chios have more than compensated for the requisitioning of foodstuffs'. The situation on German-occupied Lesvos (Mytilini) was found to be equally satisfactory. But the situation was much less satisfactory on Italian-occupied Samos: 'in regard to the question of the manner in which native produce in Samos has been disposed of . . . Monsieur Allard has particularly stressed that it has been impossible for a representative of the Swedish Government to establish how native produce in Samos was disposed of before the arrival of Monsieur Allard in April 1943'.[46] Even for the transitional period, and up until the permanent establishment of the Joint Relief Commission, its delegates made every effort to clarify the situation to the British government:

> Monsieur Allard reports that the requisitioning of olive oil and dried fruits by the German occupation authorities from the entry into force of the agreement concerning compensation imports . . . up till the last September was not on a scale to prejudice the reasonable requirements of the civilian population. Any shortage of these commodities in certain localities was due to transport difficulties and inflationary rises in prices.[47]

Another possible form of food leakage from local production to the occupation forces was that mentioned by an escapee, Major A. Tsaousopoulos, who, while in Greece, had been director of transport of the Joint Relief Commission. Referring to mainland Greece, he reported that while the Italian authorities insisted on fixing the purchasing price of wheat at only 17 drachmas when bought by the Greek government, at the same time the peasants 'were selling at 30 drachmas to military units and to dealers who toured the countryside to buy supplies for the military' and naturally refusing to sell to the Greek government.[48] If this was happening on a large scale it could indeed have had serious repercussions on the availability of food for the civilian population. This could have only occurred in the early months of the occupation as the peasants soon became aware of the seriousness of the situation and refused to use cash in their dealings.

Above all, it was plundering by individual soldiers that reduced the availability of food, especially in places of low productivity such as Syros. Such food plundering seems, from the specific case studies, to have been almost exclusively performed by Italian soldiers rather than the Germans.[49] What seems certain is that it is currently impossible, and may remain so, even to estimate the extent of 'official' requisitioning of foodstuffs by the occupying forces. It is certain that requisitioning occurred but it also seems that its extent has been hugely exaggerated, being based, to a large extent, on inaccurate information or the propaganda of the war years and the reports and diaries of individuals who lived through those years.[50] Interestingly, 'detailed records seem not to have been kept' and even an approximate 'estimation of the value of the confiscated and requisitioned goods . . . is almost impossible'.[51]

To conclude, direct food requisitions did not substantially affect local food availability. Indirect methods of 'acquiring access' to foods, such as 'purchasing' and plundering by individual soldiers, were more significant. Moreover, requisitions of non-edibles – raw materials, vehicles, boats and so on – accelerated, if not caused, the economic collapse of the country which itself affected the food situation.[52]

Levels of agricultural production

Almost without exception the decline in agricultural production during the occupation years is, at least partly, blamed for the famine and the food crisis. The cited causes of the reduction in agricultural output include, among others, the severe lack of draft animals, the weakening of those that remained due to the lack of fodder, the lack of machinery, the short-age of farm labour and fertilisers, the lack of seed, much of which was consumed during the famine, the shortage of high quality seed and the discontinuation of crop rotation during the occupation years.[53] However, labour was extensively 'imported' from towns throughout Greece since town-dwellers would readily move to the rural areas to work in exchange for food.[54] Most of the draft animals had been requisitioned by the Greek army for the war effort. Moreover, the use of machinery and fertilisers was, in any case, extremely restricted prior to the occupation and seeds for cultivation were given to farmers either by the Italians or by the local government.[55]

The figures for agricultural production for individual years – and most importantly the figures concerning wheat – cited by most authors on the subject are broadly consistent.[56] This is because, directly or indirectly, these figures originate from the official estimates of annual agricultural production that were undertaken 'by the public officials concerned', unlike the pre-war figures which were produced by the Greek statistical service.[57] Yet, how were these estimates reached? In the words of the director of the Swedish Delegation to the Joint Relief Commission, Emil Sandström: 'on the basis of the yield of 10 per cent tax in kind, it was calculated that last year's crop [1942] amounted to 350,000–400,000 tons. This year it has been very difficult to obtain an accurate estimate.'[58] In another Joint Relief Commission report the method of calculation is presented in even greater detail: 'the 1942 harvest . . . was calculated at 350,000–400,000 tons. This calculation is based on the collection carried out by the government, i.e. the exaction of 1/10 of the crops as a tax *in natura*, the tax having yielded about 40,000 tons.'[59] The final official estimates for 1942 and 1943 were 343,000 and 368,000 tons respectively. Levels of production were similarly estimated at the local level, as is illustrated by the example of Chios for which estimates of the 1941 production, prepared in 1943, are available (see Table 2.1). Two sets of such estimates are available. The first set originates from M.G. Theotokas, who must have used figures provided by local Chiots with authority and knowledge of the situation.[60] The second are the estimates of the Ministry of Agriculture based in Athens. The latter estimates are consistently lower than the first by at least a quarter. Moreover, even those of Theotokas are unrealistically low. Theotokas prepared these estimates while writing a report that was sent to the Red Cross Commission pleading for help for Chios. I suspect this explains the low productivity shown for 1941 in relation to the productivity of earlier years. Moreover, the almost halved productivity shown for potatoes bears no relation to newspaper reporting in late 1941, which referred to the expectation of a good potato harvest that 'may be as high as two million oka [approximately 2,560,000 kgs]'.[61]

It is, and it was at the time, widely acknowledged that the tax in kind collection by the Greek state was a complete failure, its yield amounting to only a tiny fraction of the required ten per cent of harvested crops.[62] Margaritis also questions the validity of official figures on agricultural production for the occupation period.[63] He speculates that the official production figures must have been 'massaged' so that they would essentially match the figures for the tax collected in kind.[64] This was not exclusively a problem of the occupation years, as the writer of a United Nations Relief and Rehabilitation Administration report explains: 'little reliable data are available regarding domestic food supplies in hand during the interval between liberation and the midsummer harvest of 1945. Greek farmers felt compelled to provide only a minimum estimate of their production in order to justify help to themselves and to cover up widespread hoarding of food supplies, which were the only safe form of investment.'[65] Thus, to put it plainly, the estimated and widely cited figures of agricultural output during the years of the occupation bear little relation to reality.

When outlining the poor production of the occupation years, comparison is invariably made with the figures of the late 1930s. However, as is acknowledged, these were years of unprecedentedly high yields, due mainly to the government efforts to achieve self-sufficiency. So, for example, the 1938–40 average annual wheat production was three times that of 1922–31.[66] For other products, the increase amounted to 75 per cent. Thus, average annual wheat production of approximately 310,000 tons between 1922 and 1931 for the whole country is comparable even

Table 2.1   Cultivated land, agricultural production and productivity on Chios, 1936–38 and 1941

Product	Average 1936–38			1941 (Theotokas)			1941 (Agricul. Statistics Office)	
	Cultivated land in stremma	Production in 1,000 oke	Productivity in oke per stremma	Cultivated land in stremma	Production in 1,000 oke	Productivity in oke per stremma	Production in 1,000 oke	Productivity in oke per stremma
Wheat	35,462	2,448	69.0	50,000	2,016	40.3	1,575	31.5
Oats	1,444	101	69.9	1,500	64	42.7	50.1	33.4
Maslin	24,318	781	32.1	20,000	754	37.7	589	29.5
Barley	13,187	1,366	103.6	15,000	1,151	76.7	599	39.9
Potatoes	3,077	3,831	1,245.0	1,300	863	663.8	673.5	518.1
Other garden products	6,655	4,510	677.7	3,500	2,436	696.0	0	0.0
Beans	573	25	43.6	200	0	0.0	0	0.0
Broad beans	16,748	1,530	91.4	22,000	548	24.9	428	19.5
Chick peas	5,106	301	59.0	6,000	102	17.0	79.7	13.3
Lentils	1,843	105	57.0	2,000	41	20.5	31.7	15.9
Oil		2,036			640			
Olives		875			384			
Total	132,683	19,870		151,700	9,690		4,025.95	

Notes: Estimates of the 1941 production are available from data collected by Theotokas himself and data from the Agriculture Statistics Office of the Agriculture Ministry in Athens. For the calculations concerning 1936–38 production Theotokas must have used published data as similar figures appear in a PRO report (PRO, WO204/8887). 1 oke is the equivalent of 1.28 kg or 2.8 lb.1 stremma = 1000 square metres.
Source: Mikhail Theotokas Archive, Korais Library, Chios, folder 7, 'Episitistikai anagkai Khiou'.

with the 1942 and 1943 published figures, although considerably lower than the 1941 figure of 566,000. It should be noted here that the occupation period figures refer to the production of the Greek state except for the areas of Eastern Macedonia, Western Thrace and the Ionian Islands. The first two, major wheat producers, were occupied by Bulgaria. The Ionian Islands, a major olive oil producing area, was cut off from the rest of Greece. Significantly, this point applies to all comparisons made between the figures for production during the pre-war and occupation periods, something that is rarely acknowledged.

To summarise, the estimated figures for production during the occupation years bear no relation to the actual production levels during those years, while comparisons with the immediate pre-war years are somewhat misleading in demonstrating the extent of production decline during the years of occupation. The estimated figures, which have been widely reproduced, were closely linked to, and reflected the level of collection of, the tax in kind. Production was probably as high as that of a 'normal' year, although cultivation was concentrated in fewer, more specific products, namely wheat and certain pulses.

What were the main causes of the famine?

The controls imposed upon existing markets were so severe – price control, controls on movement, restrictions on the shipment of food and so on – that legal trade was almost entirely curtailed. Monetary disorganisation and inflation added significantly to the price increases that occurred due to the lack of foodstuffs and the presence of the black market. The severe fragmentation of the markets is reflected in the great variation in black market prices of goods across the country. What was exceptional in this market was its extreme volatility and the fluctuation in prices that every 'shock' would bring. Such 'shocks' were events in the war that were perceived as delaying or bringing forward the end of the war; changes in the law concerning black-marketeering; the announcement of the arrival of relief food from abroad or the cancelling of such a shipment. More importantly, any rumour of any of the above was enough to 'shock' the market, leading to a concomitant fluctuation in the prices. It should be noted here that prices do not necessarily refer to monetary value alone, since barter was used not only by private individuals but also by most traders, as well as by the occupation forces and by the Joint Relief Commission itself.

It seems that it was this market fragmentation that was probably one of the most important causes of the famine. It occurred in the first year, when the 'shock' of dislocated markets also occurred, coinciding with the greatest mortality. In the following years, illegal and occasionally legal trading was established, though this was a 'new' trade, performed by 'new' people with new rules and new routes. Still, controlling the markets, especially in abnormal times, was in line with the ideology of the time. The Greek government closely controlled the market prior to, and during, the war, as was the case with the British and many other wartime economies. It was the splitting up of the country, and concomitantly the markets, into patchwork pieces; the attempt to impose very tough controls on the markets; the lack of governmental authority in imposing some of the laws/decrees (such as those referring to the collection of agricultural produce), as well as the complete lack of reliable information that led to a problem of food availability being transformed into a full-blown famine.

Short-term effects on mortality

Detailed demographic data concerning populations affected by famines are rare. As a result, estimates of famine deaths vary widely: from half to one and a half million for the Irish famine; from three to ten million for that in 1932–33 in the Ukraine; and from 15 to 30 million for the Chinese 'Great Leap Forward'.[67] Estimates of deaths resulting from the Greek famine vary from 100,000 to 200,000 and from 250,000 to 450,000 (the first two figures refer to the winter of 1941–42, the third refers to the famine victims between 1941 and 1943, and the last refers to the May 1941–April 1943 period).[68] Given that the population of Greece in 1940 was 7,344,860, the estimated percentage of famine deaths varies from 1.4 to 6.1. The cause of the uncertainty is the lack of published data for the whole country. Fortunately, civil registration did continue in some places, providing detailed and accurate data.[69] However, before commencing the study of mortality, it is first crucial to establish the duration of the famine.

Duration and severity of the famine

Prior to the famine, Greece experienced declines in both mortality and fertility. Life expectancy at birth for both sexes in 1928–29 was 48.3 for Ermoupolis, the principal town on Syros, 54.1 for Chios town, around 56 for Vrontados, above 52 for Mykonos and around 49 years for Greece as a whole (see Table 2.2).[70] The 1930s represent a decade when substantial decreases in both fertility and infant mortality rate (IMR) occurred for

Table 2.2   Life expectancy at birth, crude death rate and ratio of famine to pre-famine crude death rate on Syros, Chios, Mykonos and Athens/Piraeus (various lengths of famines)

	1928–29 e0	1938–39 CDR	Famine CDR	Corrected CDR	1949–53 CDR	Ratio
Syros island		15.7	94.6			6.0
Ermoupolis	48.3	17.3	113.8		8.4	6.6
Ano Syros		15.7	79.8			5.1
Rural Syros		8.6	25.7			3.0
Chios and Vrontados towns		15.0	54.7	68.3		4.6
Chios town	54.1	15.1	54.3	67.9	9.4	4.5
Vrontados	56.0	14.5	56.5	70.6		4.9
Mykonos island		13.1	117.6		9.5	9.0
Mykonos town		13.0	134.7		10.1	10.4
Rural Mykonos		13.3	71.1		7.5	5.3
Athens/Piraeus		12.1*	39.5			3.3

Notes: *The 1938–39 CDR for Athens/Piraeus refers to 1940. Data from P. Copanaris, *La Santé Publique en Grèce pendant la Guerre et l'Occupation 1940–1944* (Paris, 1945), pp. 4–5.
Sources: The population figure for the 1938–39 rates were estimated from the October 1940 census population figure minus the births, plus the deaths that occurred between 1 January 1939 and the census date. Similarly, for the famine rates, the population figure for the mid-point of the famine was estimated from the October 1940 census figure minus the deaths, plus the births that occurred between the two dates. The births and deaths were obtained from the civil registration database. For Syros and Mykonos, additional calculations were made where instead of the October 1940 census population figure the 'census' figures supplied by the Italian administration for January 1942 were used (General State Archives in Ermoupolis, Italian Archive, folder 203). While the estimated values of the crude death and birth rates differed from the first set, the overall trends and results were not significantly altered. For Athens and Piraeus the population figure of 1,100,000 and the death figures supplied in P. Copanaris, *La Santé Publique* are used.

the whole of Greece (from 134 in 1931, the IMR declined to 99 in 1938). Thus, by the time of the famine, life expectancy was moderately high and improving.

In defining the length of the famine, the monthly number of deaths was established for the period 1939 to 1945 for the populations of Chios town and Vrontados, Syros, Mykonos, Athens/Piraeus, Thessaloniki and the total of twenty-seven major towns (see figures 2.1 and 2.2).[71] While for the two towns on Chios the course of the famine was virtually identical, both Syros and Mykonos experienced significant local variations.

The peak of the famine occurred in the middle of a harsh winter. Interestingly, for all populations there are two peaks, one in January and one in March or April 1942 (for Thessaloniki the peak lasts for the first

28

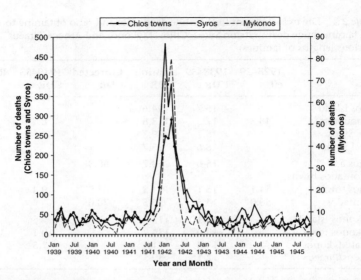

Figure 2.1   Monthly number of deaths: Chios towns, Syros and Mykonos, 1939–45
Sources: Civil registration records of Syros, Chios and Mykonos islands.

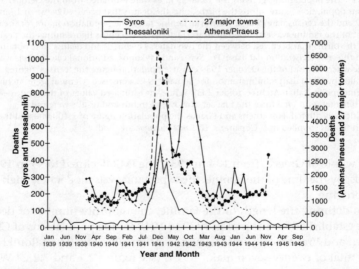

Figure 2.2   Monthly number of deaths: Syros, Thessaloniki, Athens/Piraeus and 27 major towns, 1939–45
Note: The 27 major towns do not include either Athens/Piraeus or Thessaloniki.
Sources: Civil registration records of Syros of Athens/Piraeus and 27 major towns,
P. Copanaris, *La Santé Publique en Grèce pendant la Guerre et l'Occupation 1940–1944* (Paris, 1945), pp. 4–5; for Thessaloniki, PRO, FO371/42366, W13768 'Greek relief: reports on the work of the Greek Relief Commission in Salonica'.

Table 2.3 Baseline monthly number of deaths in 'normal' times, famine period and length of famine in five Greek localities

	Baseline number of deaths	Famine period	Length of famine (months)
Syros island	52	Aug.41–Dec.42	17
		Jan.–Jul.44	7
Chios towns	66	Oct.41–Jan.43	16
Mykonos island	10	Nov.41–Jun.42	8
Thessaloniki	336	Dec.41–Mar.43	16
Athens/Piraeus	1,780	Oct.41–Dec.42	15

Note: 'Normal times' are the years 1938–39 except for Athens and Thessaloniki for which 1940 was used.
Sources: Civil registration records of Syros, Chios and Mykonos islands; for Athens/Piraeus the population figure of 1,100,000 and the death figures supplied in P. Copanaris, *La Santé Publique en Grèce pendant la Guerre et l'Occupation 1940–1944* (Paris, 1945), pp. 4–5 are used; the data for Thessaloniki are from PRO, FO371/42366, W13768 'Greek Relief: Reports on the Work of the Greek Relief Commission in Salonica'.

three months of 1942). In order to establish a baseline number of deaths, the average number of monthly deaths representing 'normality' was calculated from the 1936 to 1940 figures.[72] This was subsequently inflated by 60 per cent, except for Mykonos, whose figures were inflated by 100 per cent due to the small numbers involved (see Table 2.3). Thus, periods of elevated mortality are those months when mortality exceeded the baseline mortality figure. The beginning of the famine was as early as August 1941 for Syros, and as late as December 1941 for Thessaloniki. The mortality crisis ended in June 1942 for Mykonos, but not until March 1943 in Thessaloniki.

The period of elevated mortality was only eight months on Mykonos, though for the other localities it lasted between 15 and 17 months. The effect of the famine was found to be inversely proportionate to its duration in the localities. Here, the ratio of the pre-famine to famine crude death rate is used as a measure of the severity of the famine (see Table 2.2).[73] The ratio was nine for the island of Mykonos, and just over three for Athens/Piraeus. For Thessaloniki the ratio was 3.1, while for the twenty-seven towns it was 2.6.[74]

Significant differentiations in the evolution of the famine can be observed for all the populations listed. Interestingly, it seems that Athens/Piraeus and the twenty-seven towns are the two cases that display a similar course. Thessaloniki provides an exceptional case in that its population experienced a second, higher peak in October 1942. This was most certainly due to the outbreak of malaria in the spring and summer of

1942.[75] From the evidence provided in the death records of a number of municipalities around Thessaloniki as well as that of the town itself, the effects of the malaria epidemic in terms of mortality became evident in the period July 1942 to February 1943.[76] Though malaria was not exclusively responsible for this peak, directly and most probably indirectly and in combination with starvation, the disease had a profound effect on the levels of mortality in Thessaloniki. Still, contemporary medical observers remarked that the rate of mortality due to malaria was much higher in the rural areas of Macedonia, where starvation was minimal, compared with Thessaloniki itself.[77] The same epidemic affected parts of Thessaly, Epirus, Sterea Hellas (mainland Greece) and the Cyclades.[78] The most seriously affected areas were those where malaria was endemic.[79] Malaria continued to be a problem for the rest of the occupation period to varying degrees in some areas, but especially in the rural areas of northern Greece.[80]

For Syros, the base line monthly number of deaths was exceeded once again in the period January to July 1944. This should be noted as a secondary, less serious famine, whose causes lay in part in the interruption of the relief operations.[81] Athens also saw a secondary incidence of elevated mortality in December 1944 due to the temporary suspension of relief operations.[82] Both these instances reveal the vulnerability of these populations and their heavy reliance on relief operations.

A strong regional variation in the severity of the famine is also revealed in towns that experienced higher mortality increases, almost twice as high as those recorded in the countryside. The major determinant of this was local production patterns and access to land. For example, virtually no one in Ermoupolis, the principal town on Syros, possessed land or had links to farming.[83] A small part of the Ano Syros population did, which explains its somewhat lower mortality increases. The residents of rural Syros did have land.[84] Some rural dwellers owned small plots of land yet would also be employed as agricultural workers. The increase in mortality among the rural population is explained by the unavailability of such work during the famine. Land ownership divisions were less straightforward on Mykonos and Chios: here, a sizeable percentage of the urban population owned land, though it may not necessarily have been under cultivation in 1941, a trend that was certainly rectified in 1942. In both islands, the population of the towns would usually rent land to farmers under an agreement, dividing the produce between them. (Exceptionally, the administrative area of Chios town also included a group of farmers living in Kampos.)

The variability of the patterns observed point to the importance of local circumstances. Significantly, access to the countryside – and its produce – played an important role. On Mykonos, the links between the urban centre and the countryside were strong as a result of the owner-ship of small parcels of land by town dwellers. This not only had a posi-tive effect in alleviating the famine during the summer months of 1942, but also ensured that no further increases in mortality occurred. The same early return to 'normality' is suggested by the data for the town of Ano Syros and for rural Syros, where there was also some access to land. While both clearly experienced the famine, their populations recovered earlier than those of Ermoupolis. For Athens/Piraeus, and also for the twenty-seven major towns as a whole (except Thessaloniki) there was no excess mortality after 1942 up to the time of liberation in October 1944, due in part to relief operations.

Epilogue

This chapter has focused on the causes of the food crisis during the years of occupation and its short-term consequences for mortality. The food crisis started as an immediate consequence of the deficiency of food in the first two months of occupation. Some foodstuffs were requisitioned by the occupation forces; some foodstuffs that were on their way to Greece never arrived due to the blockade; while a country-wide panic over the food situation occurred immediately upon occupation. The harvest in the summer of 1941 did increase the availability of food but the fear of the approaching winter made producers retain as much as they could of their products. The collapse of the markets that occurred due to the dis-memberment of the country into various occupation zones and the attempt of a weak government to regulate markets closely were major factors leading to the famine in the first year of occupation. Very import-ant was the absence of established systems of welfare for the destitute and impoverished population, systems that could have possibly been modified and adapted to an emergency situation so as to protect those most in need. Such systems did not exist prior to the occupation and any attempts that were made for relief were haphazard and inefficient. The persistence of the British blockade policy as the famine unfolded served to intensify the fears of the population as to the short-term food supply. Still, if the blockade had not been lifted and relief had not arrived, the mor-tality crisis of the first year of the occupation would most certainly have been repeated. It is clear that the occupation forces did not deliberately provoke the food crisis at any stage, as the British themselves acknow-ledged: 'it is likely that their negligence last year was due less to a positive desire that the Greeks should starve, than to reluctance or incapacity to overcome the difficulties involved in providing the people with even a minimum of food. The physical difficulties are of course considerable.'[85] Transport difficulties were immense and remained so both for the Joint Relief Commission in the later years of the occupation and also for the United Nations Relief and Rehabilitation Administration (UNRRA) after the liberation in October 1944.

Looking at the short-term demographic effects of the famine, the findings demonstrate that this was a truly deadly famine, especially in the twentieth-century European context. It occurred in a population that enjoyed at the time a rather high life expectancy despite its relative economic underdevelopment. The disproportionate mortality of young adult males must have had a lasting effect on the sex ratio of the Greek population with concomitant effects on its economic development. Nonetheless, the effects of war make it impossible to assess the direct effects of the famine on any observed changes in the sex ratio. The effects of the famine surely did not fade away immediately. A study of the height of conscripted soldiers aged 20 showed that the consistent and regular annual increases that occurred for those born in the 1920s and up to 1935 were reversed for those born in the years 1936 to 1942.[86] The recorded heights reached a peak for the birth cohort of 1935, with a height of 167.52 cm and a trough of 167.11 cm for those born in 1942. Considering that these figures concerned a very significant percentage of these cohorts, these were surely indications of stunted growth, although they were soon reversed. The long-term effects on marriage must have also been significant. Considering the reduction in the number of adult males due to the war and the famine but also the significant postponement of marriages that occurred during the crisis and presumably also during the civil war, a wedding 'boom' would be expected to occur in the post-war years.[87] But Greece did not experience either a rapid recovery in levels of marriage or a post-war baby boom. In terms of fertility, Greece moved from a society that was tentatively starting to regulate its fertility in the 1930s to one that certainly did so in the 1950s. A hidden aspect of the occupation years is certainly the exchange of sex for food by Greek women to Italian and German soldiers but also to Greeks. There are brief references to this phenomenon, but it is generally passed over. One such appears in the well-known 1942 recruiting pamphlet for the resistance organisation EAM, *Ti einai kai ti thelei to EAM*. Its anonymous author (Dimitris Glinos) complained of the 'astonishing and unexpected' extent of prostitution and asked whatever had happened to traditional Greek morals.

More explicit are the rates of illegitimacy, enormous by Greek standards, recorded, for example, in Ermoupolis. Though a small number of women from Syros, presumably mostly Catholics, married Italian soldiers and moved to Italy, the majority did not do so. How did a society where virginity and sexual morality were of paramount concern cope with such a situation? What happened to the illegitimate children that resulted from these liaisons, and what happened to their mothers? Migration to Athens, I would speculate, provided an answer to their problematic presence in the restricted environment of a provincial town. In terms of life expectancy, the long-term effects are not immediately visible. Post-war Greece demonstrated significant gains in life expectancy for a number of reasons. One certainly was the selection effect of the famine. That is to say that it was the poorer sections of the urban working class, together with many of the elderly, who were the principal victims in the famine.

Notes

1. This chapter is the outcome of research that was carried out during the project 'Public health and population dynamics during the 1941–42 Greek famine'. The project was funded by the Wellcome Trust History of Medicine Panel, the support of which is gratefully acknowledged. The overall results of the project have been published in Violetta Hionidou, *Famine and Death in Occupied Greece, 1941–44* (Cambridge, 2006), in the Cambridge Studies in Population, Economy, and Society in Past Times series.
2. S. Zurbrigg, 'Did Starvation Protect from Malaria? Distinguishing between Severity and Lethality of Infectious Disease in Colonial India', *Social Science History*, XXI (1997): 54. For other definitions of famine, see, for example, W.A. Dando, *The Geography of Famine* (London, 1980). See also Alexander de Waal, *Famine that Kills: Darfur, Sudan, 1984–1985* (Oxford, 1989).
3. V. Hionidou, 'Why Do People Die in Famines? Evidence from Three Island Populations', *Population Studies*, LVI (2002): 65–80.
4. K.A. Doxiadis, *The Sacrifices of Greece in the Second World War* (Athens, 1946), Table 15 and comments.
5. Cormac Ó Gráda, *Black '47 and beyond. The Great Irish Famine in History, Economy, and Memory* (Princeton, New Jersey, 1999), p. 197.
6. Among all the published accounts and diaries utilised in this book only one was written by a woman.
7. Notable exceptions are Maria Thanopoulou, *I Prophoriki Mnimi tou Polemou. Dierevnisi tis Syllogikis Mnimis tou B Pagkosmiou Polemou stous Epizontes enos Khoriou tis Levkadas* (Athens, 2000); Janet Hart, *New Voices in the Nation: Women and the Greek Resistance, 1941–1964* (Ithaca, 1996); Pothiti Hantzaroula, 'Shame in the Narratives of Domestic Servants in Greece, 1920–1945', in R. Schulte and P. Hantzaroula (eds), *Narratives of the Servant* (European University Institute Working Paper HEC No 2001/1, Florence, 2001), pp. 83–104; Nicholas Doumanis, *Myth and Memory in the Mediterranean. Remembering Fascism's Empire* (London, 1997). Most of my own work utilises oral evidence.
8. Ó Gráda, *Black '47 and beyond*.

9. W. Diamond (1947), *Agriculture and Food in Greece*, UNRRA, Operational Analysis Paper 19, pp. 5–6; Z. Demathas, 'I Exelixi Vasikon Megethon tis Ellinikis Oikonomias, 1935–1939', in H. Fleischer and N. Svoronos (eds), *I Ellada 1936–44. Diktatoria, Katokhi, Antistasi. Praktika A Diethnous Synedriou Synkhronis Istorias* (Athens, 1989), p. 151.

10. Mark Mazower, *Greece and the Inter-war Economic Crisis* (Oxford, 1991), pp. 79–81.

11. Sokratis Petmezas, 'I Anaptyxi tis Agrotikis Oikonomias', paper presented at the conference on The Greek Economy in the 19th Century (1830–1914), Hydra, Greece (October 2004), pp. 10–12; personal communication.

12. D. Delivanis and W.C. Cleveland, *Greek Monetary Developments 1939–1948* (Bloomington, 1950), pp. 22–4.

13. Delivanis and Cleveland, *Greek Monetary Developments*, p. 23.

14. Delivanis and Cleveland, *Greek Monetary Developments*, pp. 44–7.

15. Mark Mazower, *Inside Hitler's Greece: the Experience of Occupation 1941–44* (New Haven and London, 1993), p. 50; *The Times*, 7 May 1941.

16. L.M. Kalvocoresis, *Khronikon Katokhis tis Khiou para ton Germanon 1941–1944* (Athens, 1958), p. 3.

17. General State Archives, Chios, ABE 1411, 'Phrourarkheio limenos Khiou. Vivlio antigraphon epistolon tou 1941'.

18. John Hondros, *Occupation and Resistance: the Greek Agony 1941–1944* (New York, 1983), p. 52.

19. Informant No 8, Chios; Informant No 14, Chios; Informant No 17, Syros.

20. Mazower writes that 'to travel from the capital to the Peloponnese required a permit from the *carabinieri* and a booking several days in advance' and that 'the voyage by caique [small boat] from Piraeus to Chios took fifteen to twenty days, and could only be managed at a price beyond most people's reach' (Mazower, *Inside Hitler's Greece*, p. 33). By January 1942, the Bulgarians and Italians refused to recognise the passes provided by the Germans, further restricting population movements (*The Times*, 10 January 1942).

21. Mazower, *Inside Hitler's Greece*, pp. 24–7; John Hondros, 'Greece and the German Occupation', in David Close (ed.), *The Greek Civil War, 1943–1950: Studies of Polarization* (London, 1993), p. 45.

22. Kalvocoresis, *Khronikon Katokhis*, p. 73. The seizure of shipping by the Axis authorities was considered by *The Times* correspondent as a reason for the extreme severity of the famine on the islands (*The Times*, 28 October 1941).

23. *The Times*, 22 January 1942. Mazower emphasises the especially strict prohibition imposed by the Italians on trade between the islands in the Aegean sea and the 'notoriously strict surveillance of fishing boats, which could carry information or even passengers as well as fish' (Mazower, *Inside Hitler's Greece*, p. 55). At a later stage, fisherman were permitted to fish, provided that Italian soldiers accompanied them, D.N. Khalaris, *Ta Katokhika* (Athens, 1997, II, p. 129). Much of the catch was routinely requisitioned.

24. Doxiadis, *The Sacrifices*, Table 16 and comments; *The Times*, 22 January 1942.

25. According to Hondros, the 1941 harvest was especially poor, having produced less than half of the normal output, J. Hondros (1969), 'The German Occupation of Greece 1941–44', PhD thesis, Vanderbilt University, p. 67. Diamond, citing Varvaressos, suggests that the wheat produced in 1940–41 was 80 per cent of that of 1935–37. For other cereals and for pulses it was 36 and 45 per cent respectively (Diamond, *Agriculture*, p. 12).

26. K. Delopoulos (ed.), *To Imerologio Katokhis tou Minou Dounia* (Athens, 1987), p. 26; D. Phaphalios in a letter of 20 June 1941, Argenti Archive; *Syriana Grammata* 1991, p. 241 citing the diaries of a local school. *The Times* reported on 5 May 1941 that 'the scarcity of food, which has always existed in Greece, now threatens to reach catastrophic proportions'.

27. P. Hoffmann, 'Roncalli in the Second World War: Peace Initiatives, the Greek Famine and the Persecution of the Jews', *Journal of Ecclesiastical History*, XL (1989), p. 77; Argenti Archive, Korais Library, Chios, Documents relating to the German occupation of Chios 1941–44, 'War Diaries and Associated Documents of the 164th Infantry Division and other German units in Greece', p. 18.

28. Argenti Archive, Korais Library, Chios, Documents relating to the German occupation of Chios 1941–44, 'War Diaries and Associated Documents of the 164th Infantry Division and other German units in Greece', p. 18.

29. Hondros, 'Greece', p. 46.

30. Mazower, *Inside Hitler's Greece*, p. 31 citing US National Archives (Washington, DC), T-821/249/829-32, 'Situazione economica e organizzazione civile nei territori occupati', 1 November 1941; Heinz Richter, *1936–1946: Dyo Epanastaseis kai Antepanastaseis stin Ellada* (Athens, 1975), pp. 155–6.

31. Hagen Fleischer, *Stemma kai Svastika: I Ellada tis Katokhis kai tis Antistasis 1941–1944* (Athens, 1986), pp. 204–6.

32. J.O. Iatrides (ed.), *Ambassador MacVeagh reports: Greece, 1933–1947* (Princeton, 1980), p. 374.

33. *The Times*, 16 August 1941.

34. D. Kitsikis, 'La Famine en Grèce (1941–42): les Conséquences Politiques', *Revue de l' Histoire de la Deuxième Guerre Mondiale*, LXXIV (1969): 30–1.

35. The report of Junod, a Red Cross representative, was one of the most powerful early accounts of the situation in Athens (PRO, FO371/32460, 'Rapport sur la situation en Grèce, par A. Junod', 31 January 1942).

36. Kitsikis, 'La Famine', p. 30.

37. Hondros, 'German Occupation', p. 85.

38. International Committee of the Red Cross Archives, Geneva, SG.11 Secours à la Grèce. Pays: Grèce. Notes-memos-rapports-questions diverses, Box 1223, 'Rapport sur la situation alimentaire en Crete', Bengt Helger, 10 October 1942. Harry Ritter also stressed the limited 'use of Greek agricultural produce by the Wehrmacht', Harry Ritter Jr (1969), 'Hermann Neubacher and the German Occupation of the Balkans, 1940–1945', PhD, University of Virginia, p. 144.

39. PRO, FO371/32475, 'Preliminary Survey of the Olive Oil Situation in Greece', 1 October 1942.

40. Part of the 1940 tobacco crop of Samos was sold to the Germans (ACI, folder 69, 1 October 1941, 15172, Al Comando superiore forze armate delle isole Italiane dell'Egeo, Ufficio servizi, 'Risorse agricole'). Etmektsoglou-Koehn mentions that olive oil was confiscated in the Ionian islands and in Crete, although the Joint Relief Commission's accounts indicate that the Italians 'purchased' Cretan olive oil (Gabriella Etmektsoglou-Koehn (1995), 'Axis Exploitation of Wartime Greece, 1941–1943', PhD thesis, Emory University, p. 415; International Committee of the Red Cross Archives, Geneva, SG.11 Secours à la Grèce. Pays: Grèce. Notes-memos-rapports-questions diverses, Box 1223, 'Rapport sur la situation alimentaire en Crete', Bengt Helger, 10 October 1942.)

41. Etmektsoglou-Koehn, 'Axis Exploitation', pp. 410–11.
42. PRO, FO371/32475, no 494, letter to the British Legation, Stockholm, 16 October 1942; FO371/32475, 'Preliminary Survey of the Olive Oil Situation in Greece', 1 October 1942.
43. International Committee of the Red Cross Archives, Geneva, SG.11 Secours à la Grèce. Pays: Grèce. Notes-memos-rapports-questions diverses, Box 1223, 'Rapport sur la situation alimentaire en Crete', Bengt Helger, 10 October 1942.
44. Tsouderos Archive, General State Archives, Athens, Despatch E, Folder 2, 1941–1944, Episitismos, 'First Report of the Swedish Inspection Committee'.
45. PRO, FO 371/33176, 1942 Greece, R6750/281/19, 'Seizure of Greek Harvest', telegram from War Cabinet to Switzerland, 21 October 1942.
46. Argenti Archive, Korais Library, Chios, Chios during Second World War 1941–1945, Dossier I, Memorandum, Stockholm 19 July 1943, 34.
47. PRO, FO371/36507, Greece, file no 3, 'Aide-Memoire to the Royal Ministry of Foreign Affairs, Enclosure in Stockholm Despatch No 230 E.W. 15 December 1943'.
48. PRO, FO 371/36585, Relief in Greece 1943, 'Exposition of the Food Situation in Greece by Major A. Tsaousopoulos', 5 January 1943. For a similar remark see Etmektsoglou-Koehn ('Axis Exploitation', p. 416).
49. In mainland Greece during the last year of the occupation and in relation to guerrilla warfare, it seems that German soldiers were also engaged in food plundering, K. Papakongkos (ed.), *Arkheio Persson: Katokhika Dokoumenta tou DES Peloponnisou* (Athens, 1977), pp. 172, 206, 221–2.
50. An interesting example of the restricted nature of information and possibly of its manipulation is provided by the occupation of Samos by the Germans. Following a short period of occupation by the British in the autumn of 1943, British reports state that the Germans requisitioned all the foodstuffs left behind by the British. Yet a local inhabitant in his memoirs describes the thorough and organised looting of the British depots by the local population (Nikos Noou, *Ta Paidia tis Thyellas* (Athens, 1993), pp. 173–7).
51. Etmektsoglou-Koehn, 'Axis Exploitation', pp. 414–15.
52. Hondros, *Occupation and Resistance*, pp. 61–7; for an in-depth discussion see Etmektsoglou-Koehn, 'Axis Exploitation', pp. 308–43.
53. See, for example, PRO, WO304/8592, Appendix B, Report dated 10 April 1944; B. Helger (ed.), *Ravitaillement de la Grèce pendant l'Occupation 1941–1944 et pendant les Cinq Mois après la Libération* (Athens, 1949), p. 27.
54. Informant No 9, Informant No 17, Chios; Maria Manolakou, *Apo to Imerologio enos Paidiou tis Katokhis* (Athens, 1985), second edition, pp. 53–4; P. Karousis, *Mnimes apo tin Katokhi stin Khio* (Athens, 1985), p. 77.
55. Giorgos Margaritis, *Apo tin Itta sti Exegersi. Ellada: Anoixi 1941–Phthinoporo 1942* (Athens, 1993), p. 79; Helger, *Ravitaillement de la Grèce*, p. 2; ACI, folder 86, 19 February 1942, 'Comando militare delle Cicladi, Ordinanza N.55'; ACI, folder 31, 6 June 1941, 'Bando che disciplina la raccolta dei cereali per l'anno 1941 nelle isole Greche occupate dalle truppe Italiane'.
56. The 1941 output of wheat was approximately 500,000 tonnes according to Margaritis, *Apo tin Itta*, p. 64. According to Hondros it was 'less than half the normal average' (the average for 1937–40 was 901,719 tonnes), p. 67. Heinz Richter's figure for 1941 is 566,000 tons (Richter, *1936–1946: duo Epanastaseis*, p. 152). For Mazower, 'the 1941 harvest of most crops was between 15 and 30

per cent lower than it had been before the war' (Mazower, *Inside Hitler's Greece*, p. 26).

57. M. Negreponti-Delivanis, *Greece in Transition 1821–1971* (Thessaloniki, 1979), p. 147, citing A. Bacalbasis, *The Greek Economy 1941–4* (Athens, 1945).
58. PRO, FO371/36507, 'Memorandum on a Meeting at the British Legation on 6th December, 1943'. One reason for this difficulty was clearly that in the specific year production up to 2000 okes (5460 lbs) was not subject to taxation.
59. PRO, WO204/8594, 'Swedish-Swiss Red Cross Commission. Policy and correspondence aide-mémoire regarding increased food import to Greece'.
60. M. Theotokas Archive, Koraes Library, Chios, folder 7, 'Episitistikai anagkai Khiou'.
61. *Proodos*, 18 November 1941.
62. Mazower, *Inside Hitler's Greece*, p. 28; Margaritis, *Apo tin itta*, pp. 69–76.
63. Margaritis, *Apo tin Itta*, pp. 179–82.
64. Margaritis, *Apo tin Itta*, pp. 147–8.
65. Diamond, 'Agriculture', p. 23.
66. Helger, *Ravitaillement de la Grèce*, p. 22. The annual average wheat production figures were 310,000 tons for 1922–31, 930,000 tons for 1938–40, 566,000 tons for 1941 and 300,000 tons for 1942–43.
67. Ó Gráda, *Black '47 and Beyond*, p. 85.
68. Fleischer, *Stemma kai Svastika*, p. 196; M. Black, *A Cause for our Times: Oxfam, the First 50 Years* (Oxford, 1992), p. 8; Mazower, *Inside Hitler's Greece*, p. 41 citing Helger, *Ravitaillement de la Grèce*, p. 625; V.G. Valaoras, 'Some Effects of the Famine on the Population of Greece', *Milbank Memorial Fund Quarterly*, XXIV (1946): 225.
69. A serious drawback for this study is the unavailability of an age structure for the populations under examination. The closest census to the famine, that of 1940, provides only population figures disaggregated by sex. The censuses of 1928 and 1951 do provide age structure but both are too distant from the famine to be of value.
70. The life expectancies of Chios town, Vrontados and Ermoupolis have been calculated using the age structures recorded in the 1928 population census. The average numbers of births for the years 1928 and 1929 were used to calculate the infant mortality rate (IMR), while for the rest of the age groups the published mortality data for 1928 and 1929 have been utilized. Unfortunately, an age structure is not available for the rest of the populations examined here. The life expectancy for Greece is taken from S. Preston, N. Keyfitz and R. Schoen, *Causes of Death: Life Tables for National Populations* (New York, 1972), pp. 324, 326. For Mykonos, see V. Hionidou, 'The Demography of a Greek Island, Mykonos 1859–1959: a Family Reconstitution Study' (PhD thesis, University of Liverpool, 1993), Table 6.8.
71. For Athens/Piraeus, Thessaloniki and the twenty-seven towns only aggregate data are available and that only for the period 1940 to 1944. These were drawn from archival sources rather than from the original certificates. The twenty-seven towns do not include Athens/Piraeus or Thessaloniki.
72. For Athens/Piraeus, Thessaloniki and the twenty-seven towns the average number of deaths in 1940 has been used to establish the baseline.
73. For an estimate of the base population figures see Table 2.2.

74. This estimate is based on the number of deaths only. The population of Thessaloniki was 226,486 in 1940 but the arrival of large numbers of refugees during the occupation period complicates the matter.

75. Vasilis Gounaris, K. Vasilis and Petros Papapolyviou, 'Ekteleseis, Via kai Asitia sti Thessaloniki tis Katokhis. Erevna kai Katagraphi', in Vasilis Gounaris and Petros Papapolyviou (eds), *O Phoros tou Aimatos stin Katokhiki Thessaloniki. Xeni Kyriarkhia, Antistasi kai Epiviosi* (Thessaloniki, 2001), pp. 135–40. By 1939, the mortality rate in Greece due to malaria was as low as four per 100,000 population (PRO, WO204/9003, Health conditions in Greece, 9). Still, this rate disguised the high geographical and annual variation of malaria incidence within the country (K. Dimissas, 'Peri tis Ektaseos kai Entaseos tis Epidimikotitos tis Elonosias kata tin therinophthinoporinin Periodon 1942', *Praktika Iatrikis Etaireias Athinon*, 5 December 1942: 505).

76. Gounaris and Papapolyviou, 'Ekteleseis, Via kai Asitia', pp. 136–40.

77. Athanasios Mantekos, 'I ex Asitias kai Elonosias Thnesimotis eis Thessalonikin kai agrotikas Periokhas tis Makedonias (1940–1943)', *Praktika Akadimias Athinon*, Athens, 23 March 1944: 75–87.

78. Dimissas, 'Peri tes Ektaseos', pp. 507–9.

79. Dimissas, 'Peri tes Ektaseos', p. 509.

80. Dimissas, 'Peri tes Ektaseos', pp. 505–22.

81. Helger, *Ravitaillement de la Grèce*, p. 388; International Committee of the Red Cross Archives, Geneva, G; Secours aux population civiles, Sg 11 pays Grèce, box 1225, correspondence avec la délégation en Grèce, 1941–1944, 'Aide mémoire from Stockholm, 10 December 1942'; International Committee of the Red Cross Archives, Geneva, Sg.11 Secours a la Grèce. Pays: Grèce. Notes-Memos-Rapports-Questions diverses, box 1223, Aide mémoire ravitaillement des Cyclades, des îles Ioniennes et de l'Epire', Berne, 24 May 1944.

82. A. Laiou-Thomadakis, 'The Politics of Hunger: Economic Aid to Greece, 1943–45', *Journal of the Hellenic Diaspora*, VII (1980): 27.

83. I. Travlos and A. Kokkou, *Ermoupolis. I dimiourgia mias neas Polis sti Syro stis Arkhes tou 19ou Aiona* (Athens, 1980).

84. Moreover, the population of Ano Syros had a much closer relationship with the countryside – a relationship present at both the personal level, with family ties connecting the two, but also at the level of religion. Catholics inhabited Ano Syros and the countryside whereas Ermoupolis was predominantly Orthodox.

85. PRO, FO371/36490, 'Monsieur Allard's Arrangements for Control of Greek Native Produce'.

86. V. Valaoras, 'To Anastima kai o Typos Aimatos (ABO) ton Ellinon', *Elliniki Anthropologiki Etaireia* (1968), Table 2.

87. During the famine young adult males experienced proportionately higher mortality compared to other age groups and compared to females (Hionidou, 2006, pp. 165–78). Marriages were rare during the famine years due to social conditions, see, for example, V. Hionidou, 'The Demography of a Greek Famine: Mykonos 1941–1942', *Continuity and Change*, X (1995): 285.

3
The Politics of Famine Relief for Occupied Greece

George Kazamias

Introduction

From the autumn of 1941 onwards, the Western Allies were faced with the developing famine conditions in Greece. The aim of this chapter seeks to examine the politics of famine relief for occupied Greece. Specifically, it focuses on the process whereby the Western Allies reached the decision to grant permission for the relief effort to take place, as well as on the reasons why such permission was granted.

To look first at the information available to the Allies regarding the famine in Greece. If the Allied governments had some initial doubts regarding the magnitude of the problem, by the autumn of 1941 the deterioration of conditions in Greece was clearly dramatic. A small sample indicating the intelligence available to the British government before the end of December 1941 is set out below. All the sources stress the gravity of the situation. The dates of these communications also indicate that the British government was aware from a very early stage of the urgency of the food situation in Greece:

4 July 1941, R 6763/96/19 tel. Cairo to FO: 'The food situation is extremely grave . . .'

24 July 1941, PRO, FO 371 /29840, R7070 'Summary of outstanding Greek Questions': 'All reports state that starvation conditions prevail and that there is acute danger of epidemics. Cholera is stated to have already broken out in Piraeus and other coastal towns. Children are dying of hunger and women waiting in the food queues are seen fainting from weakness. The streets are littered with dead horses, dogs and cats.'

PRO, FO 371 /29840, R 7308, tel. no. 300 SAVING: '. . . Famine conditions are making themselves felt in Greece . . .'

PRO, FO 371 /29840, R 7349, 'Statement by Lincoln McVeagh, the U.S. Minister in Greece, who left the country on 5th June 1941': '. . . The people is starving and the Germans seize all foodstuffs.'

26 July 1941, FO 371 /29840, R 7401, U.S. Chargé d'Affaires, Athens: 'conditions . . . terrible and the population is practically starving'.

R 8523, 17 Sept. 1941, from Censorship: 'the food situation is disastrous'.

W 13428/49/49 tel., 12 Nov. 1941 Berne to FO: 'More people have died in the past week (from starvation) than in the preceding month . . .'

Based on the above, the Foreign Office had almost predicted a famine as early as 16 July 1941. In a summary of this date of outstanding Greek questions, Edward Warner of the Southern Department of the Foreign Office, had written that: 'this [the food situation] is likely to be the most difficult question of all. Greece produces little food and is almost entirely dependent on imported cereals.'[1]

The United States administration was in possession of similar information at much the same time. This was for two main reasons: first, the large Greek-American community in the US and second, the later entry of the US into the war. As early as July 1941 – some five months before the US entered the war – appeals had started flowing into Washington. The US administration received information on Greece mainly from Greek-American circles, both persons and organisations. Of the latter, the most prominent were the Greek War Relief Association (GWRA) and the American Hellenic Educational Progressive Association (AHEPA) (see Chapter 4). The GWRA had brought the food situation inside occupied Greece to the attention of the US government as early as July 1941. A separate appeal by Emmanouil Tsouderos, prime minister of the Greek government-in-exile, had reached President Roosevelt in late December 1941.[2] The large Greek-American presence in the US also meant that (at times considerable) information would reach the federal authorities through news from home sent in letters from relatives. It also meant that news coverage of events in Greece would be received by a comparatively large and anxious lobby, eager to act in aid of its homeland.

The US had the added advantage that, until December 1941, it was not at war with the Axis. Lincoln McVeagh, the US minister in Greece, was withdrawn from the country soon after the beginning of the occupation, together with the small embassy staff. However, Burton Berry, the Second

Counsellor of the Legation, was posted to Rome, charged with representing American interests in Greece. Throughout the summer, autumn and early winter of 1941, Berry returned to Greece on a number of occasions. In subsequent reports to the State Department he described the appalling conditions in Greece and urged action.[3] In one such report, dated 20 September 1941, he stated that: 'Greece today is dangerously near starvation. The people urgently need wheat, rice, sugar and fats . . . The hope of all Greeks is for supplies from abroad.'[4]

Similar reports were also available from the Red Cross; from appeals originating in the Vatican; and also from numerous appeals and *démarches* by the Greek government-in-exile and its diplomatic representatives.[5] Further information on the famine was also forthcoming from other US diplomatic missions in Europe (in Turkey, Germany, Italy, Bulgaria and Romania), as well as from the stream of US citizens who started to leave Greece after the occupation and continued to do so for some months until the entry of the US into the war.[6] Thus, the government of the US was well informed during the critical months of 1941 from sources that were both diverse and reliable, sources that relayed first-hand information both directly and indirectly from occupied Greece.

In addition to the above, there were also the representations of the Greek government-in-exile. It is true that Tsouderos' handling of the matter between June 1941 and the end of the year left much to be desired. Though apparently aware of the problem, Tsouderos initially accepted the validity of British arguments in favour of the blockade.[7] Furthermore, he concurred in the sale to the British authorities of Australian wheat purchased by Greece before its fall (the cargoes had been stopped at Suez). It was only late in 1941, when the crisis had reached its peak, that he pressured both the British and the US governments for action.[8]

Policy

(a) British blockade policy

Forms of blockade have been used in war since antiquity. More recent antecedents of organised large-scale blockade were the continental blockade during the Napoleonic wars and the blockade imposed on Germany during the First World War.[9] On the outbreak of the Second World War, Britain once again imposed a blockade of enemy territory. The aim was to stop any form of supplies from reaching the enemy. Since the Germans controlled the occupied countries of Europe, goods traded with enemy or enemy-occupied countries were declared contraband and either confiscated or prevented from proceeding to their destination.

After a shaky and not altogether effective beginning, blockade policy was outlined by Winston Churchill in a speech of 20 August 1940 in the House of Commons. The blockade was placed in the context of total war against Germany and was considered one of the vital steps needed to win the war. Beside the goods necessary for German industry, the blockade also included foodstuffs, which were not to be allowed through the blockade into continental Europe. The aim was to put pressure on the food stocks of the occupiers. Thus, the policy stipulated that no food would be allowed into Europe until its liberation, when 'food and freedom' would go hand in hand into the liberated countries.[10]

(b) The Axis

Faced with the developing famine, the position of the Axis was quite simple. The German view was that Greece was the responsibility of Italy. Therefore no action appears to have been recommended and none was taken (at least until much later when the Axis authorities realised that the delivery of famine relief in Greece was boosting the cause of the Allies). Italy on the other hand, even though it may have wanted to help, could not do so, as food shortages were already developing at home. The Italians were rather more inclined to accept their responsibility (after all they were in nominal control of the greatest part of Greek territory) but they were fully aware of their inability either to help Greece (because of food supply problems in Italy itself) or to force Germany to take measures in this direction.[11]

On the other hand, from early on during the occupation, the German authorities in Greece publicly declared that the suffering of the Greeks was simply the result of the British-imposed continental blockade. The Germans carefully avoided replying to the British allegation, based on their interpretation of international conventions, that the provisioning of an occupied country was the responsibility of the occupying power. Nonetheless, the German authorities in Greece were prepared to allow relief to be sent to Greece and guaranteed that they would not interfere with the ships involved and further guaranteed that they would not confiscate any such supplies.[12]

(c) Greece

It was clear that the situation in Greece made necessary, indeed imperative, some form of initiative on behalf of the country, and that this would have to come from its allies. Beyond its humanitarian dimension, Greece's plight had valuable propaganda content: there were fears in some British circles that the Greeks might turn xenophobe or even pro-Axis. The question that Edward Warner of the Foreign Office put was very clear:

> ... can we view with equanimity the reduction of the Greek population by famine, its health, particularly in the case of children, ruined and in outlook violently anti-British?[13]

With the benefit of hindsight, we can say that that the famine (even in the darkest days of 1941–42) does not appear to have given rise to increased collaborationism in Greece (though this area needs further study[14]). However, the fear that the Greeks' will to resist the occupier would be undermined by famine was well founded: the main wave of large-scale armed resistance begins in earnest from 1942 onwards. In any event, the argument that Britain had abandoned its ally and was hiding behind legalistic arguments at the expense of Greek lives was certainly a powerful one. As Konstantinos Logothetopoulos, Prime Minister of the second collaborationist government during the occupation, claimed in his memoirs:

> Even when the issue was the life of the Greek people which was in danger of death from famine, (England) instead of hastening to its aid, exhausted all the legalistic arguments on the international responsibility of the occupier to provide food for the occupied country; [these arguments] would [certainly] allow the dead Greeks and the undernourished younger generation to sue the ... dictators.[15]

Thus both sides in the conflict saw propaganda value in the problem of relief for Greece. For the Axis, it was an occasion to try and prise the Greeks away from their pro-British sympathies. For the British, it was a case of maintaining the will of the people to resist (a question of some military significance) and also of maintaining the traditionally strong influence exercised by Britain in the country in the post-war world.

Untying the Gordian knot: the reaction of the Western Allies

What we mean by the 'Gordian knot' is the complex of relationships between different groups in Britain and the US that interacted in dealing with the problem of famine relief for Greece. We can distinguish different groups in the two countries, operating at different levels. Thus in Britain there are two government departments that mainly dealt with the problem, the Ministry of Economic Warfare and the Foreign Office. In the US, the government agency that dealt mainly with policy (and thus with the question of famine relief for Greece) was the State Department. However, in the US, there was a proliferation of other agencies that also dealt with relief (including relief for Greece).[16]

Both in Britain and in the US there were also extra-governmental agencies pressing for relief for Greece. In Britain, some pressure in favour of relief for Greece gradually built up, as is demonstrated by questions in the House of Commons[17] and press coverage of the famine, as well as by the activities of the public at large, notably the famine relief committees that were established in Britain (see Chapter 10). Some have seen these outside pressure groups as the continuation of groups supporting pacifism or international brotherhood, both causes that had been marginalised by the advent of war.[18] In any event, wartime conditions allowed the British government to control closely the information that was made available to the press and the general public.

In the US, outside the Roosevelt administration, pressure in favour of relief originated among the Greek-American community and also, to an extent, in both the Congress and the press (see Chapter 4). Both within and outside the administration, there existed a multiplicity of actors: numerous government departments and sub-groups, the Congress, the Greek-American community and individual citizens. All exhibited some interest or attempted in one way or another to influence policy, with varying degrees of success. At the same time, while communication channels were to some degree restricted, they were not necessarily monopolized by the state. A flow of information, as well as considerable communication and cooperation, was effected by means of the links offered by channels such as the Greek-American community. Information was received and disseminated among its members as well as outside the community through family links with Greece itself. When the United States' entry in the war in December 1941 limited these contacts, considerable information could, and did become available to Greek-American circles through the channels available to the Greek government-in-exile. As a result, in the United States there existed a relative diffuseness of information, with nothing like the quasi-monopoly of information enjoyed by Whitehall in Britain.

(a) The British government

By the end of 1941, conditions in Greece were fast making it clear that, since Britain had instituted and upheld the blockade, the ball was mainly in the British court. At this point, a tug of war within the British government developed between the Foreign Office (under Anthony Eden, the Foreign Secretary, who was generally in favour of relief for Greece) and the Ministry of Economic Warfare (MEW, under Hugh Dalton, who was in favour of maintaining the blockade).

The Foreign Office, a long-established government department, with long-standing links with Greece, was at the time acting as the patron of the Greek government-in-exile. As a result, the Foreign Office appears to have acquired a good idea of the situation in Greece as early as July 1941. It did consider the possibility of allowing Greece to starve and rejected it. For the Foreign Office, it was clear that anything other than the lifting of the blockade, at least for wheat, of which Germany had no shortage, was inadequate.[19]

On the other hand we have the Ministry of Economic Warfare.[20] Under Dalton, this pursued a policy of actively supporting, and even strengthening, the blockade. Dalton favoured a hard-line policy. In his own words, he was 'against all moderation in this [the blockade] and in all the other forms of economic pressure which my Ministry was supposed to exercise' and sought 'firm and total enforcement'. With 'great singleness of purpose', he was all for a 'hard boiled policy'. This was in line with his overall policy, which had – very appropriately – as its motto the phrase 'belligerency at all times'.[21] According to Dalton, the

> passage [in Churchill's speech of 20 August 1940] on Blockade and on Food and Freedom going into Europe together . . . was lifted almost bodily from my brief supplied to him before the weekend. It could not have been better put.[22]

What is more, the blockade was probably the single most effective weapon in the hands of the Ministry of Economic Warfare and probably the main reason for its existence as a government ministry. On the specific question of the Greek famine, the Ministry of Economic Warfare seems to have favoured a hard line. This is indicated by the answers to parliamentary questions that had been tabled as well as by internal correspondence both in the ministry itself and with other departments, principally with the Foreign Office. The line followed was roughly that, although the gravity of the situation in Greece was clear and recognized and although all the moral arguments in favour of relief for Greece were accepted, the decisive factor was that no precedent should be established in providing relief for an occupied country. Feeding the population was the occupier's responsibility and no help should be given to aid it in fulfilling this responsibility. This aggressive, utilitarian approach seems to have been much in line with Dalton's character and disposition and in keeping with the policy he advocated.[23]

(b) The US government

On the other hand, the United States came to the problem with fewer preconceptions. In the US, there was no government department to defend blockade. The US had no need to uphold such a rigid policy. The Roosevelt administration was not a coalition government and it was clearly in the 'driver's seat' as far as a number of issues were concerned (including financial issues). Furthermore, parts of the US administration did have an axe to grind as far as Britain was concerned and wished to make sure that the preponderance in decision-making shifted from London to Washington. In the words of the Weekly Political Summary compiled at the British Embassy (14 May 1942):

> On the one hand the Board of Economic Warfare under Vice-President Wallace and his alter ego Milo Perkins, are dreaming of a kind of world New Deal. This group of self-confident, country-bred liberal reformers have prepared blueprints to reorganize the world in order to secure the best distribution of persons and things with a bold programme for spending the vast natural resources of the United States upon world reconstruction.
>
> The Wilkie-Welles-Luce group . . . see the world as a vast market for the American producer, industrialist and trader. They are believers in the American Century, energetic technicians and businessmen filled with romantic, equally self-confident, economic imperialism, eager to convert the world to the American pattern.
>
> Besides these there is the Farm Bloc, powerful but with no foreign policy except the belief the food will win the war, and the various movements advocating forms of neo-Wilsonian international organization.
>
> The clash between those who plan world social and economic arrangements and the dynamic militant technocrats is perhaps the most important political manifestation at the moment.[24]

In the United States, policy did not necessarily come (or even pretend to come) from a single source. A host of services, departments and associations (among them the president, the State Department, the Lend-Lease Administration, the GWRA, the American Red Cross and the army, to cite only some) were at one or another time invited to offer suggestions on ad hoc actions, or had to interpret the 'policy' to the extent that there was one. Each of these sources of policy apparently followed its own way, with minimal interference from the others. In this vein, President Roosevelt, in the opinion of Sked and Cook:

> presented a picture of perfect aimlessness . . . He objected to Churchill's old fashioned 'power politics' and relied on his fellow-republican and anti-imperialist, Stalin, to help him create a world of 'democracy and peace'.[25]

This situation sharply contrasted with the clear policies of the 'economic royalists' within the United States administration, who demanded an ever bigger share of United States trade in the world market at the expense of Britain. The Foreign Economic Administration – under whose aegis relief for Greece was managed for part of the period examined – was an 'economic royalist' princedom.[26]

What then of decision-making in this climate? Across the Atlantic, matters were less clear-cut. The Roosevelt administration tended to react to pressures, internal and external. Roosevelt himself was aware of the problem, as were most (if not all) of the relevant departmental heads in the State Department. Their reaction appears from the start to have been in favour of relief. This reaction is difficult to explain in terms of a friendly personal or political background or preconception in favour of Greece because these do not appear to have been particularly significant. Some importance may be attributed to the stereotypes of United States' altruism and philanthropy, compounded with a native and long-established pragmatism and self-interest. However, these essentially moral influences, do not appear, by themselves, to account for the pressure in favour of a pro-relief policy. It is when they are considered within the framework of overall *attitudes* towards policy that these factors take on their true dimensions.

The solution: lifting the blockade

The stumbling block was clearly British blockade policy. Despite the disagreements within Whitehall and with the transatlantic partner (which were not made public), attempts were made to find a solution that would allow relief into Greece without – somehow – breaking the blockade. A number of schemes were discussed; threatening to starve Italian civilians in Abyssinia was one; secret deliveries of food carried in small boats from the Middle East was another; even evacuating some 10,000 Greek women and children from 'high risk areas' was discussed. However, by

September 1941 only one scheme was actually in operation. This was dubbed the 'Turkish Scheme' and provided for a limited amount of food-stuffs (some 50,000 tons) to be purchased in Turkey and shipped to Greece, assuming of course that this amount was available (see Chapter 5). However, it soon became clear that the amounts available were pitifully small and wholly inadequate. Rather than 50,000 tons by January 1942, when the scheme was wound up, only around 6,500 tons in total had been transported to Greece in two small Turkish steamers (the *Kurtuluş* and the *Dumlupınar*).[27]

Discussions between the British government departments continued for the rest of 1941. Yet, despite evidence presented by the Foreign Office to the Ministry of Economic Warfare on conditions in Greece, the reaction of the Ministry of Economic Warfare remained firmly negative. A telegram to the British Embassy in Washington clearly demonstrates the position:

> The Cabinet considered the question ('that we should allow the Turks to supply wheat which we should substitute from our own stocks in the Middle East') here on December 24th and unanimously supported the view of the Minister of Economic Warfare that the suggested supply of wheat to Greece through the blockade . . . was . . . unacceptable.[28]

However the situation in Greece was so serious that policy clearly had to change. Despite the public show of unanimity, since Dalton seemed unwilling to allow a change in policy, a group of government officials from other departments seem to have resolved to do it for him.

On 10, 13 and 14 January 1942, a series of telegrams arguing strongly in favour of relief for Greece to be admitted through the blockade (headed 'HUSH-MOST SECRET') were exchanged between the Minister of State for the Middle East (Oliver Lyttleton), the Lord Privy Seal (Clement Attlee), the Foreign Secretary (Eden) and the Prime Minister (Winston Churchill). These seem to have decided the issue.[29] After some deliberation as to the wording of the statements to be made, the British government, in a surprising reversal of official policy up to that time, publicly announced the first shipment of 8000 tons of wheat to Greece. The public statement indicated that this was a one-off initiative, not to be followed by any others; the FO and the MEW, however, had already started working on the details of a permanent settlement of the issue. The 'Swedish scheme', as it was called, provided for Canadian wheat (and later other foodstuffs as well) to be transported on Swedish-owned ships from Canada and the US to Greece through the continental blockade.

The plan, though largely hatched in the Foreign Office, was brokered by the Swedish government and, for reasons of tact, presented to Berlin as a Swedish initiative. Relief was to be administered by a specially instituted Swedish-Swiss Relief Committee, headed by a Swede, and under the auspices of the International Committee of the Red Cross (see Chapter 6).[30] Guarantees were to be sought (and were given) by the Axis authorities that they would not interfere with the supplies or their distribution. It is no exaggeration to say that a large number of Greeks especially in urban centres either directly (through the soup-kitchens) or indirectly (through the easing of pressures on food stocks and the stabilisation of prices) owed their survival to this scheme.

The two ministries seem to have agreed on the terms to be proposed to the Germans as early as 18 February 1942.[31] In a 'Memorandum by the Minister of Economic Warfare' to the War Cabinet, dated 14 February 1942, the Swedish scheme was discussed for the first time, as the guidelines for a permanent supply arrangement were put forward. This document appears to have been Dalton's last involvement in the matter of the blockade of Greece. Only a few days later, he was 'promoted' to the Board of Trade. The Dalton approach to the blockade had been abandoned. It is noteworthy that there is no mention of this rather stunning change of policy in Dalton's memoirs.[32] The agreement on Greek relief that developed was the only major and long-term agreement between the belligerents that proved workable. It breached the lines of confrontation and allowed for food to be shipped to Greece throughout the period of Axis occupation.

Why did the policy change? An interpretation

Britain

We should finally look at the reasons why the policy changed. Let us first look at Britain. The question to answer is why was there a change in policy? Regarding Greek relief in early 1942, the problem for Britain is multi-faceted. Allowing relief into Greece under Nazi occupation was potentially the beginning of a process that could dismantle the whole apparatus of economic warfare. Although not in any way comparable to the plight of the Greeks, Belgians were also suffering shortages and there were some fears regarding conditions in Norway.

It is also true that since the forceful speech of Churchill of 20 August 1940, economic warfare had not lived up to expectations: it had not brought the Axis to its collective knees and it had failed to cause the occupied populations to rise up. On the other hand, the blockade of

Greece was offering the Axis considerable material for propaganda (in Turkey as well as in Greece) and it appeared to be undermining (or at least endangering) the traditional British position. The shape the question acquired was thus how the longer-term interests of Britain could be preserved while also saving at least a part of the blockade policy. Indeed, the concession to Greece allowed Britain to maintain its hard line on relief intended for other parts of occupied Europe for the rest of the war.[33] On the issue of longer-term interests, according to the Foreign Office, the change was necessary so that Greece, a country traditionally friendly to Britain, would continue to be so: it seems that the FO *did* consider it 'important to us to have a healthy population of seven and a half million Anglo-phile Greeks to reinforce our position in the Eastern Mediterranean after the war'.[34] Yet post-war geopolitics were not the only reason. Other considerations were also present: domestic public opinion, as evidenced in parliamentary questions submitted to the House of Commons and also by other expressions of sympathy for Greece: the Oxford Committee for Famine Relief, subsequently to evolve into Oxfam, was created in 1942 with the express purpose of 'the relief . . . of famine and sickness arising as a result of the war'[35] (see Chapter 10). Numerous other similar committees and dignitaries were also active.[36]

However, probably equally important for the Foreign Office and also for the prime minister, who took the final decision on lifting the blockade of Greece, was public opinion in the US, as well as the US position vis-à-vis the blockade in general. In the US, Greek-American organisations were already applying pressure on the Roosevelt administration and appealing to the American public for aid to Greece, regardless of British objections (see Chapter 4). Even Eleanor Roosevelt seems to have taken the matter up in one of her newspaper articles that were syndicated throughout the US.

If Dalton and the Ministry of Economic Warfare were insensitive to such pressures from abroad, other policy-makers were not. Luckily for Greece, it was these others that carried the day. While looking at the American angle, it is also interesting to note that once the scheme was under way, although Britain officially had the major say in it, the scheme was in effect largely run or overseen by the US. Indeed, it was used as an experimental pilot scheme in advance of the return of the Allies to continental Europe. This de facto American dominance may perhaps be interpreted as yet another early precursor of the shape of the post-war world.

Returning to the British government, its efforts displayed an interesting mixture of feelings and intentions. Until early 1942 at least, the British government was not prepared to move in the direction of outright concessions. A struggle seemed to be taking place as to whether to enforce the blockade or make concessions. The British government also appeared to consider thoroughly the possible effects any concession to Greece might have: Greece should not be seen to be favoured above the other Allies. The visible, outward manifestation of this struggle was the wandering course from one inadequate scheme to another: from the 'Turkish scheme' to the evacuation plan to secret shipments.

Thus, in theory the blockade remained in force until September 1942, when the Swedish scheme began operating. In essence, however, the blockade was lifted in September 1941, when the first relief shipments from Turkey were authorized and shipped to Greece. In the meantime, throughout the tragic and critical winter of 1941–42, British reaction to any concession (essentially from Dalton's Ministry of Economic Warfare) was strong enough to prevent any plan from maturing to a point where it might provide adequate relief for Greece.

To sum up, we should say that the British government as a whole was not insensitive to the crisis created by the war and the effects of the naval blockade imposed on Greece. However, it was equally not prepared to go all the way in any particular direction. It was not unscrupulous enough either to abandon Greece to its fate or retaliate against Italy (the weaker and more ineffective Axis partner) by deliberately starving Italian civilians in Abyssinia in order to achieve its goal of squeezing food out of Italy for the Greek population.[37] By themselves the numerous plans and attempts mentioned above provide enough positive evidence to this end. It may be said, however, that in its attempts to find a solution, the British government could not (at least until 1942) overcome the stumbling block created by its own earlier policy declarations. The blockade policy, as set out in Churchill's speech of 20 August 1940 and repeated in the declaration of 10 March 1941,[38] ruled out any concessions to countries (even Allied countries) overrun by the enemy. The crucial period from June 1941 to February 1942 was spent in attempts to find a formula that would enable the British government both to alter its policy and keep it unchanged at the same time. Needless to say, this attempt proved to be self-defeating.

The US

In the United States, however, in contrast with Britain, both the input to policy and its output varied. The approach of the personalities involved was also different. They do not appear to have exhibited the streak of stark, cold realism witnessed in Britain. Some rhetoric with altruistic and 'idealistic' undertones is evident, primarily in public statements. Otherwise, an apparently cool, 'sanitized' approach is apparent.

The policy referred to above, may be explained by reference to the strength of US 'economic royalism'. Proliferation of sources of policy may have led to clashes strong enough to prevent the formation of an official policy. On the other hand, this lack of official policy makes studies of issues that are specific (albeit marginal to the overall grand strategy such as the Greek famine) more relevant to policy matters. It is in such areas, it may be argued, that some of the strongest trends that had a potential to develop into policies were most obvious.

In this respect, United States policy towards the Greek famine may again be considered as a foretaste of things to come. Relief to Greece was a form of intervention, a line of policy that fitted with the viewpoint of the interventionist lobby in America. At the same time it appealed to idealists. It was a step away from isolationism, without appearing to be so. Cloaked in its 'moral' dimension, it gave rise to few objections. It provided the 'economic royalists' with access to a new market, and one that traditionally belonged to the sterling area. It also appealed to the worldwide New Dealers, adherents of the line of thought that America had to redistribute some of its wealth to less fortunate nations, for the simple reason that this was the only way to stimulate their recovery (and subsequently trade) and avoid future economic crises.

This is not to say that all American action in Greece was part of a larger plan, with the United States taking a longer-term view of its strategic and security interests. Such a view does not appear to be justified, at least in the case of Greek relief. The actions of the United States were apparently governed by ad hoc measures; these, in turn, were the application of a very general attitude that can scarcely be called a 'policy', being apparently no more than a general outline of principles. The principles were there. None of them, however, may be considered to have been the predominant one in shaping policy on Greek relief.[39]

Concluding remarks

In conclusion, we can say that Britain used all its accumulated skills and experience to attain its goals in Greece and to reconcile its policy with wider wartime demands. Initially Britain appeared prepared to go so far as to leave Greece to its fate; later it was ready to use relief as a means to maintain its dominant position in Greece. The fact that it did not achieve political domination and that its position was (soon after the war) eroded is only a reflection of the progressive limitation of Britain's role. The seat of power was swiftly shifting westwards, across the Atlantic, to the United States. At least a part of the British elite was unable to appreciate this fact. Wartime Greek relief is an area where this trans-atlantic predominance, from an early stage, was obvious to anybody who examined the subject closely. Britain wanted the United States to help it win the war; it recognized that the United States would be vital in this effort and realized that it would have to play a major role in determining the post-war order. What was not as clearly recognized by officials, especially at the time in the US, was that the case of the famine foreshadowed the inevitable involvement of the United States in Greece after the war.

The United States attitude was at the other extreme. Its behaviour was based on an ad hoc approach which was understandable perhaps in view of its inexperience. At times it could be described as impulsive, if not instinctive. Indeed, the fact that it gravitated towards relief could be interpreted as a somewhat clumsy and ill-defined attempt at involvement. In an admirably idealistic but hopelessly naive way, it attempted to deal with the case in hand in a detached, sterilized manner, appearing to believe that relief could be isolated from the political and other realities of the day. This detachment was to continue until 1947, when the sudden decision of Britain to disentangle itself from responsibilities in Greece, jolted the United States into action. It need not have been so; the suddenness of the action could have been anticipated. In the developing bi-polar divide, increasing United States' involvement in Greece was in direct relationship to the decline of British strength and influence. As demonstrated by US involvement in Greek relief, the decline in British influence was evident from an earlier stage: throughout the war the vast majority of assistance to Greece (and Britain) came from across the Atlantic. What fed the Greeks throughout the occupation was mostly Canadian wheat, and pulses, dried fish, vitamins and powdered milk produced in the United States, transported in Swedish ships and paid for (mainly) with United States Lend-Lease money. What flooded Greece after its liberation was United Nations Relief and Rehabilation Administration supplies, mostly of United States origin. To this wholesale 'invasion', Britain, exhausted by years of war, had little to add. During the occupation, Britain sent relatively little to Greece in the way of food. The most tangible (and effective) British contribution consisted of the British Liaison Officers (BLOs) scattered all over Greece working with the Greek resistance organisations. However in most cases, apart from paying with *khryses lires* (gold sovereigns) for goods and services in Greece, the BLOs had little involvement in wartime relief.

For each of the two countries involved, the case of Greek relief had something to illustrate. For Britain, a country with a traditionally major global role and a long tradition of active involvement in Greek affairs, it could be said that this series of events was the precursor of an imperial sunset. For the United States, the fledgling superpower, still struggling to reconcile itself with its newly-acquired power and world role, it was but the beginning of the journey of an 'innocent abroad'.[40]

Notes

1. See PRO FO/371, 16 July R 7038/96/19, 'Outstanding Greek Questions' (drawn up by Edward Warner).
2. The appeal from Tsouderos was submitted to the State Department on 22 December 1941. See 868.48/2012, letter, from the Greek minister in Washington, Kimon Diamantopoulos, to the Under-Secretary of State, Sumner Welles, also printed in *Foreign Relations of the United States* (henceforward *FRUS*), *Diplomatic Papers, 1942*, volume II, *Europe* (Washington, 1962), p. 726. The appeal was transmitted to President Roosevelt and a draft reply was prepared on 31 December 1941. The draft was signed by the president on the same day. See 848.68/1194 and 868.48/2012, also in *FRUS*, pp. 727–30.
3. Berry went so far as to take the initiative in approaching the Red Cross representatives in Marseilles and Bern to this end; see 868.48/1178, tel. no 1903, 5 December 1941. For this initiative he was reprimanded by the State Department and told not to repeat such approaches; see 868.48/1178, State Department tel. of 9 Dec. 1941.
4. See Roosevelt Presidential Library, Hyde Park, New York, President's Secretary File (PSF), Box no. 70, PSF-Vatican: M. Taylor, *The Food Situation in Greece, A Memorandum Requested by Mr. Taylor*, signed by Burton Y. Berry, Rome, Italy, 20 September, 1941.
5. For an example of a report from the Vatican see previous footnote. See, for example, 868.48/2011, appeal by Tsouderos to Roosevelt, 22 December 1941; also 868.48/2012, from Diamantopoulos to Welles, 24 December 1941, and 27 April 1942.
6. These included the missions to *Germany* (868.5018/9, tel. no. 1918 of 15 May 1941, see also 860h.5018, also /14, tel. no. 3237 of 21 August 1941 and /18, 3863 of 23 October 1941; and see 868.5018/15, tel. no. 1271 of August 26, 1941, /16 tel. no. 1433 of 17 September, 1941, also in 868.00/1128, /17, tel. no. 1630 of 20 October, 1941, also /27, tel. no. 2609 of 20 April 1942, also in 868.48/3027); *Bulgaria* (see 868.5018/10, tel. no. 286 of 21 June, also in 740.0011 EW 1939-/12281; and 22 December 27 1941, also in 740.0011 EW 1939-/17921); *Romania* (see 868.5018/12, tel. no. 662 of 17 July 1941). Among the neutral countries, *Switzerland* (see 868.48/3523, 3442 and 3318 also 868.5018/28, tel. no. 3442 of 2 October, 1942, also in 868.5017/10 and /29, tel. no. 4915 of 31 October 1942 also in 868.48/3315); and numerous communications from

Turkey (see 868.5018/19, tel. no. 141 of 9 December 1941, /24, tel. no. 87 of 16 February 1941, /25, tel. no. 22 of 7 January 1941).

7. See Emmanouil Tsouderos, *O Episitismos 1941–44, Mesi Anatoli* (Athens, 1948), p. 17.

8. For Tsouderos' eventual threat to resign see also Lena Divani, *I Politiki ton Exoriston Ellinikon Kyverniseon 1941–1944* (Athens, 1991), p. 195.

9. For a review of blockade and its effects during the Napoleonic Wars see, for example, F. Crouzet, 'Wars, Blockade, and Economic Change in Europe, 1792–1815', *Journal of Economic History*, XXIV (1964): 567–88. For economic warfare and blockade during the Crimean war, see Olive Anderson, 'Economic Warfare in the Crimean War', *Economic History Review* (new series), XIV (1961): 34–47. For the blockade of Germany during the First World War, see for example, A.C. Bell, *A History of the Blockade of Germany and of the Countries associated with Germany in the Great War: Austria-Hungary, Bulgaria and Turkey, 1914–1918* (London, 1937). During the First World War, the blockade enforced by the Entente Powers (Britain, France and Russia) had led to the creation of the Commission for the Relief for Belgium (headed by Herbert Hoover), which brought relief supplies for Belgium and Northern France, mainly through neutral Holland. The Second World War blockade is examined in detail in William N. Medlicott, *The Economic Blockade*, 2 vols (London, 1952–59) (reference to Greece is made in vol. II). For the US and economic warfare, see David L. Gordon and Royden Dangerfield, *The Hidden Weapon, the Story of Economic Warfare* (New York, 1947) (for Greece, see particularly pp. 131–6).

10. See Ben Pimlott (ed.), *The Second World War Diaries of Hugh Dalton, 1940–45* (London, 1986), p. 76.

11. According to the terms of the 1936 Berlin-Rome Axis Agreement, Greece, Albania and Yugoslavia belonged to the Italian sphere of interest, while Austria, Czechoslovakia and Yugoslavia belonged to the German sphere. See Barbara Jelavich, *History of the Balkans*, vol. II, *The Twentieth Century* (London, 1976). See also Malcolm Muggeridge (ed.), *Ciano's Diplomatic Papers* (London, 1948), pp. 375–9, for Ciano's conversation with Hitler on 5 July 1940, where Ciano was assured that the Mediterranean was a 'purely Italian matter'. On the limitations on Italian policy, see O. Chadwick, *Britain and the Vatican during the Second World War* (Cambridge, 1987), p. 193: 'Italy was technically responsible for the Greek famine but had no food to help, and the Germans who had food would not help.'

12. On the differences in the interpretation of the Hague Convention of 1907, see Lena Divani, *I Politiki ton Exoriston Ellinikon Kyverniseon*, pp. 187–8. K. Logothetopoulos, *Idou i Alitheia* (Athens, 1948), p. 85 writes that the German guarantee was given as early as July 1941.

13. See PRO, FO 371/29840, R 7038/96/19, dated 11 July 1941. It is noteworthy that in the original version of Warner's memo, the words '. . . a Greece with a population reduced to five million' [underlined in the original] have been deleted and replaced by 'the reduction of the Greek population by famine, its health . . . ruined . . . etc.'

14. For a recent study of collaborationism in Thessaloniki see Str. Dordanas, *Ellines enantion Ellinon* (Thessaloniki, 2006).

15. K. Logothetopoulos, *Idou i Alitheia*, p. 11, quoting from the article 'Kakhypopsiai' by the deputy Alexandros Vamvetsos in the Athenian daily *Ethnikos Kyrix*,

5 September 1948. In another passage he claims that permission to lift the blockade 'was not secured in time by the circles abroad [who were] close to the Allies, who, in a superficial manner and without much thought had put forward the idea that famine would force the Greek people to revolt', *Idou i Alitheia*, p. 85.

16. The body initially responsible was the Board of Economic Warfare. This was dissolved on 15 July 1942 and replaced by the Office of Economic Warfare (OEW). In addition and operating parallel to these, there existed the Office of Foreign Relief and Rehabilitation Operations (OFFRO) and the Foreign Economic Administration (FEA). Both the Office of Foreign Relief and Rehabilitation Operations and the Office of Economic Warfare were in turn consolidated into the Foreign Economic Administration on 25 September 1943.

17. On this subject see G. Kazamias, 'Polemos kai Koinovoulio: I Vretaniki Vouli ton Koinotiton kai o Episitismos tis Elladas', *Neoellinika, Deltio Erevnas Istorias Neoterou Ellinismou Akadimias Athinon*, VII (2007), forthcoming.

18. See Maggie Black, *Oxfam, the First 50 Years. A Cause for our Times* (Oxford, 1992), p. 1.

19. For a detailed analysis of the position of the Foreign Office, see George Kazamias, *Allied Policy towards Occupied Greece, the 1941–44 Famine* (PhD Thesis, Bradford, 1991), particularly Chapter 5.

20. For an analysis of the Ministry of Economic Warfare viewpoint see Kazamias, *Allied Policy towards Occupied Greece*, particularly Chapters 4 and 6.

21. Hugh Dalton, *The Fateful Years, Memoirs 1931–1945* (London, 1957), p. 325. Also, Medlicott, *The Economic Blockade*, vol. II, p. 558. It is interesting that Dalton himself refers directly to the last two phrases used by Medlicott in his official history of the Ministry of Economic Warfare to describe his attitude towards the blockade. He more or less says so in so many words in a note on p. 325 of his *Memoirs*.

22. Pimlott, *The Second World War Diaries of Hugh Dalton*, p. 76.

23. See, for example, Dalton's position as presented in Parliament on 10 February 1942. On this date, a question was asked in the House of Commons on 'the manner in which the Germans and Italians have carried out their legal and moral responsibility to feed the Greeks'. This question was planted by Hugh Dalton, in order to give publicity to his view of 'famine as an instrument of German policy'. See Hansard, *Parliamentary Debates, Commons*, Fifth Series, 10 February 1942, vol. 377, p. 1368. See also Pimlott, *The Second World War Diaries of Hugh Dalton*, pp. 366–7.

24. See H.G. Nicholas (ed.), *Washington Despatches 1941–45, Weekly Political Reports from the British Embassy* (London 1981), pp. 38–9.

25. See Alan Sked and Chris Cook, *Post-War Britain: a Political History* (London, 1979), p. 57.

26. See Sked and Cook, *Post-war Britain*, p. 58.

27. On these as well as other relief schemes and plans, see G. Kazamias, 'Turks, Swedes and Famished Greeks: Some Aspects of Famine Relief in Occupied Greece, 1941–44', *Balkan Studies*, XXXIII (1992): 293–307.

28. See PRO, FO 837/1233, tel. No. 7320, from FO to Washington.

29. See FO 837/1231, tels. HUSH-MOST SECRET, TAUT Nos 456 and 457 of 10-1-1942, TAUT nos. 505 and 513 of 13-1-42 and GREY no. 336 of 14-1-42.

30. An account of the working of this scheme in Greece is given by Paul Mohn, the first chairman of the joint Swedish-Swiss committee that administered it in Greece. See Paul Mohn, *Inter Arma Caritas, Anamniseis apo tin Ellada stin Katokhi* (Nicosia, 1968).

31. See PRO, FO 837/1231, T550/29/Z, headed 'DRAFT CONDITIONS'. In the top left-hand margin there is, handwritten (probably by Drogheda himself), 'agreed by Lord Drogheda and Sir O. Sargent at F.O. 18/2'.

32. PRO, FO 837/1231, W.P.(42) 80. 'Memorandum by the Minister of Economic Warfare' to the War Cabinet, headed 'Greece: The Blockade'. The document is probably back-dated. Dalton only mentions some small concessions to Vichy France. See Dalton, *The Fateful Years*, p. 355.

33. See, for example, Ronald W. Zweig, 'Feeding the Camps: Allied Blockade Policy and the Relief of Concentration Camps in Germany, 1944–45', *Historical Journal*, XLI (1998): 825–51.

34. PRO, FO 371/29840, R 7038/96/19.

35. See Canon T.R. Milford, 'The War Years and After', in *The Oxfam Story* (Oxford, 1965), p. 2. Oxfam was from its beginnings as the Oxford Committee for Famine Relief especially interested in relief for Greece (see Chapter 10).

36. For a list of some of the Famine Relief Committees see PRO, FO 837/1250 and FO 837/1251.

37. See Kazamias, 'Turks, Swedes and famished Greeks'.

38. See PRO, FO/837 1221, W6503/49/49, Statement on the Blockade Policy of the British Government: communicated by the Washington Embassy to Ministry of Economic Warfare. (Received May 29), dated Washington, March 10, 1941.

39. For a more detailed account see Kazamias, *Allied Policy towards Occupied Greece*, particularly Chapter 8.

40. The phrase is borrowed from Mark Twain, *The Innocents Abroad* (first edition: Hartford, Conn., 1869).

4
The Greek-American Community and the Famine in Axis-occupied Greece

Alexandros K. Kyrou

The Greek-American response to the famine and humanitarian crisis in Axis-occupied Greece reflected the enduring identification of the Diaspora with the welfare of Greece and the Greek people. The Greek-American community was not unique insofar as it, like other ethnic groups in the United States, demonstrated an ardent interest in events that affected its homeland, but the extent to which Greek-Americans turned their group concern into successful lobbying of government and policy formation was arguably without rival during the Second World War. Indeed, this largely ignored aspect of Greek and American wartime history points to the importance of Diaspora groups in influencing the strategic calculus of the belligerent Great Powers whose support for humanitarian needs was interpreted against strategic, realpolitik considerations. The few studies heretofore that have examined the famine and subsequent relief effort in occupied Greece have tended to emphasize state actors to such an extent that the more nuanced, sub-textual, but critical and decisive role of the Greek-American community and its international relief organisation, the Greek War Relief Association, has been either misunderstood or altogether overlooked. This chapter will present a corrective to this conventional narrative by exploring Greek-American efforts to intercede in the international environment as a non-state, non-governmental actor on behalf of humanitarian imperatives in Greece during the Second World War.[1] Within that framework, this inquiry will discuss the establishment of the Greek War Relief Association, the association's response to the famine in Greece, the impact of Greek-American activism on wartime international politics, and the consequences of these events for a broader transformation of the Greek-American community, as well as in the nature and relations of Greece and the Greek Diaspora in America.

The establishment of the Greek War Relief Association

On the very day that Mussolini launched his abortive invasion of Greece on 28 October 1940, the Greek-language media in the United States urged the country's half-million Greek Americans to rise to the support of their homeland.[2] Within hours of newspaper reports and radio broadcasts about Italy's attack, an outpouring of concern drove Greek-Americans to converge spontaneously in church basements, society halls, coffeehouses, and schoolrooms in large and small Greek communities scattered across the United States. Just as quickly, Greek-American voluntary associations circulated calls for meetings to bring together members of all community organisations. Little time was wasted in organising such efforts on a local level. On 29 October, for example, representatives of forty Greek-American organisations in New York met, elected a coordinating committee, and established an agenda to unite all Greek-American organisations in New York for the purpose of sending aid to Greece. Similar developments to those in New York took place in other parts of the United States, especially in metropolitan areas, such as Boston, Chicago, and Detroit, where particularly large Greek-American communities were concentrated. While working to coordinate their efforts with other organisations, several groups, especially the *topika somateia*, the mutual aid organisations bringing together migrants from the various regions of Greece, also launched independent efforts to send help, in the form of money, to their respective *patrides*, their communities of origin in Greece. Setting an example that other organisations followed, in the first ten days after the outbreak of hostilities between Italy and Greece, immigrants in New York from Kastoria in northern Greece, through their charitable organisation *Omonoia* (Concord), established the National Greek Relief Fund of Kastorians and collected 50,000 dollars as the first instalment of a general fund earmarked to aid their native city near the Greek-Italian lines. The Society of Kastorian Jews in Manhattan donated the first 4000 dollars, while more money poured in from Kastorian fur workers in New York's Garment District, who collectively pledged one day's wages to the effort.[3]

Despite the energetic efforts of the Kastorians and others, it soon became apparent that a national structure would be necessary to coordinate any large-scale relief campaign. Accordingly, and in response to a call by Archbishop Athenagoras, the head of the Greek Orthodox Archdiocese of North and South America and subsequently Ecumenical Patriarch, hundreds of representatives from Greek communities and voluntary associations convened in New York on 7 November. Guided by

Athenagoras' proposals, the representatives agreed to merge their efforts under one panhellenic and pan-American organisation to be known as the Greek War Relief Association (GWRA). The representatives established the basis for the executive administration of the new organisation, elected the influential Hollywood movie magnate, Spyros Skouras, as national chairman, resolved to adopt a policy of putting aside the political divisions of the inter-war period, and launched an immediate drive for 10,000,000 dollars to aid Greece.[4]

Two days after the meeting that established the GWRA, the state government of New York officially recognized the GWRA as an incorporated organisation, and shortly thereafter the association was chartered as a humanitarian relief group by the United States Department of State and legally empowered to raise and distribute funds for the relief of Greece.[5] Immediately, the nationwide networks of organisation and communication developed earlier by the Greek Orthodox Archdiocese, major community organisations such as the American Hellenic Educational Progressive Association (AHEPA), the Greek American Progressive Association, and other bodies mobilized themselves to support the GWRA.[6] Archbishop Athenagoras issued an encyclical on 11 November that was read and distributed in all of the approximately 350 Greek Orthodox parishes in the United States, which announced the formation and goals of the GWRA. He followed this formal announcement with personal appeals to community leaders to promote the GWRA. Athenagoras urged the archdiocese's hierarchy, clergy, and parish councils to put aside all other projects and devote themselves and their communities entirely to the relief cause. Underscoring his own commitment to this effort, Athenagoras placed the faculty and students of the Holy Cross Theological School in Pomfret Center, Connecticut, in the service of the GWRA, while effectively transforming the archdiocese's offices in New York into an organising centre for the GWRA.[7]

Working in concert with Athenagoras, Spyros Skouras embarked upon a nationwide speaking tour of Greek-American communities to promote the GWRA. The greatest source of community activism at the crucial local level of organisation was generated by the AHEPA, which, as Skouras acknowledged, provided the GWRA with most of its leadership. The American Hellenic Educational Progressive Association was established in 1922 by a small group of Greek immigrant entrepreneurs in Atlanta, Georgia. The organisation was created to serve as a community bulwark against the powerful American nativist movement, which targeted Greeks along with other Mediterranean and East European groups for prejudice and exclusion because of their supposed racial and cultural inferiority to Anglo-Saxon Americans. The AHEPA's official message of group survival and prosperity through middle-class acculturation, but not assimilation, appealed to many Greek immigrants. By the late 1920s, the organisation had expanded to create a nationwide web of chapters, making it the largest and most omnipresent institutional feature, after the church, in the life of most Greek-American communities. In short, the AHEPA's well-organized chain of chapters, coupled with the wide constellation of Greek Orthodox parishes integrated into a single archdiocese, provided the GWRA with a pre-existing nationwide structural network that it could graft itself onto. Furthermore, the parishes and voluntary associations making up the formal structures of the Greek-American community contained virtually unlimited and diverse human resources that enthusiastically lent themselves to the service of the GWRA.[8]

In terms of its organisational structure, the GWRA operated through a hierarchy of chairmen and committees, each working at different levels of responsibility. In ascending order, these committees operated on a community, district, state, regional and, ultimately, a national level.[9] By 19 November, all the members of the national executive committee had been appointed to their posts, and a nationwide system of administration was in place. The national executive committee included Spyros Skouras, the national president, Archbishop Athenagoras, the national chairman, George Vournas, who was national vice-president of the GWRA and also vice-president of the AHEPA, and the prominent philanthropist, Harold S. Vanderbilt, who served as honorary national chairman of the GWRA. The GWRA's national headquarters were located in Manhattan offices made available by the City Farmers Bank of New York. Answering to the national executive leadership, nine regional directors and their committees operated out of their respective headquarters in metropolitan New York, upper New York state, Boston, Chicago, Washington, DC, Philadelphia, San Francisco, New Orleans, and Dayton, Ohio. Most of the regional directors were also leading members of the AHEPA, including AHEPA president Van Nomikos, who led the GWRA's important Chicago-based operations.[10]

Not surprisingly, the organisation of the GWRA paralleled to a considerable extent AHEPA's administrative structure throughout the United States. Nonetheless, in preparing its organisation and fund-raising tactics the GWRA leadership also looked outside the Greek-American community for inspiration. In this regard, the Finnish-American community's mobilization and successful campaign to deliver humanitarian relief to Finland during the 1939–40 Soviet-Finnish Winter War, a conflict in many ways analogous to the Italo-Greek War, provided the GWRA with a working organisational model in the form of the Finnish Relief Fund. Moreover, the recent, successful example of the Finnish-Americans – an immigrant community that was much smaller and less prosperous than the Greek-American community – gave added confidence to Greek-Americans that they could achieve their relief goals.[11]

The GWRA successfully attracted many prominent Americans into its membership, thus enhancing the organisation's public image. The Association's Greek-American leadership made a deliberate effort to bring celebrities and prominent community leaders from outside the Greek-American community into its ranks in order to promote public awareness and support for the organisation and its cause. This initiative was largely successful, drawing many notable philanthropists, academics, and performers, into the GWRA who, in turn, lent their influence to the promotion of Greek relief.[12]

In this particular effort, the GWRA benefited immeasurably from the business assets at the disposal of Spyros Skouras. As president of 20th Century Fox Films, Spyros Skouras, along with his brother George, who would become head of United Artists, wielded enormous clout in the entertainment world in general, and the motion picture industry in particular. Skouras was determined to commit his considerable influence to the service of the GWRA. Using Hollywood's powerful studio system to his advantage, Skouras enlisted scores of major film stars and hundreds of entertainers and other artists to contribute their celebrity to the Greek cause. Thanks to Skouras, film premieres and other highly publicized Hollywood events became occasions for GWRA fund-raising drives, while GWRA rallies benefited from the participation and support of entertainment personalities. This policy, which aimed to associate respected, popular, and patriotic American public figures with the GWRA, was also intended to produce positive American attitudes towards Greece and its need for humanitarian aid. Broader American involvement in the GWRA was, therefore, important in that it helped promote Greek-American objectives while framing those interests as humanitarian and not parochial. Furthermore, in the view of Greek-Americans, the participation of non-Greek-American elites in the GWRA marked a social watershed for Greeks as an ethnic community.[13] The willingness of large numbers of influential Americans to work alongside Greek-Americans for the benefit of a Greek cause was regarded as a critical threshold in the Greek-American community's acceptance and respectability. These facts further emboldened Greek-Americans to act freely and openly in a public space that until recently would have viewed their actions on behalf of Greece as a sign of questionable loyalty to the United States.[14]

Although celebrities, high profile events, and media coverage in support of Greek war relief were instrumental in generating public support for the Greek cause, grassroots efforts within the Greek-American community were the most crucial factor behind the GWRA's success. The initiatives undertaken to gather money and other resources for relief were as diverse and varied as the Greek-American community itself. These projects were simply too vast in number to identify here, but some deserve mention as representative examples of both their resourcefulness and the extent to which the relief cause captured the attention and energies of the Greek-American community writ large. Beginning in November, local parish communities throughout the United States met to hold one-hour pledge-drives, raising hundreds of thousands of dollars for the GWRA. Inspired by the example of students at the St Demetrius Greek Orthodox School of Jamaica, New York, who in December donated their candy and allowance money to the GWRA, the roughly 500 Greek-language schools in the United States launched local neighbourhood and community fund-raising campaigns.[15] Seeking donations from passers-by, and dressed often in traditional folk costumes, Greek-American schoolchildren and older youth from the AHEPA's junior auxiliaries became a regular presence on busy downtown street corners throughout the country's cities.[16] At Columbia University, Greek-American college students formed a fund-raising organisation for the benefit of the GWRA, and similar groups which emerged on other campuses throughout the country matched its success.[17] Across the United States, sewing circles were established by the Greek Orthodox women's philanthropic organisation, the Philoptochos Society, in which women and girls produced tens of thousands of pieces of clothing for Greek civilians. In a move that would be repeated in other cities, the members of the Greek Restaurateurs Association of New York pledged to make weekly donations to the GWRA, to use their premises to publicize the GWRA's cause, and to solicit donations from patrons.[18] Greek-Americans owned over 40,000 restaurants, coffeehouses, confectioners, and other food service businesses in the United States, patronized by millions of customers daily, making these ubiquitous establishments ideally positioned to promote the Greek relief cause.[19] In addition, the GWRA gained considerable public attention through national and local press reports, advertisements, and community-sponsored radio broadcasts and cultural events.[20]

Regardless of their type or location, all fund-raising efforts were subject to standardized GWRA regulations, which emphasized uniform management and accounting methods, transparency, and the highest ethical standards. During the war and into the liberation period, the GWRA acquired a well-earned reputation with the United States government for uncompromising integrity and efficiency. Indeed, underscoring the GWRA's efficiency and demonstrating the Greek-American community's ability to work effectively in the broader organisational context of international humanitarian assistance, an early wartime study by the Department of State concluded that the Association's operating expenses were the lowest among all the many American organisations involved in humanitarian relief in 1940–41.[21]

Within a matter of days of its establishment, the GWRA and its cause had been embraced by virtually every segment of the Greek-American community. Indicative of both the scope and intensity of the Diaspora mobilization, by 15 November over 350 Greek Orthodox parish communities and over 2000 Greek-American voluntary associations had joined the GWRA. Within a few months of its founding, the GWRA had organized 964 local chapters.[22] These organisational accomplishments were important insofar as they enabled Greek Americans to achieve their primary objective – the collection and dispatch of aid for Greece. In the five-month period between the Italian attack and the subsequent German invasion of Greece in April 1941, the GWRA succeeded in sending significant aid to Greece. By the end of November, the GWRA's national executive committee in New York had established a central committee in Athens, led by the American minister to Greece, Lincoln MacVeagh, to administer services and distribute aid in Greece primarily through the Greek Red Cross.[23] Prior to the German occupation of Athens, the GWRA had raised approximately 4,700,000 dollars, 80 per cent of which had been cabled to its central committee in Athens.[24] These funds were used for a range of philanthropic assistance channelled carefully to civilians; such aid included the distribution of food, heating fuel, clothing and medical services, and financial support to distressed families of soldiers who had lost their lives. Under MacVeagh, the GWRA central committee continued to distribute aid until the last possible moment before the Germans entered Athens on 27 April.[25]

Occupation, famine, and early relief efforts

No amount of humanitarian aid could save Greece from German aggression. Intervening to rescue Mussolini from his humiliating fiasco in Greece and in order to secure his Balkan flank before the invasion of the Soviet Union, Hitler invaded Greece and Yugoslavia in early April 1941. Overwhelmed by the combined Axis armies, Greece was overrun and occupied by German, Italian, and Bulgarian forces. Once the occupation began, Britain imposed a naval blockade of Greece's ports and sea-lanes[26] (see Chapter 3). The blockade was intended to close Greece's shipping lanes and prevent their use for the German war effort. The implementation of the blockade would soon lead to famine in Greece.[27]

Greece was a net importer of wheat and relied on foreign sources for more than one-third of its food needs. The Axis occupation and the subsequent British blockade ended the normal means of securing the foodstuffs vital to Greece's survival. This situation was worsened by Greece's poor grain harvest of 1940, which produced roughly one-third less than the pre-war average. The Axis expropriation of food stocks intensified the crisis, and the division of the country into Italian, German and Bulgarian occupation zones disrupted the pre-war systems of supply and distribution of food. Soon after the start of the Axis occupation these conditions combined to strain Greece's already acutely diminished resources to breaking point.[28]

Reports of food shortages in Greece appeared in the Greek-American press in June 1941 and predictions of famine surfaced as early as July.[29] Rather than discouraging Greek-Americans from pursuing efforts to deliver aid, the Axis occupation magnified the need to provide immediate relief to the Greek population. In short, the serious deterioration of conditions in Greece drove Greek-Americans to expand their relief objectives.[30] The Greek-language press led the discussion in the Greek-American community on the widening crisis in Axis-occupied Greece. The press boldly asserted that Britain's blockade should and could be changed to accommodate the delivery and distribution of food to the threatened Greek population. The leading figure in this movement was Basil Vlavianos, the publisher and editor of the influential New York Greek-language daily, *Ethnikos Kiryx*.[31] Through a multitude of fiery public appearances, as well as countless editorials, Vlavianos called for a lifting of Britain's blockade against Axis-occupied Greece. Vlavianos insisted that Greece's severe food shortage, in combination with the country's staunch resistance against the Axis, demanded that Allied strategists find some means of re-opening the vital shipping lanes to Greece. Vlavianos implored Britain not only to alter its total blockade policy, but also to lend all available support in dispatching food and other humanitarian aid to Greece.[32]

Encouraged by Vlavianos and other community leaders, Greek-Americans began a grassroots lobbying campaign. Through the mass dispatch of telegrams and letters to their elected representatives in Washington, the Greek-American community worked to enlist the support of the United States government to apply pressure on Britain to alter its blockade policy against Axis-occupied Greece.[33] Meanwhile, working behind the scenes, the GWRA had learned from its contacts with the Greek government-in-exile that Britain had declared that it was in principle willing to allow relief supplies to be sent to Greece from Turkey. Britain had previously agreed that neutral countries within the strategic blockade zone could send supplies to occupied countries in the same region. Turkey, an official neutral, which fell in the larger British blockade zone, was already trading with the Axis (see Chapter 5). London thus saw no reason to forbid some of these supplies from going to the Greek population. However, no additional resources from outside the blockade zone could be shipped to Greece, and Britain was determined to silence any demands to lift the blockade. Armed with this information, Spyros Skouras, after outlining a relief strategy with the help of Norman Davis, the executive director of the American Red Cross, met with representatives of the Department of State on 21 August 1941.[34] With the backing of Davis and Ambassador MacVeagh, Skouras presented a proposal to the Department of State's Division of Near Eastern Affairs for a trial shipment of wheat to Greece. Skouras' plan called for the GWRA to charter a neutral vessel, load it with wheat in Turkey, the United States, or any other willing country, and dispatch it to Greece. In order to ensure proper distribution of the intended cargo, the GWRA would send a representative oversight group to accompany the relief shipment. If the proposed pilot shipment proceeded satisfactorily, the GWRA would follow it with others. In addition, Skouras' plan envisioned the assistance of the Department of State in securing from the belligerents assurances of safe passage for the relief ship.[35]

With the understanding that neither the American Red Cross nor the United States government would be directly involved in the operation, the Division of Near Eastern Affairs recommended Skouras' proposal and forwarded it to Assistant Secretary of State Sumner Welles for official approval. The GWRA plan was endorsed for both humanitarian and diplomatic reasons. The State Department's intelligence sources had concluded that the food crisis was more severe in Greece than in any other occupied country, and that it was generally the view that Britain, and secondarily the United States, had a distinct obligation to save a country in the Allied camp from famine. Moreover, the Division of Near Eastern Affairs reported that the failure to send aid to Greece had created a perception in the Turkish government that Britain had cynically abandoned Greece after Athens had served its purposes to the fullest and was no longer useful to the Allied war effort. Consequently, analysts in the Near East Division concluded that as long as the Greek crisis was met with indifference by Britain, Ankara would not be receptive to any overtures from London to enter the war on the side of the Allies.[36]

Given the Allies' hopes that Turkey might eventually enter the war on their side, Turkey's interest in the Greek situation created an opportunity for helping Greece. With encouragement from Washington to put into practice its willingness in principle to allow some aid to enter Greece, London accepted a plan whereby food purchased in Turkey by a British commercial corporation acting on the behalf of, and funded by, the GWRA and the Greek government-in-exile would be shipped to Greece and distributed under the supervision of the International Red Cross (IRC).[37] While the British Embassy in Ankara began negotiations with the Turkish government for a trial programme of aid to Greece, and as approval for such a plan languished in the Turkish Ministry of Commerce for more than a month, the GWRA began transferring funds to the International Red Cross in Geneva and to its own representatives recently sent to Turkey from the United States. These funds, beginning with an instalment of 300,000 dollars sent to the IRC in Geneva, were to be used for the purchase of foodstuffs, vitamin concentrates, and medical supplies, as well as for the costs of transport.[38] Preparations for cargo distribution were entrusted to the IRC Committee in Athens. Acting officially under instructions from Geneva, and in concert with GWRA planning, the Athens IRC consulted with the occupation authorities in Athens, and, with their consent, appointed an administrative committee of prominent Athenian philanthropists to deal with the logistical needs arising out of the distribution of the intended cargo.[39] The IRC also formed an executive steering committee consisting of representatives of the German, Greek, and Italian Red Cross organisations.[40] In a meeting held on 21 October 1941, the executive committee formulated a management plan for food distribution based on community and institutional needs. Moreover, the committee garnered assurances of cooperation from the occupation authorities.[41]

Shortly after the executive committee outlined its relief agenda, a Turkish steamship, the *Kurtuluş*, or *Liberation* (fortuitously also the name of a predominantly Greek-inhabited district of Istanbul), arrived from Istanbul and anchored off Piraeus. The unloading and distribution of the *Kurtuluş'* cargo began on 29 October. Three days earlier, the occupation censors had authorized a press release, which announced that 'the generosity of American relief organisations has made it possible to make distribution among the Greek population of large food supplies which have been purchased and transported from abroad'.[42] The GWRA was not mentioned by name in the statement and the Greek public apparently remained unaware of the organisation's role in the delivery of the aid shipment.[43] Nonetheless, the occupation authorities honoured their pledge to the IRC by aiding them in the transfer of the foodstuffs. As an unprecedented operation in exceedingly precarious circumstances, the GWRA's shipment was a remarkable success – almost 3,000,000 lbs of food had been sent to, and distributed in, occupied Greece without Axis interference.[44]

Once Allied intelligence reports confirmed that the occupation forces had seized none of the shipment, the *Kurtuluş* was dispatched on a second relief voyage. After taking on another 3,000,000 lbs of food purchased in Turkey, the *Kurtuluş* arrived in Piraeus on 10 November.[45] Thus began a regular pattern whereby food and medical shipments arrived in Greece during the early winter of 1941–42. The *Kurtuluş* made several relief voyages between October 1941 and January 1942, carrying over 6700 tons of food to Piraeus before it sank in the Sea of Marmara on its sixth voyage. A replacement ship, the *Dumlupınar*, was sent on two more voyages, delivering an additional 2400 tons of food to Greece through March 1942. During the winter of 1941–42, the IRC established 450 feeding centres located primarily in the Athens-Piraeus area and fed approximately 150,000 people daily. While improving its operations in Athens, the IRC began to develop plans for an expansion of its activities to other parts of the country.[46]

The famine as an international political problem

The IRC's preparations for implementing larger aid operations were, however, soon dashed. Although Ankara had initially given assurances that it was prepared to sell 50,000 tons of food for Greek relief, excluding wheat, Turkish military officials soon began to restrict the export of all foods. Subsequently, Ankara announced in early December 1941 that because its own food reserves were insufficient for the winter, it would be forced to reduce and probably cut off its supply of food to Greece in January 1942 or soon thereafter.[47] Confronted by this new obstacle, the GWRA sought the permission of both the British and United States governments to agree to the use of a source other than Turkey for the purchase of food for Greece. London, however, objected to any shipment of goods to Greece if the relief materials did not originate in Turkey.[48]

This position was, of course, the result of Britain's strategic blockade policy, and it also represented an adroit subtext and secondary objective of that policy. Once London acquiesced in Washington's insistence on allowing food to be shipped from Turkey to Greece, British strategic planners worked to take advantage of this small-scale exception to their overall blockade. There is no evidence to indicate that London would have allowed food to be sent to Greece were it not for pressure from Washington, which was acting largely at the behest of the GWRA. Quite to the contrary, British inaction before the application of American pressure on this front would suggest that humanitarian imperatives did not figure prominently, if at all, in London's approach to the Greek problem. Consequently, when London agreed to permit the shipment of relief supplies from Turkey to Greece, it did so not only to placate Washington, on which it depended to sustain its own war effort, but as an acceptable application of a strategic contingency. In short, Britain saw the GWRA plan involving Turkey as a means of reducing Ankara's surplus resources. More precisely, the British Foreign Office and Ministry of Economic Warfare were concerned that Turkey, one of Germany's largest economic partners outside the theatre of war and Berlin's chief supplier of chromium, indispensable to Germany's steel armaments production, was contributing more to the German war effort than its official neutrality offered to the Allies. As a result, London accepted arrangements that diverted any Turkish resources, including food, to Allied nationals who would consume supplies that might otherwise become available to the Axis.[49] Having to some extent accomplished this aim, at least in the short term, the British were now apparently indifferent to renewed pleas for direct aid to Greece.

Meanwhile, conditions in Greece reached startling levels by mid-winter 1941–42. In late December and early January, the German military authorities recorded 300 deaths per day from starvation in Athens. The IRC reported a higher number of approximately 400 deaths per day in Athens, and on some days as high as 1000 in Attica. Even before the beginning of winter, the American and Greek-American press were reporting the onset of wide-scale famine in Athens and other urban areas, the islands, and parts of the countryside.[50] In response, the GWRA intensified the urgency of its demand that food be sent to Greece immediately.[51] Due, in large part, to the ongoing and concerted Greek-American lobbying campaign, as well as to mounting intelligence reports confirming the severity of the crisis, the United States government began to show signs of serious concern over the situation in Greece. Moreover, President Roosevelt and the Department of State began to express political misgivings about Britain's blockade policy. Apart from the risk of alienating Ankara, the blockade gave German propaganda an unparalleled opportunity to attack Britain for the apparently mercenary abandonment of a gravely imperilled ally.[52] Sufficiently motivated by these facts to intervene on behalf of Greece, on 3 December 1941, the United States government invited London to supply information about its blockade of Greece and to confirm or deny allegations of responsibility for the famine.

The British did not reply to the request and were asked again on 5 January 1942, to provide a response to the United States government's inquiry. After more than a week, British Foreign Secretary Anthony Eden answered with a message seeking to exonerate Britain from any role in, or responsibility for, the famine. Eden stated, furthermore, that London's policy was being implemented on behalf of the Greek government-in-exile. Eden's assertions, however, appeared disingenuous, for the Greek government-in-exile had earlier dispatched a series of desperate pleas to the GWRA and Washington, asking the United States to take direct action to alleviate the famine.[53] When confronted with this contradiction, Eden simply insisted that it was not Britain's obligation but Germany's responsibility, as an occupying power, to care for the welfare of the Greek people. Eden made it clear that Britain was not prepared, as his government saw it, in effect to help the Germans cope with their occupation problems.

Eden's belated defence of the British blockade had no impact on the United States government's decision to support the GWRA position. In fact, on 31 December 1941, the American Secretary of State, Cordell Hull, had urged President Roosevelt to speak directly to Churchill and persuade him of the merit of lifting the blockade. Hull recommended that the United States government allow the GWRA to transfer funds to the IRC in Geneva for food and medical supplies to be sent to Greece. The IRC apparatus in Athens would again supervise distribution of relief supplies, some of which the Turkish Red Crescent had offered to contribute to the project.[54]

Pressure against the blockade mounted in early January 1942, when the British Minister of State for the Middle East in Cairo, Oliver Lyttelton, a man as close to the Greek problem as perhaps any British official, expressed support for the GWRA's demands to lift the blockade.[55] Lyttlelton was not unfamiliar with the GWRA. In June 1941, the association had established a liaison committee in Egypt that distributed financial support to Greek refugees in the Middle East and helped to coordinate other aid projects with the National Greek Committee of Egypt, the Egyptian Greek community's wartime organisation. Lyttelton's mission in Cairo had already benefited from the activities of both the GWRA and the National Greek Committee. In fact, the National Greek Committee carried out the first actual relief operation in occupied Greece. In breach of its own blockade policy, London permitted the Greeks in Egypt, with financial and organisational support from the GWRA, to hire neutral Swiss ships to deliver food, medical supplies, and even medical personnel from Alexandria to Crete for a limited period under IRC supervision and with German approval. The recipients of this first humanitarian intervention in occupied Greece, which took place in June 1941, were not primarily Cretan civilians, but, instead, the thousands of wounded and captured British and Commonwealth forces on Crete who had not yet been transferred to prisoner-of-war camps in Central Europe.[56] At any rate, on 9 January 1942, Lyttleton pleaded with Churchill personally to end the blockade, pointing out that the extreme suffering of the Greek people would have serious consequences and that history would judge the British harshly for their policy. Furthermore, he warned Churchill that the British abandonment of the Greeks would rupture their historic friendship with Britain and make them susceptible to communism, a fear that would increasingly drive British policy towards wartime Greece.[57]

In an effort to quell the unwelcome scrutiny and criticism that its blockade was producing, the British government announced on 12 January 1942, that pending the availability of transport ships, which were in scarce supply, it would send 8000 tons of wheat to Greece as a first instalment towards relief. However, London also stated that the blockade would remain in force.[58] This pronouncement satisfied none of the parties interested in bringing relief to Greece and it produced a storm of protest from the Greek-American community. Finally acknowledging that the blockade policy was no longer politically viable, on 16 February Churchill accepted the proposal to permit the renewal of major aid shipments to Greece and to allow them to originate from outside the blockade zone. Accordingly, on 22 February London notified Washington that it was willing to lift its blockade of relief convoys.[59] After securing the consent of both the American and British governments, the GWRA prepared the first relief shipment from the United States that would go directly to Greece.[60] With donations from the American Red Cross and the Medical Surgical Relief Committee of America, the GWRA chartered the Swedish vessel *Sicilia* to transport relief supplies to Greece. Loaded with over 2,500,000 lbs of food and 9 tons of medicines, the *Sicilia* left New York for Piraeus in late March.[61]

'Operation Blockade', or the 'Swedish Plan', and sustained relief

Although the *Sicilia* mission, and another ship chartered by the GWRA, the *Industria*, helped to alleviate the food crisis in Greece in the short term it was obviously insufficient to end the famine. The GWRA leadership understood that the success of any long-term strategic relief programme would require the cooperation of the belligerent governments and a coordinated international effort. After considerable preparation, the GWRA submitted to the Department of State a proposal for relief it dubbed 'Operation Blockade'. At its centre, Operation Blockade proposed the use of a neutral plan, which envisaged the shipping of cargoes of food, medicine, and clothing from the United States or Canada to Greece, provided that safe passage could be assured by the belligerent nations. Following discussions with President Roosevelt, Assistant Secretary of State Welles, and Red Cross Chairman Davis, the GWRA leadership expanded the outline of its proposal by adopting the former individuals' suggestions, which emphasized the importance of a neutral international commission within Greece, presumably the IRC, which would administer the distribution of relief.[62] While waiting for a response from London to its Operation Blockade proposal, which now enjoyed the backing of Washington, the GWRA set aside funds for the cost of the plan's initial implementation. The GWRA also used this period to coordinate planning with its Greek-Canadian counterpart, the Greek War Relief Fund (GWRF), and to solicit donations of wheat and other foodstuffs from various Allied and neutral governments, as well as initiating negotiations with the representatives of a Swedish shipping company for the use of its vessels to transport relief.[63]

Britain accepted the outline of Operation Blockade in principle, but concern over the potential repercussions and the troubling political precedent that lifting the blockade under American, let alone indirect Greek-American pressure, might pose, led London to insist that a neutral party such as Sweden appear as the originator of the relief initiative.[64] The GWRA accepted London's conditions and agreed to defer public recognition to Stockholm and effectively participate in a face-saving ploy for Churchill's government.[65] Thus, on 2 March, the British and United States ambassadors in Stockholm, Victor Mallet and Herschel Johnson, met with the Swedish Foreign Minister Erik Boheman and Prince Carl discreetly to invite the Swedish government to undertake the relief scheme, which would become known to the public as the 'Swedish Plan'. Boheman, who had already received a memorandum from Mallet outlining the proposal and conditions, and Prince Karl, the chief of the Swedish Red Cross, at once reacted favourably to the plan. In order to promote the illusion that Sweden was the sole architect of the relief plan, London insisted that the Germans should not be made aware of the origins of the initiative. The Swedes themselves were apparently not informed of the GWRA as a factor in the formulation of the plan.[66]

Stockholm accepted the proposal, and on 19 March Foreign Minister Boheman presented the relief scheme to the Axis. The Italians responded favourably to the 'Swedish Plan' on 7 April, and Rome's acceptance was followed by a positive reply from Berlin on 27 April. Implementation of the plan, however, was forestalled by differences over the structure of the commission that would preside over the relief apparatus in occupied Greece. After several months of complicated wrangling between Germany and Italy on one side, Britain on the other side, and the IRC and the Swedish Foreign Ministry in the middle, the impasse was broken in August 1942.[67] Consequently, that same month Stockholm officially established the so-called Joint Relief Commission in Athens, made up of Swedish and Swiss personnel, and led by the Swedish national Paul E.A. Mohn (who would be succeeded by Emil Sandstrom in March 1943), which began implementation of the relief plan originally envisioned by the GWRA. Steadily extending its network of local committees and relief distribution throughout most of Greece, the Joint Relief Commission operated with considerable success during the remainder of the occupation and in the first several months after liberation in October 1944.[68]

Of course, sustained relief in Greece would not have been possible without the kind of regular shipments of relief supplies that the GWRA and GWRF made possible beginning in August 1942. Carried by three Swedish vessels, and containing 15,000 tons of wheat donated by the Canadian government, as well as 50 tons of medical supplies which the GWRA and GWRF jointly purchased from the American Red Cross, the first of these aid shipments left Montreal for Greece on 7 August 1942.[69] Thereafter, relief cargoes originating in Canada, the United States, and Argentina were transported on a monthly basis by a fleet of initially eight, later 12, and ultimately, by the summer of 1944, 16 Swedish vessels.[70] From August 1942, the relief project delivered a minimum monthly shipment of 15,000 tons of wheat, 3000 tons of dried vegetables, and 100 tons of powdered milk to Greece.[71] Ambulances and transport vehicles were also included in some of the shipments.

The GWRA and the Greek government-in-exile paid the costs for the relief supplies and their shipment through 1942. Helping to sustain this enormous humanitarian initiative, beginning in January 1943, the United States government assumed most of the costs for the relief shipments, excluding the 15,000 tons of wheat, which, subsequent to persuasive appeals made to Ottawa by the GWRA and the GWRF, were donated by the Canadian government every month to the relief effort.[72] By March 1945, the GWRA had dispatched 101 relief convoys to Greece, which delivered approximately 647,000 tons of wheat and other foodstuffs, 3000 tons of clothing, and 20,000 tons of medicines and other relief goods.[73] In financial terms, the Greek-American-led relief effort delivered to Greece supplies valued at more than 100,000,000 dollars.[74] Through this humanitarian intervention, the GWRA's Operation Blockade prevented a repetition of the catastrophic winter famine of 1941–42 during the rest of the occupation and during the winter immediately following liberation. Thus, the Greek-American community's humanitarian concern for Greece, the political corollary of which was the concerted lobbying for a change in Allied policy, helped produce the conditions necessary for ending the famine in occupied Greece.[75]

Conclusions and implications

In the final analysis, apart from the single-minded commitment of Greek Americans, the GWRA was successful in its effort to end the famine in Greece because it was equipped with enormous structural resources. The GWRA possessed significant organisational advantages in the form of local, regional, and national networks that had developed as integral institutions within the Greek-American community before the Second World War. In short, by marshalling the Greek Orthodox Church, voluntary associations, and other organisations, the GWRA was able to combine the Diaspora's diverse community networks into a formidable national movement with, ultimately, international clout. The structures of the Greek Orthodox archdiocese and AHEPA, for example, which had evolved into impressive institutions during the 1920s and 1930s, helped prepare the Greek-American community for successful activism in the 1940s, and the GWRA propelled that activism by effectively consolidating the various grassroots organisations into an influential national pressure group.[76]

The energies directed at providing relief to famine-stricken Greece necessarily took into account not only the financial and organisational needs attendant on such intervention, but the complex political and diplomatic challenges also involved in such an effort. Undaunted by seemingly insurmountable obstacles, the effectiveness of the GWRA as a lobbying force helped to produce a level of success that no similar organisation achieved during the war. In other words, the GWRA effectively compelled the belligerent states to alter their policies in the interests of humanitarian imperatives. Thanks to the GWRA, Greece became the only occupied country in Europe to benefit from a large-scale, prolonged relief programme planned and originating in the Allied camp.[77] The involvement of the Greek-American community in the international effort to relieve Greece from famine had been enormous and decisive. Clearly, at no point since the Diaspora's central role in the development of a modern Greek national identity, had Greeks outside Greece been such a crucial factor in the life of the Greek nation as was the Greek-American community during the Second World War.

In the pursuit of relief goals, Greek-Americans came to realize that they could affect international conditions. Encouraged by their success, and conscious of their potential to influence official policy through organized advocacy, Greek-Americans turned their organisations into a force for the lobbying of government. Greek national pride was invoked with great urgency during the Italo-Greek War, and guided by their own sense of nationalist vigilance during the occupation period, Greek-Americans, through domestic lobbying, as well as the application of political pressure and the use of international structures, prevailed upon Allies and Axis alike, directly and indirectly, to allow the delivery of humanitarian relief to Greece. To what extent Greeks or others in Europe ever became aware of the central, driving role played by the Greek-American community in putting into motion and sustaining this international relief effort is largely moot. What is clear is the fact that the Greek-American community demonstrated both remarkable initiative and political acumen in lobbying on behalf of Greece, all without the inducement, control, or involvement of Greek officialdom and the Greek state. This fact points to a major transformation in the relationship between Greece and the Greek Diaspora in America produced by the wartime relief experience.

By independently initiating the championing of humanitarian relief, concurrent with the collapse of an official Greek authority, the Greek-American community reaffirmed its connection to Greece while simultaneously reframing the power balance between Greece and the Greek Diaspora, or the Greek centre and periphery. The Greek-American community realized it could act autonomously and effectively for the collective good, without direction and/or permission from the homeland. This realization and the shifting balance of power – or, at least, recalibration in terms of more equal distribution between centre and periphery – created the conditions for a gradual reconsideration of the nature of the bond between Greece and Greek America. Of course, it is not clear whether from Athens' perspective the GWRA experience implied a Greek-American capacity and right to autonomous action by the periphery on behalf of the centre. In many ways, this is a question that remains unresolved.

Notes

1. An important and highly detailed work on the famine and relief is found in Georgios A. Kazamias, 'Turks, Swedes and Famished Greeks: Some Aspects of Famine Relief in Occupied Greece, 1941–44', *Balkan Studies*, XXXIII (1992): 293–307. For an earlier work which breaks with conventional interpretations

by placing the Greek War Relief Association at the centre of the international relief operation, see Alexandros K. Kyrou, 'Ethnicity as Humanitarianism: the Greek American Relief Campaign for Occupied Greece, 1941–1944', in Dan Georgakas and Charles C. Moskos (eds), *New Directions in Greek American Studies* (New York, 1991), pp. 111–27. For an expanded version of the latter publication, see Alexandros K. Kyrou, 'Operation Blockade: Greek-American Humanitarianism during World War II', in Eugene T. Rossides (ed.), *Greece's Pivotal Role in World War II and its Importance to the US Today* (Washington, DC, 2002), pp. 109–27.

2. *Atlantis*, 28 October 1940; *Ethnikos Kiryx* (National Herald), 28 October 1940.
3. *Ethnikos Kiryx*, 9 November 1940.
4. Ibid., 19 November 1940; George Papaioannou, *From Mars Hill to Manhattan: the Greek Orthodox in America under Athenagoras I* (Minneapolis, 1976), p. 135; George Papaioannou, *The Odyssey of Hellenism in America* (Thessaloniki, 1985), pp. 176–7. For biographical information on Spyros Skouras, see *The Ahepan*, XV (January–June 1941): 40–2; and Theodore Saloutos, *The Greeks in the United States* (Cambridge, 1964), pp. 278–80. Although there were some personnel changes within the GWRA's executive committee, the organization's national leadership remained largely as originally constituted, as follows: Harold S. Vanderbilt, Honorary National Chairman; Thomas J. Watson and Howell W. Murray, Honorary National Vice-Chairmen; Mrs Lytle Hull, Honorary Chairman, Women's Auxiliary; Archbishop Athenagoras, National Chairman; George C. Vournas, National Vice-Chairman; Spyros P. Skouras, National President; William Helis, National Vice-President; Joseph Larkin, National Treasurer; K.P. Tsolainos, National Secretary; Mrs L.J. Calvocoresse, Chairman, Women's Auxiliary; Oscar Broneer, Executive Vice-President. The National Executive Committee consisted of Winthrop W. Aldrich, Archbishop Athenagoras, William Helis, Charles D. Kotsilibas, Joseph J. Larkin, Thomas A. Pappas, Spyros P. Skouras, Stephen C. Stephano, S. Gregory Taylor, K.P. Tsolainos, Harold S. Vanderbilt, and George C. Vournas. For more information on the GWRA's most prominent national officers, see Bobby Malafouris, *Ellines tis Amerikis 1528–1948* (New York, 1948), pp. 218–19.
5. *Ethnikos Kiryx*, 11 November 1940; 19 January 1941.
6. Saloutos, *The Greeks in the United States*, p. 345. An official, yet highly useful, well-documented history of the largest and most influential Greek-American voluntary and fraternal association is found in George J. Leber, *The History of the Order of AHEPA (The American Hellenic Educational Progressive Association), 1922–1972: including the Greeks in the New World, and Immigration to the United States* (Washington, DC, 1972).
7. Papaioannou, *From Mars Hill to Manhattan*, pp. 135–6; Papaioannou, *The Odyssey of Hellenism in America*, p. 177.
8. Saloutos, *The Greeks in the United States*, pp. 345–6.
9. *Ethnikos Kiryx*, 19 January 1941.
10. See Demetrios J. Constantelos (ed.), *Agones kai Agoniai tis en Ameriki Ellinikis Orthodoxou Ekklisias: Engkyklioi kai Eggrapha ton Eton 1922–1972 [Encyclicals and Documents of the Greek Orthodox Archdiocese of North and South America Relating to its Thought and Activity, the First Fifty Years 1922–1972]* (Thessaloniki, 1976), pp. 283–5. The GWRA's executive national offices were located at 730 Fifth Avenue in the Heckscher Building of New York, and the City Farmers

Bank of New York City donated the entire premises to the organization. See
Ethnikos Kiryx, 20 November 1940.

11. In response to the outbreak of the 1939–40 Winter War, Finnish-American
communities and voluntary associations throughout the United States successfully merged their initial, multiple grassroots relief movements into one
nationwide confederation known as the Finnish Relief Fund. As a centralized
national coordinating organization, the Finnish Relief Fund was able to maxi-
mize the Finnish-American community's potential for humanitarian action,
ultimately sending over 3,400,000 dollars in aid to Finland. See *Ethnikos
Kiryx*, 30 October 1940. For a comparative discussion of wartime humanitarian
aid projects pursued by the largest Eastern European ethnic group in the United
States, see Donald E. Pienkos, *For Your Freedom Through Ours: Polish American
Efforts on Poland's Behalf, 1863–1991* (Boulder, Colorado, 1991), pp. 73–104.

12. For a contemporaneous discussion of methods to be used for soliciting main-
stream American support for the GWRA cause, see *Ethnikos Kiryx*, 9 January
1941. Much of the GWRA executive staff in New York was, in fact, provided
by influential American public figures, several of whom had lived in Greece
before the war. For more information, see Saloutos, p. 346. The American
Friends of Greece, a philanthropic and cultural organization founded in 1923
to aid Greece in its postwar refugee crisis, played an especially significant role
in promoting the GWRA among American intellectuals and other elites. The
organization's members, including the well-known Princeton University professor T. Leslie Shear, and other prominent scholars, especially those forming
an influential elite of classicists, historians, and archaeologists, who, like
Shear, had been associated with the American School of Classical Studies in
Athens during the interwar period, offered the public an erudite perspective
on the importance of the GWRA's mission. Shear was elected chairman of the
Committee for Aid to Greece, formed at Princeton University on 15
November 1940, by members of the American Friends of Greece and scholars
associated with the American School of Classical Studies in Athens. Acting in
concert with the GWRA, Shear's Committee for Aid to Greece initiated its
humanitarian efforts by dedicating, on the day of the committee's establishment, funds for the purchase and maintenance of an ambulance in Athens.
See *Ethnikos Kiryx*, 16 November 1940.

13. Greek-Americans' public image and group status benefited enormously from
Greece's successful resistance to Italian aggression. The Greek army's unexpected and stunning victories against Italy produced laudatory reporting in the
American press, as well as praise from public officials. The Greek-American community capitalized on the media's lionization of Greece's resistance against fascist Italy, the first Allied victory in Europe, to acquire for itself a level of group
acceptance and prestige previously unrepresentative of the Greek social experience in the United States. For additional discussion, see Charles C. Moskos,
Greek Americans: Struggle and Success (New Brunswick, New Jersey, 1989),
pp. 49–50; Saloutos, p. 344. For examples of philhellenic press reporting, see
Frank Daley (ed.), *Greece, Gallant – Glorious* (Haverhill, Massachusetts, 1941),
pp. 26–37. Apart from relevant articles originally published in the *Baltimore Sun*,
the *Boston Herald*, the *Los Angeles Times*, the *New York Times*, and other major
newspapers, this compilation includes a number of official proclamations made
by elected officials illustrating the diverse American support for the Greek cause.

14. Saloutos, p. 344.
15. *Ethnikos Kiryx*, 6 December 1940.
16. Leber, p. 330. Impetus was given to youth involvement in the relief campaign with the organization of the GWRA National Youth Division. Originally formed through the merger of 52 local New York City youth organizations on 28 November 1940, the youth division soon thereafter expanded throughout the United States. The National Youth Division's executive offices were chaired by Soterios V. Papanikas, National Chairman; George T. Gavaris, Chairman; Aristides Lazoros, Vice-Chairman; Anne Anthony, Secretary; Anthony Kourtos, Treasurer; Stathy N. Pandiri, Adviser (*Ethnikos Kiryx*, 12 January 1941).
17. *Ethnikos Kiryx*, 30 December 1940.
18. Ibid., 21 January 1941.
19. Ibid., 7 November 1940, 21 January 1941.
20. Ibid., 4 May 1941.
21. For a discussion of GWRA management and accounting procedures, see Saloutos, pp. 347–8. Whereas overhead costs for such organisations, according to the National Information Bureau, which investigated national and international agencies engaged in humanitarian relief, philanthropic, social, and civic work, typically exceeded 25 per cent, the GWRA expended only 4 percent (see *New York Times*, 2 May 1941).
22. *Ethnikos Kiryx*, 20 November 1940; Saloutos, p. 349. For more information on the development and expansion of the GWRA, as well as the organisation's relief activities in Greece before the Axis occupation of the country, see Constantelos, pp. 281–97, 303–6, *passim*; Greek War Relief Association, *$12,000,000* (New York, 1946); Malafouris, pp. 218–26; Papaioannou, *The Odyssey of Hellenism in America*, pp. 176–81; and Saloutos, pp. 345–50. In terms of its national-level organisation, the GWRA was divided into nine regions, each with its own administrative director and headquarters, as follows: Greater New York (Gregory Taylor, New York); Upper New York State (Dean Alfange, New York); New England (Antonios Pappas, Boston, Massachusetts); Midwest (Harry A. Reckas, Chicago, Illinois); East Central (George Vournas, Washington, DC); Middle Atlantic (Stephanos Stephanou, Philadelphia, Pennsylvania); Ohio (Vasileios Chibithes, Dayton, Ohio); West (Peter Boudouris, San Francisco, California); and South (William Helis, New Orleans, Louisiana). For more related information, see 'Archbishop Athenagoras to Archdiocese's clergy, community councils, and the Philoptochos Sisterhood, December 13, 1940', in Constantelos, pp. 283–5.
23. *Ethnikos Kiryx*, 20 November 1940.
24. The GWRA central committee in Athens expended approximately 3,336,000 dollars in relief aid prior to the German occupation of the city on 27 April 1941. On 14 April 1941, the central committee returned, by cable, 255,000 dollars to the GWRA headquarters in New York in order to safeguard the money from potential confiscation by the Axis. Likewise, the remainder of the funds originally dispatched to the Athens committee, totalling 175,000 dollars, was deposited in a special pharmaceutical reserve account under the protection of the International Red Cross (IRC) (*Ethnikos Kiryx*, 5 May 1941).
25. Malafouris, p. 220; Saloutos, p. 349.
26. Detailed studies of the military phases of Greece's involvement in the Second World War during the period preceding the Axis occupation of the country are

found in Mario Cervi, *The Hollow Legions: Mussolini's Blunder in Greece, 1940–1941* (Garden City, New York, 1971); Greek Army General Staff, *O Ellinikos Stratos kata ton Defteron Pangkosmion Polemon: Ellenoitalikos Polemos, 1940–1941,* volumes I–V (Athens, 1966); and Alexandros Papagos, *The Battle of Greece* (Athens, 1949). For an examination of the connection of the Axis campaign in Greece and Yugoslavia to German grand strategy, see Andrew Zapantis, *Hitler's Balkan Campaign and the Invasion of the USSR* (Boulder, Colorado, 1987).

27. See John Louis Hondros, *Occupation and Resistance. The Greek Agony 1941–44* (New York, 1983), pp. 67–70; Saloutos, p. 349. One of the most detailed studies of the onset of the wartime famine is found in Dimitri Kitsikis, 'La Famine en Grèce (1941–42): Les Consequences Politiques', *Revue d'Histoire de la Deuxième Guerre Mondiale,* LXXIV (1969): 17–41. For a discussion of the famine and the political dimensions of relief during the last stages of occupation, see Angeliki Laiou-Thomadakis, 'The Politics of Hunger: Economic Aid to Greece, 1943–1945', *Journal of the Hellenic Diaspora,* VII (1980): 27–42. The chapter entitled 'The Famine', in Mark Mazower, *Inside Hitler's Greece: the Experience of Occupation, 1941–44* (New Haven, 1993), pp. 23–52, combines multiple case insights with an excellent review of the famine within the larger framework of Axis occupation.

28. Karl Brandt, in collaboration with Otto Schiller and Franz Ahlgrimm, *Germany's Agricultural and Food Policies in World War II,* vol. II, *Management of Agriculture and Food in the German-occupied and other Areas of Fortress Europe, a Study in Military Government* (Stanford, 1953), pp. 235–8; Hondros, p. 67. A useful analysis of economic conditions in Axis-occupied Greece is found in Stavros B. Thomadakis, 'Black Markets, Inflation, and Force in the Economy of Occupied Greece', in John O. Iatrides (ed.), *Greece in the 1940s: a Nation in Crisis* (Hanover, 1981), pp. 61–80.

29. *Atlantis,* 8 July 1941; *Ethnikos Kiryx,* 7, 8 July 1941.

30. *Ethnikos Kiryx,* 1, 22 July 1941. Blocked from dispatching aid directly to Greece, the GWRA temporarily shifted its efforts to respond to the humanitarian needs of Greeks outside Greece. In short, the GWRA national executive committee resolved to send aid to Greek refugees who had fled the Axis occupation for safety in Egypt and elsewhere in the Middle East. These refugees also included a significant number of Greek-Americans who had repatriated to Greece before the war. With the consent of the United States Department of State, the GWRA established a committee of representatives in Cairo. By the end of July 1941, the GWRA Egyptian Committee had received 10,000 dollars from the GWRA headquarters in New York. These funds, and others which followed, were used to aid in the settlement of growing numbers of Greek refugees in the Middle East.

31. The *Ethnikos Kiryx* began publication in 1915 and soon achieved prominence in the Greek-American community as the chief rival to the older, conservative New York Greek-language daily newspaper, *Atlantis.* The two most authoritative studies of the Greek press in the United States are found in Andrew T. Kopan, 'The Greek Press', in Sally M. Miller (ed.), *The Ethnic Press in the United States: a Historical Analysis and Handbook* (New York, 1987), pp. 161–76; and Victor S. Papacosma, 'The Greek Press in America', *Journal of the Hellenic Diaspora,* V (1979): 45–61. For a cross-cultural examination of the press, see Charles Jaret, 'The Greek, Italian and Jewish American Ethnic Press: a Comparative Analysis', *Journal of Ethnic Studies,* VI (1979): 47–70. Brief

biographical information on Basil Vlavianos, emphasizing his role as a community leader during the Second World War, is found in Malafouris, pp. 370–1.

32. *Ethnikos Kiryx*, 9 August 1941.
33. Ibid., 7 August 1941.
34. United States Department of State 868.48/1143, 'Memorandum of Conversation' Shipment of Food to Greece by Greek War Relief Association acting for the Greek Red Cross, 21 August 1941; United States Department of State 868.48/1144, 'Memorandum', Proposed Shipment of Wheat to Greece by the Greek War Relief Association, 22 August 1941. The GWRA was able to confirm independently the outbreak of the famine and routinely provided Washington with detailed reports on its severity. This field reporting was accomplished through the services of a Portuguese agent, Antonio Gomes, who operated as an intelligence source for the GWRA in Athens from 1941 to late 1943. See British Archives R 13659/4/19, Political Memorandum, From Ridley Prentice to the Political Intelligence Department, n.d. (From the British Archives File of the Michael Matsas Collection, RG 500; Center for Holocaust Studies Documentation and Research, Brooklyn, New York). The latter materials were relocated, beginning in 1997, in the Museum of Jewish Heritage – a Living Memorial to the Holocaust, Library and Archive, Manhattan, New York.
35. United States Department of State 868.48/1144, 'Memorandum', Proposed Shipment of Wheat to Greece by the Greek War Relief Association, 22 August, 1941.
36. Ibid.
37. United States Department of State 868.48/1163, the London Embassy to the Secretary of State, Food Supplies for German-Occupied Territories, 18 October 1941.
38. United States Department of State 868.48/1181, official Greek War Relief Association correspondence from Spyros Skouras to Assistant Secretary of State Breckinridge Long, 15 October 1941.
39. United States Department of State 868.48/1187, the Rome Embassy to the Secretary of State, Food Shipments for Greece from Turkey Financed by the American 'Greek War Relief Association', 14 November 1941; United States Department of State 868.48/1187, Second Secretary of the Athens Embassy, Burton Y. Berry, 'Memorandum' (enclosure to No. 2510 of 14 November, from the Rome Embassy), condensed account of the preparation for and distribution of the first food shipment received from Turkey on the SS *Kurtuluş*, together with an annex showing in tabular form the quantity of foodstuffs distributed to the various types of organizations, 14 November 1941.
40. Ibid.
41. Ibid.
42. United States Department of State 868.48/1171, Special Assistant to the Secretary of State to the Greek War Relief Association, 25 November 1941.
43. Saloutos, p. 349.
44. United States Department of State 868.48/1187, Second Secretary of the Athens Embassy, Burton Y. Berry, 'Memorandum', 14 November, 1941; United States Department of State 868.48/1171, Special Assistant to the Secretary of State to the Greek War Relief Association, 25 November 1941.
45. United States Department of State 868.48/1171, the Rome Embassy to the Secretary of State, 15 November 1941.

46. Hondros, p. 72; United States Department of State 868.48/1187, the Rome Embassy to the Secretary of State, Food Shipments for Greece from Turkey Financed by the American 'Greek War Relief Association', 14 November 1941; United States Department of State 868.48/1187, the Rome Embassy to the Secretary of State, 15 November 1941; United States Department of State 868.48/1171, in reply to SD 868.48/1171, 14 November 1941, Confidential Report for the Secretary of State from Joseph C. Green, Special Assistant to the Secretary in Charge of the Special Division, 25 November 1941 .

47. Hondros, pp. 68, 72. The likelihood of a winter wheat export shortage in Turkey had been foreseen by the GWRA as early as August 1941. With an anticipated decline in Turkish agricultural production, coupled with Ankara's policy of low price-fixing that often led to hoarding by farmers, the GWRA had prepared an alternative contingency for maintaining the flow of food supplies that would not depend on Turkish markets. United States Department of State 868.48/1143, 'Memorandum of Conversation', Shipment of Food to Greece by Greek War Relief Association Action for the Greek Red Cross, 21 August 1941; United States Department of State 868.48/1144, 'Memorandum', Proposed Shipment of Wheat to Greece by the Greek War Relief Association, 22 August 1941. Shortly before the German invasion, the Greek government had purchased approximately 50,000 tons of wheat from Australia to fill the country's needs through the summer of 1941. The ships carrying the wheat did not reach Greece in time to deliver their cargoes and, following the Axis occupation, remained at anchor in Egypt. Consequently, in concert with the GWRA's new contingency, the Greek government-in-exile planned to transfer the undelivered wheat languishing in Egyptian ports to Turkey where it would be used to replenish state stores of grain to levels required by Ankara to re-open access to its larger domestic wheat reserves. This proposal was necessarily complicated because it took into account the British demand that all relief supplies originate in Turkey. United States Department of State 868.48/1172, telegram sent by the Department of State to the London Embassy, 26 November 1941; United States Department of State 868.48/1172, Wallace Murray from the Division of Near Eastern Affairs to Assistant Secretary of State Welles, 3 December 1941.

48. United States Department of State 868.48/1172, report from the Division of Near Eastern Affairs to Berle, and received by Assistant Secretary of State Acheson, 6 December 1941.

49. Ibid. For an analysis of the importance of Turkish agricultural and mineral markets to both belligerent camps during the Second World War, see Selim Deringil, *Turkish Foreign Policy during the Second World War: an 'Active' Neutrality* (Cambridge, 1989), pp. 21–2, 128–32. The most authoritative treatment of Turkey in international affairs during the Second World War is found in Frank Weber, *The Evasive Neutral: Germany, Britain and the Quest for a Turkish Alliance in the Second World War* (Columbia, Missouri, 1979). An excellent analysis of Turkish foreign policy objectives is found in Alexis Alexandris, 'Turkish Policy towards Greece during the Second World War and its Impact on Greek-Turkish Détente', *Balkan Studies*, XXIII (1982): 157–97. Turkish diplomacy during the latter half of the war is examined in Edward Weisband, *Turkish Foreign Policy 1943–1945: Small State Diplomacy and Great Power Politics* (Princeton, 1973).

50. United States Office of Strategic Services, Foreign Nationalities Branch, 14/GR-178, 19 January 1942. The IRC counted over 90,000 deaths throughout Greece during the winter famine of 1941–42, approximately 50,000 of which took place in the greater Athens area. For more statistical details, see Hondros, p. 71.

51. United States Office of Strategic Services, Foreign Nationalities Branch, 14/GR-178, 19 January 1942; United States Office of Strategic Services, Foreign Nationalities Branch, 14/GR-178, 6 March 1942.

52. United States Office of Strategic Services, Foreign Nationalities Branch, 14/GR-178, 23 March 1942.

53. Hondros, p. 73. For the official British position on London's responses to the famine, see W. N. Medlicott, *The Economic Blockade*, vol. II (London: Her Majesty's Stationery Office, 1959).

54. Communication from the Secretary of State (Hull), 31 December 1941, published in United States Congress, House of Representatives, *Foreign Relations of the United States: Diplomatic Papers, 1942*, vol. II, *Europe* (Washington, DC, 1962), pp. 727–9.

55. Procopis Papastratis, *British Policy towards Greece during the Second World War 1941–1944* (Cambridge, 1984), p. 117; telegram from the Greek Minister (Diamantopoulos) to the Under Secretary of State (Welles), 24 December 1941, published in United States Congress, House of Representatives, *Foreign Relations of the United States: Diplomatic Papers, 1942*, vol. II, *Europe*, pp. 726–7; telegram from the King of the Hellenes (George II) to President Roosevelt, 6 February 1942, published in United States Congress, House of Representatives, *Foreign Relations of the United States: Diplomatic Papers, 1942*, vol. II, *Europe*, p. 736.

56. *Ethnikos Kiryx*, 3 June 1941. For background on the Greek community of Egypt, see Alexander Kitroeff, *The Greeks in Egypt, 1919–1937: Ethnicity and Class* (London, 1989).

57. Papastratis, p. 117; telegram from the Greek Minister (Diamantopoulos) to the Under Secretary of State (Welles), 24 December 1941, published in United States Congress, House of Representatives, *Foreign Relations of the United States: Diplomatic Papers, 1942*, vol. II, *Europe*, pp. 726–7; telegram from the King of the Hellenes (George II) to President Roosevelt, 6 February 1942, published in United States Congress, House of Representatives *Foreign Relations of the United States: Diplomatic Papers, 1942*, vol. II, *Europe*, p. 736.

58. *New York Times*, 7 February 1942; Papastratis, p. 117.

59. Hondros, p. 74.

60. United States Department of State 868.48/3028, 6 March 1942; United States Office of Strategic Services, Foreign Nationalities Branch, 14/GR-178, 17 March 1942.

61. See Greek War Relief Association, *A Statement by the Greek War Relief Association, Inc., to its Chapters and Co-Workers* (New York, 1943); Malafouris, p. 221.

62. Saloutos, p. 349.

63. For detailed information on the use of the Swedish vessels employed in Operation Blockade, see Malafouris, p. 222. For a history of the GWRF, see Florence MacDonald, *For Greece a Tear, the Story of the Greek War Relief Fund of Canada* (Fredericton, New Brunswick, 1954). Major studies of the Greek Canadian community are found in Leonidas C. Bombas (ed.), *O Ellinismos tou Montreal/Montreal Hellenism: 1843–1985* (Montreal, 1985); Peter D. Chimbos,

The Canadian Odyssey: the Greek Experience in Canada (Toronto, 1980); and Stephanos Constantinides, *Les Grecs du Quebec* (Montreal, 1983).

64. Hondros, p. 74; United States Department of State 686.48/3157, 'Memorandum', 13 June 1942; United States Department of State 868.48/3168, the London Embassy to the Secretary of State, 30 June 1942.

65. At this stage in the planning process, the GWRA's 'Operation Blockade' proposal became known as the 'Swedish Plan' (see Hondros, p. 74).

66. Hondros, pp. 74–5; Telegram from the Minister in Sweden (Johnson) to the Secretary of State, 6 March, 1942, published in United States Congress, House of Representatives, *Foreign Relations of the United States: Diplomatic Papers, 1942*, vol. II, *Europe*, pp. 743–4; United States Department of State 868.48/3157, 'Memorandum', 13 June 1942; United States Department of State 868.48/4892, Board of Economic Warfare, Blockade and Supply Branch, Reoccupation Division Confidential Report, *Greece: Relief Food Distribution by the Joint Relief Commission*, 12 June 1943.

67. The German and Italian governments assumed the existing IRC authorities in Athens, which had administered relief operations since the *Kurtuluş* period, would manage the distribution of any future relief shipments. The British government, openly antagonistic towards the IRC apparatus, demanded that the original committee in Athens should not participate in any expanded relief operations and that the Swedish authorities be given exclusive responsibility for the execution of the programme. None of the belligerent powers showed any inclination to compromise and the relief deliberations reached an impasse that lasted until the beginning of August. Under pressure from the United States, the British government finally accepted a compromise plan drafted by Swedish Foreign Minister Boheman to establish a so-called Action Committee (ultimately known as the Joint Relief Commission), composed of Greek, Swedish, and Swiss personnel, and to make the new organization solely responsible for relief distribution. The original IRC Committee in Athens would continue to operate, but only as a liaison between the Action Committee and the Axis authorities. See Hondros, pp. 74–5; United States Department of State 868.48/3157, 'Memorandum', 13 June 1942; United States Department of State 868.48/4892, Board of Economic Warfare, Blockade and Supply Branch, Reoccupation Division Confidential Report, *Greece: Relief Food Distribution by the Joint Relief Commission*, 12 June 1943.

68. The headquarters of the Joint Relief Commission were located in the Marasleion School in the Kolonaki district of Athens. The relief apparatus was coordinated between two main centres: the Athens general administrative headquarters; and the Piraeus office, which oversaw the processing and transportation of relief shipments. The Athens general headquarters included two subordinate divisions responsible for the distribution of relief. One of these divisions directed provincial distribution, and maintained representatives and major relief centres in Kalamata, Patras, Thessaloniki, and Volos, while the second division served the Athens-Piraeus area. The supervision of distribution on the islands was administered by a commission field office in Crete and by two mobile representatives assigned to Chios, Lesbos, and Samos. At the local level, a network of committees and subcommittees, numbering approximately 1600 by 1943, expanding to 3000 in 1944, and reaching over 5300 by 1945, were established to manage the apportionment

of supplies in the country's towns and villages. In terms of official personnel, by the end of 1942, the Commission included 25 Swedish and Swiss executive administrators, almost 50 Greek and Swiss physicians, some 1000 nurses and medical volunteers, approximately 3000 labour volunteers, and over 1200 employees. See Brandt, Schiller and Ahlgrimm, pp. 240; Kazamias, p. 304; United States Department of State 868.48/4892, Board of Economic Warfare, Blockade and Supply Branch, Reoccupation Division Confidential Report, *Greece: Relief Food Distribution by the Joint Relief Commission*, 12 June 1943. For local case studies of the administration and activities of the relief apparatus, see Philip Argenti, *The Occupation of Chios by the Germans and their Administration of the Island, 1941–1944* (Cambridge, 1966), pp. 170–5, *passim*; and Greek War Relief Association, *A Letter from Issari* (New York, 1943).

69. Malafouris, p. 222. United States Department of State 868.48/4892, Board of Economic Warfare, Blockade and Supply Branch, Reoccupation Division Confidential Report, *Greece: Relief Food Distribution by the Joint Relief Commission*, 12 June 1943; United States Office of Strategic Services, Foreign Nationalities Branch, 14/GR-178, 24 April 1942. Instrumental in the success of the GWRA's medical aid projects were the efforts of Chicago physician Speros Demetriou Soterakos. Soterakos was responsible for organizing the Medical Division of the GWRA and helped raise 340,000 dollars in relief donations from his colleagues. Soterakos and other prominent Chicago Greek-American professionals and intellectuals are discussed in Andrew T. Kopan, 'Hellenic Letters in the New World: the Greek Pioneer Intellectual in Chicago', in Fotios K. Litsas (ed.), *Hellenika Grammata: Essays in Tribute to Hellenic Letters* (Chicago, 1985), pp. 206–13.

70. Brandt et al., p. 240; United States Department of State 868.48/4892, Board of Economic Warfare, Blockade and Supply Branch, Reoccupation Division Confidential Report, *Greece: Relief Food Distribution by the Joint Relief Commission*, 12 June 1943.

71. Ibid. Beginning in the summer of 1944, the minimum monthly delivery of food shipments rose to 35,000 tons.

72. Ibid., Hondros, p. 75.

73. Malafouris, p. 222.

74. Greek War Relief Association, *$12,000,000*, pp. 8–9; Saloutos, p. 350.

75. Many estimates anticipated one million deaths if relief had not arrived in Greece before the onset of winter in 1942, while others credited the GWRA for having saved as many as two million lives by the end of the occupation. See Greek War Relief Association, *$12,000,000*, pp. 8–9; Hondros, p. 75; Saloutos, p. 350; United States Department of State 868.48/3136, Assistant Secretary of State to President Roosevelt, 15 April 1942.

76. Informative discussions and analyses of Greek-American society, community formation and institutional development, especially relating to the centrality of the local parish and its relationship to the Greek Orthodox archdiocese of North and South America, are found throughout the studies above by Moskos, Papaioannou, and Saloutos. A useful compilation of works on multiple aspects of archdiocesan history and organizational structures is found in Miltiades B. Efthimiou and George A. Christopoulos (eds), *History of the Greek Orthodox Church in America* (New York, 1984).

77. See Saloutos, p. 350.

5
The Turkish Contribution to Famine Relief in Greece during the Second World War

Elçin Macar

Greece entered on arguably the bitterest era of its history during the Second World War, when it came under Italian, German and Bulgarian occupation. Domestic food production did not meet the country's needs and the British blockade prevented food imports. This gave rise to a devastating famine during the winter of 1941–42. According to Mark Mazower there were a minimum of 49,188 deaths in the Athens-Piraeus area during the twelve months after October 1941, as opposed to 14,566 during the previous year.[1]

Early Turkish relief efforts

The first moves in Turkey to help Greece began a matter of days after the attempted Italian invasion of Greece on 28 October 1940. An announcement published by the Greek Consulate-General in the Istanbul Greek newspaper, *Apoyevmatini*, on 12 November 1940, read:

> The Greek Consulate of Istanbul announces an invitation to Greek sub- jects from the wife of the Crown Prince, Princess Frederiki: 'Greeks of foreign lands – our children who fight for our independence are also fighting with the cold! That's why I have established the organization, "Comforts [literally flannels] for soldiers". Help me with that effort.'

At the same time, the wife of the Greek ambassador Raphail Raphail, who had taken up his post in Ankara in 1939, told the Ministry of Foreign Affairs that she proposed to establish an association among Greeks in Turkey (some 17,642 members of a Greek minority totalling 125,046 were Hellenic nationals in 1935[2]) and asked for permission to transfer the goods collected to Greece. Although Turkey was gratified by the initial Greek victories over the Italians, because Greece served as a buffer between Turkey and the

Axis, such permission was given only on 18 November 1940.[3] In addition, Ambassador Raphail's wife collected and sent fifteen tons of sugar for Greek soldiers fighting the Italians. Turkey assumed a particular importance for Greece following the outbreak of hostilities with Italy. Turkey gave some limited help to the Greek army, for example the Red Crescent donated humanitarian help worth 4,163,000 drachmas to the Greek Red Cross.[4] On 17 December 1940, a women's committee in Istanbul gave 14,000 aid packages to the Red Crescent for delivery to Greek soldiers[5] and later afforded shelter for Greek soldiers fleeing from the occupation. Most of these refugees made their way to Egypt in order to enlist in the Greek armed forces in the Middle East.[6] An instance of Turkish help to Greece at this time was the making available at no cost 10,000 phials of tetanus serum, following a cabinet decision on 26 March 1941, in response to a request by the Turkish Embassy in Athens.[7] The Red Crescent, which had an agreement with the International Red Cross Committee, besides sending aid to the value of 4,163,000 drachmas to the Greek Red Cross, donated three ambulances, together with 15,000 phials of tetanus and gangrene serum, to Thessaloniki.[8]

According to Dimitri Kitsikis, writing on the basis of documents in the Greek Ministry of Foreign Affairs, Prime Minister Emmanouil Tsouderos, evacuated a few days previously to Alexandria with the King, George II, sent a telegram on 4 June 1941 to the Greek Embassy in London. This said that: 'We left Crete without food', adding that the situation in the rest of the country was scarcely any better.[9] His comments were based on the following five basic facts: the country was under occupation by Italy, Germany and Bulgaria; much of the rural population had migrated to the cities; internal communications and transportation were badly disorganized; food and material had been confiscated from the beginning of the occupation; and imports from the Allies had been cut off due to the blockade.

Günther Altenburg, appointed by Hitler as the Plenipotentiary of the Reich in Greece (*Bevollmächtiger des Reiches für Griechenland*), emphasised in messages to Berlin that Greece should not be allowed to fall into chaos, political or otherwise. But the response he received from Hitler in July 1941 was only a vague directive to 'do what you can'. The German Ministry for Foreign Affairs for its part insisted that it was Italy's responsibility to supply food for Greece. But Italy had no surplus of food for this purpose and had itself been dependent on Germany for supplies during the winter of 1940–41. Field Marshal Hermann Goering's four-year plan was the final blow. If food had to be supplied to the occupied countries then the priority was not Greece but rather Belgium, the Netherlands or Norway. Greece was well down the hierarchy of Nazi concerns. Berlin repeatedly reminded Rome that Greece was Italy's responsibility.[10] The Axis powers repeatedly emphasised that famine in Greece was the result of the British blockade in the Mediterranean and called for the lifting of the blockade of Greece in order to secure grain from non-European countries.

Britain eventually agreed that food could be exported from Turkey to Greece because it was situated 'within the blockade territory', so there would be no need to lift the blockade.[11] The suppliers of the aid would be the Greek government-in-exile, the British and US governments with the Swedish, Swiss and Turkish governments in less central roles. Non-governmental organisations, such as the Red Cross, and Greek relief organisations in the US were much involved[12] (see Chapter 4). The United Kingdom Commercial Corporation would buy food in Turkey, while the Greek War Relief Association in the United States would supply most of the money needed. Three companies were established in Turkey, Greece and the United States in order to procure and transfer food to Greece: *Türk-Ellas* (in Istanbul), *Ellas-Türk* (in Athens) and Triand. M. Fufas (in New York).[13]

The aid campaign in the Turkish press

Meanwhile, the Turkish press had also been focusing attention on the famine in Greece. It was emphasized that Greece had contributed generously to the relief effort that had followed the 1939 earthquake in Erzincan in eastern Turkey. Some 700,000 people had contributed to the raising of 2 million drachmas and now it was Turkey's turn to help.[14] Dimitri Kitsikis has written that it was *Cumhuriyet* that started the campaign, although in reality it was *Vatan* that took the lead.

In an article of 14 July 1941, entitled 'We are true friends', Ahmet Emin Yalman,[15] the editor-in-chief of *Vatan* wrote that 'we have to prove that we are true friends'. Reminding his readers of the aid from Greeks and Greek-Americans following the Erzincan earthquake, Yalman emphasised that Turkey should pay its moral debt to Greece in these days of disaster. He proposed two means of repaying this debt. Firstly, the Red Crescent should establish soup-kitchens in Greece, especially for children. Secondly, there should be commercial consignments to Greece, taking advantage of Turkey's good relations with Germany. Four days later, Necmettin Sadak, a future Minister of Foreign Affairs, replied to Yalman's article in the newspaper *Akşam*, writing that Turkey's resources were inadequate, that establishing kitchens was an 'like an American dream' and that the only answer was to obtain aid from the richer countries, Britain and the US, which had given abundant promises.

Yalman replied two days later that 'if Sadak studied our export statistics, he would see that we have a surplus of food in our country. We export to anyone who is willing to pay. So if we export to Greece, we will both be conducting business as usual while expressing our friendship and affording a remedy for their troubles.' A month later, on 12 August 1941, Yalman published a further article entitled 'Both Duty and Opportunity'. In this he wrote that Greece was a long-standing food importer; that the country's wheat-growing areas were mainly under Bulgarian occupation; that the occupiers had confiscated and consumed all available goods during the first months of the occupation with the result that the difficulties in the country had become unbearable. He added that Turkey had limited means, but that, nevertheless, the Red Crescent had a duty to impress on other states the need to assist.

Later in the year, in an article entitled 'Famine in Greece' in *Cumhuriyet*, Yunus Nadi wrote that in children's hospitals the patients did not receive even half of the milk they needed. Greece's sufferings should be made known in particular in Britain and the United States, while he emphasised that South America was an area rich in grain. Furthermore, he stressed that Europe could not help Greece because it was preoccupied with its own troubles as a consequence of the blockade. Help, he believed, could only possibly come from overseas.[16]

The beginning of large-scale aid

The Turkish government had received approval from Germany and Italy regarding which foods it could export and had made it clear that only those permitted could be sent. The Red Crescent officially undertook an aid campaign, following discussions with the International Red Cross. Late in September 1941, P. Mavromikhalis, a former Greek Minister of Foreign Affairs, Reppas, a retired air force general, and Nikopoulos, manager of Greece's airline, came to Istanbul, to discuss how the organisation would work.[17]

A commission to achieve coordination and manage operations was formed with representatives from the ministries of trade and transport, together with customs. A senior Turkish diplomat in the Ministry of Foreign Affairs and future minister, Feridun Cemal Erkin, headed the commission. Erkin was later to be awarded the Order of the Phoenix by the Greek government for his efforts.[18] At the same time, on 12 September 1941, the Red Crescent dispatched 75 tons of salt to Western Thrace.[19]

According to a document, dated 15 September 1941, of the Minister of Foreign Affairs, Şükrü Saracoğlu, it was planned to transport food by the steamship *Adana*.[20] The Greek ambassador requested that the same vessel also deliver food parcels from Greeks in Turkey for relatives and acquaintances in Greece. This request was allowed because there was at the time no postal service to Greece. In granting approval, the Ministry to the Prime Minister stated that 'the vessel will be the steamship *Kurtuluş* according to information provided by the Sea Transportation General Directorate'.[21] A symbolic choice because one translation of *Kurtuluş* is, appropriately in the circumstances, salvation.

According to the plan, there would be two voyages per month from Turkey. Turkey was chosen as the centre for the aid, because it was the only neutral state within the region and shared a border with Greece. In fact, the British government permitted land transportation despite the blockade. But the Greek-German war of April 1941 had destroyed much of the railway system. Roads had also been destroyed and were frequently impassable, while there was a shortage of trucks. The Allies could not control such traffic in practice. The blockade was essentially a naval matter, with British submarines being ordered to sink any ships they encountered in the Mediterranean.[22] So the most dangerous means of transport became the most convenient and practical way of dealing with the matter.

The voyages of the *Kurtuluş*

According to Lloyd's register of shipping, the *Kurtuluş* was built in Britain in 1882 and first operated in Britain under the name *Euripides* and presumably under Greek ownership. It was bought by the Taviloğlu family in 1930, when its name *Bülent* was changed to *Kurtuluş* in 1936.[23] On 25 September 1941, the Ministry of Foreign Affairs contacted the German, Italian and British embassies, and informed them of the *Kurtuluş'* first departure date and its intended route. Replies from both Germany and Italy indicated that the vessel's safety on the proposed route could not be assured.[24]

The *Kurtuluş* departed with its first cargo on 13 October 1941, decked out with the Red Crescent in order to be noticed by planes and submarines. On this voyage, it carried 800 tons of pulses, 240 tons of onions, 45 tons of egg and fish paste, medical materials and clothing bought with funds supplied by the American Greek War Relief Association (see Chapter 4). It was welcomed with great enthusiasm, as well as with Turkish flags, when it arrived in Piraeus two days later. It was considered to be 'a single ray of hope' for the suffering Greek nation. Newspapers in Istanbul saw the *Kurtuluş'* arrival in Piraeus as an opportunity to draw attention to the famine in Athens. They reported that 80 per cent of stores in Piraeus were closed because they did not have any goods to sell. Dock workers took any pulses they could salvage and hid them in their pockets, only to have them confiscated when they were checked at the harbour entrance. The Greek Medical Association sought the permission of the Holy Synod of the Church of Greece to bury corpses on account of the drastic increase in the number of deaths. Besides concerns about health conditions there was a shortage of coffins.[25] Moreover the amount of black bread distributed daily was less than 50 grams per person.[26]

The *Elliniki Enosi Konstantinoupoliton* (Union of Greeks of Constantinople) started collecting money from the Greeks of Istanbul. According to reports on 22 November, the Red Crescent would accept packages from Greeks who had relatives in Greece. Packages would be opened on being handed over and would be sealed after customs inspection. The Red Crescent stipulated the conditions for sending packages as follows. Permission should be sought from the ministries of customs and trade. Packages would be handed over to the Red Crescent with such a permission certificate. The maximum weight of a package would be 5 kg and the maximum value would be 10 liras per person. The ministry would determine limitations on content.

Meanwhile, Greeks in Istanbul requested an increase in the maximum amount they could send by the *Kurtuluş*. The inter-ministerial commission accepted a maximum of 500 packages per month, 3000 in total. But that number was reduced to 1000 by the Ministry to the Prime Minister. Furthermore, it was declared that soap, olive oil and sweets could not be sent.[27] Packages from Istanbul were handed over to their recipients in Piraeus and receipts were given to representatives of the Red Crescent.

As a result of publicity in the press, the campaign for aid to Greece gained momentum. At the request of professional societies in Athens, employees in various sectors (press, municipality, museums and so on) prepared packages for their Greek colleagues. Every voyage of the vessel became an event. The journalist Faruk Fenik, on returning from the *Kurtuluş'* November voyage, recounted that the vessel's crew had insisted upon leaving their own provisions in Greece and had made do with stale bread on the trip home.[28]

Public food distribution in Athens started in November 1941, thanks to the *Kurtuluş*. But, as wartime conditions worsened, the harder it became to obtain food for relief of the Greek famine in Turkey. The cabinet decided to stop the export of food at the request of the army on 26 December 1941. The *Kurtuluş* voyages were stopped. The Greek ambassador, Raphail Raphail, wrote to the foreign minister of the Greek government-in-exile: 'the market in Turkey is worsening. The government continuously takes measures to try to prevent exports.'[29]

Thereupon the British and American ambassadors stepped in and started to put pressure on Ankara; even the German ambassador joined them. The ambassadors requested permission for the *Kurtuluş* voyages to continue and promised that, in return, a Greek vessel in Egypt would start voyages from Port Said to Turkey's southern ports. The 2500 ton vessel *Margarita*, was in the Suez Canal and the agreement required that it would be at Turkey's service from the beginning of February 1942.[30] So the *Kurtuluş* voyages started again.

Kurtuluş took food parcels and grain to Piraeus. As a result of its shipments, 250,000 people were fed in soup kitchens and 14,000 children were provided with eggs, beans and salted tuna in orphanages. There was an increase in packages sent by individuals. The Association of Journalists and the Association of Doctors obtained 60 and 700 tons of food supplies respectively.[31] The Turkish Press Association declared that it would donate income from their annual dinner to Greek journalists. The press reported that an Athens street would be named Kurtuluş.

The sinking of the *Kurtuluş*

Although it had been announced that the sixth *Kurtuluş* voyage would be delayed to the 3, 4 or 5 January 1942,[32] the voyage could only be undertaken on the 19 January 1942. The cargo of 1800 tons consisted of food shipped by the *Türk-Ellas* Company (haricot beans, chickpeas, potatoes and onions), 350 packages of grain weighing 5 kg each from journalists to their Greek journalist colleagues and 800 packages shipped by Greeks of Istanbul. The *Güven* and *Anadolu* insurance companies insured its cargo for 700,000 lira, and *Milli Reasürans* insured the vessel for 40,000 lira. The captain was Ridvan Kaptan and the crew of twenty-three was accompanied by ten Red Crescent officials.

However, in the early hours of 20 January, the vessel struck rocks and ran aground due to poor weather. It was at first believed that the *Kurtuluş* had run aground on Hayırsız Ada. But later, it became known that the accident took place at Domuzburnu on Marmara Island. According to accounts by the crew, the accident took place near the village of Saraylar (Palatia). After radio reports to Istanbul, the salvage vessels *Trak* and *Saros* departed to help, but, again because of the weather, *Saros* was forced to seek shelter in the port of Silivri, while the *Trak* did the same in Tekirdağ.[33] Another vessel sent from Çanakkale, the *Hora*, was unable to find the *Kurtuluş* and managed only to reach the island of Marmara. The *Trak* departed from Tekirdağ the next day and, following information from the *Murat Reis* about the location of the wreck, it managed to reach the scene a day later. *Kurtuluş* had withstood the waves only for four hours and she had then sunk; so the *Trak* picked up the crew and the Red Crescent officials and brought them back to Istanbul.[34]

The news of the sinking of the *Kurtuluş* occasioned much anguish in Greece where its fate gave rise to many rumours. Some said the vessel had been torpedoed. The collaborationist prime minister, General Tsolakoglou, declared his sadness about the fate of the *Kurtuluş* and stated his belief that Turkey would replace her with a new one. The Red Crescent immediately started working on the issue and the name of a new vessel, *Tunç*, was mentioned in the press.

The second vessel: the *Dumlupınar*

The *Kurtuluş* had transported a total of 9800 tons, of which 6735 tons consisted of food, 140 tons of private packages and the rest was made up of medicine and clothing. The *Dumlupınar*,[35] a vessel of 2800 tons (see Illustration 6.2) soon replaced the *Kurtuluş*. Its first voyage, on 21 February 1942, was welcomed by crowds in Piraeus as 'O Khristos O Defteros', the Second Christ. City transport, cinema and entertainment venues were all free for the crew – with only alcohol available.[36]

The daily number of rations distributed in Athens-Piraeus during the winter of 1941–42 was 200,000, reaching 400,000 by March 1942. There were also kitchens administered by the Italians, but according to one Greek writer, these involved proselytism.[37] A year previously, Greece had paid for 70,000 tons of wheat from Australia but the cargo had never arrived because of the blockade. There had been many such instances. Ambassador Raphail in Ankara wrote on 14 of March 1942 that German propaganda had been exploiting the fact that Britain had confiscated 350,000 tons of wheat, which had already been paid for by the Greek government.[38]

After March 1942, the Swedish vessels *Sicilia*, *Radmansö*, *Hallaren* and *Stureborg* – which would later be sunk by Italy – delivered 13,500 tons of wheat and 10,000 tons of flour per month from New York and Haifa, paid for by Greek organisations in the USA and Canada. At the same time, the Greek War Relief Association bought food – most of it dairy produce – from the Swiss firm Migros through the Swiss Red Cross. After its second voyage on April 24, the *Dumlupınar* could not obtain potatoes and pulses to ship because the Ministry of Commerce on 2 February 1942 had prohibited the export of basic foodstuffs. Even the Turkish army did not have sufficient supplies of food.[39] In January 1942, Ambassador Raphail had already written to the government-in-exile describing how the Turkish economy had gradually been worsening with the result that black markets had emerged.[40]

The *Dumlupınar* could therefore ship only raisins, walnuts, hazelnuts and olives. Turkey could never have hoped to meet Greece's need for wheat. According to Raphail's letter, Turkey had not exported wheat for two years, while it had imported 50,000 tons of wheat with help from Britain.[41]

The Mayor of Athens wrote a letter to the Mayor of Ankara in April 1942, asking for help for some 1500 employees of the Athens municipality. The municipal assembly accepted his request.[42] Over and above that aid, on the 24 April, the *Dumlupınar* shipped packages for members of the Greek parliament, at the request of the president of the Turkish Assembly, Abdülhaluk Renda.[43]

In May 1942, public reaction intensified in Turkey when the daily ration of bread was reduced to 150 grams per capita. Meanwhile, a member of the Red Crescent returning from Greece on the *Dumlupınar* reported that the situation in Greece had improved. The daily portion of bread per head for the first four days of the week was 158 grams in Athens and Piraeus, and 254 grams for the remainder of the week. It had become clear that the situation in Turkey in this respect was actually worse than in Greece.[44]

The *Dumlupınar* departed on its fifth and the last voyage on 24 August 1942, with a cargo of 1800 tons of beans and 300 tons of potatoes, after which it returned to Istanbul. The total amount shipped in all the ten voyages made by the *Kurtuluş* and the *Dumlupınar* between October 1941 and August 1942 amounted to just 17,000 tons of food, when the agreement had been 50,000 tons. After August 1942 there were no regular voyages from Turkey to Greece. The Greek War Relief Association had paid Turkey a total of 1,400,000 dollars.[45]

The attempt to evacuate Greek children to Turkey

The press in Turkey frequently reported that it was the children in Greece who were suffering most from the misery. Konstantinos Logothetopoulos, the Minister of Health and Social Welfare and a future collaborationist prime minister, wrote to the Turkish Embassy in Athens on the 10 January 1942 asking that a group of Greek children aged between six and thirteen should be invited by Turkey and accommodated by families in Istanbul. The number of children was to be decided by Turkey. He said: 'I am sure you will give this special attention since you well know the difficulties in providing food that our state is experiencing.' The first news that the Red Crescent would bring some 1000 children to Istanbul appeared on 16 February 1942. After Turkey declared that it would receive some 1000 children, South Africa announced that it would also accept a few thousand children. At the same time, the press wrote that 1000 children would be sent to Syria and 5000 to both Egypt and Switzerland.[46]

The Ministry to the Prime Minister declared on 12 February of the same year that it was prepared to accommodate 1000 children. A directive 'for Greek children to be accommodated in our homeland' was prepared. Responsibility for the organisation of the move was left to the Red Crescent. Meanwhile, the sending of 3000 children to Egypt was also discussed, but the idea was abandoned as a result of objections by the president of the Greek Red Cross, the octogenarian Ioannis Athanasakis. He believed that the climate did not make Egypt a suitable destination for the children but, nonetheless, requested food and clothing for 1000 children aged four to ten from the Red Crescent.[47]

It was proposed that the *Dumlupınar* would embark the children on its return after its voyage of 5 March 1942 and the state-owned Maritime Lines had places for children prepared before the vessel departed, but bureaucratic formalities prevented the children from travelling.[48] It was expected that the *Dumlupınar* would return with the children – departing after 20 March – and furthermore, it was agreed that a second party of children would be accepted. A building was found and prepared for 1000 children and it was reported that two more houses in Buca (Izmir) were allocated for the housing.[49] In April 1942, an empty building in Baltalimanı on the Bosphoros in Istanbul, belonging to the Ministry of Transportation – which once housed the Fisheries Institute – was assigned to the Red Crescent and preparations were made to accommodate the children.[50] But in the end, for reasons that are unclear, the idea of sending children to Turkey was abandoned. The Greek Red Cross announced on 25 May 1942 that the scheme would not be implemented.[51] In spite of this, the press continued to report stories to the effect that the *Erzurum* would bring the children in July and that they would be accommodated in Baltalimanı.

Later aid and conclusion

In August 1942, the Swedish vessel *Hallaren* brought wheat to the port of Izmir, to be distributed to the Greek islands and the *Arslan* was assigned to assist it.[52] Furthermore, it was declared that the same vessel would transport 3000 tons of food purchased in Lebanon to Greece. Meanwhile, Argentina was able to ship 10,000 tons of wheat. The Turkish press contended that the situation had improved.

After the regular voyages of the *Kurtuluş* and the *Dumlupınar* had ceased, Turkish humanitarian aid did continue although it gradually declined. Some food was supplied in exchange for Greek olives. Turkey was in particular involved in the distribution of provisions to the Aegean islands from abroad. The *Tunç*, the *Konya* and *Güneysu* were occasionally involved in shipping aid to Greece.[53] Turkey allowed Greece to control Turkish charitable (*vakıf*) properties in Greece until the end of the war. After the liberation of Greece, Hasan Saka, the Minister of Foreign Affairs, declared that he 'acknowledged Greece's liberation with great joy'. The cabinet accepted the request of the government of Greece – which had been communicated by its embassy in Ankara – to buy food from Turkey. In a decree, dated 7 December 1944 it approved a one-off purchase by the Red Crescent of food to the maximum value of 500,000 liras to be sent to Greece.[54] In acknowledgement of the assistance provided by Turkey, gifts of a vase and a plate produced in an Athenian tile factory were sent to the Turkish president İsmet İnönü. Turkey had thus continued during the Second World War the friendship that had been established by Atatürk and Venizelos in the early 1930s.

Notes

1. Mark Mazower, *Inside Hitler's Greece: the Experience of Occupation* (London 1993), p. 38.
2. Alexis Alexandris, *The Greek Minority of Istanbul and Greek-Turkish Relations 1918–1974* (Athens, 1992), p. 178.
3. The Republican Archive of the Prime Ministry-Turkey (RAP) (30 10 256 723 17).
4. Xenophon L. Pantazidis, *I Istoria tou Ellinikou Erythrou Stavrou*, vol. 1, (Athens,1987), p. 275.
5. Gotthard Jaeschke, *Türkiye Kronolojisi (1938–1945)* (Ankara, 1990), p. 40.
6. Pantazidis, *I Istoria*, p. 336.
7. RAP (30 18 1 94 24 16).
8. Pantazidis, *I Istoria*, pp. 275 and 265.
9. Dimitris Kitsikis, *Ellas kai Xenoi, 1919–1967. Ta Arkheia tou Ellinikou Ypourgeiou Exoterikon* (Athens, 1977), p. 144. For Tsouderos' own account of the relief efforts of the government-in-exile, see *O Episitismos 1941–1944* (Athens 1946).
10. Mazower, *Inside Hitler's Greece*, p. 31.
11. Ibid., p. 46.
12. Georgios A. Kazamias, 'Turks, Swedes and Famished Greeks. Some Aspects of Famine Relief in Occupied Greece, 1941–44', *Balkan Studies*, XXXIII (1992): 293.
13. RAP (30 10 256 725 1).
14. Zeynel Abidin Ersoy, *II. Dünya Savaşi Sirasinda Türkiye'nin Yunanistan'a Yaptiği İnsani Yardımlar (1935–1945)* (unpublished MA thesis), Yildiz Technical University-Institute of Social Sciences (Istanbul, 2001), p. 77.
15. See Yalman's earliest articles: *Vatan*, 14 July 1941, 20 July 1941, 12 August 1941. Yalman was a prominent *dönme*, a descendant of the followers of the Jewish false 'Messiah' Sabbatai Zevi, who converted to Islam in the seventeenth century. Most of the *dönme* had lived in Thessaloniki and were among

the Muslims of Greece exchanged for the Orthodox Christians of Turkey in the 1923–24 population transfer. This may have made them particularly sensitive to accounts of famine in their ancestral home.

16. *Cumhuriyet*, 7 November and 20 December 1941.
17. *Vatan*, 1 October 1941.
18. Feridun Cemal Erkin, *Dışişlerinde 34 Yıl-Anılar Yorumlar*, I (Ankara, 1980), pp. 129–30.
19. RAP (30 10 179 235 6).
20. *Vatan*, 12 and 14 September 1941; *Cumhuriyet*, 12 and 14 September 1941.
21. RAP (30 10 179 235 30).
22. Kitsikis, *Ellas kai Xenoi*, p. 150.
23. RAP (30 10 191 311 17).
24. RAP (30 10 179 235 8).
25. *Cumhuriyet*, 19 November 1941.
26. *Cumhuriyet*, 25 October 1941.
27. RAP (30 10 179 235 11).
28. *Vatan*, 20 November 1941.
29. Dimitris Kitsikis, *Istoria tou Ellinotourkikou Khorou apo ton E. Venizelo ston G. Papadopoulo (1928–1973)* (Athens, 1981), p. 138.
30. Kitsikis, *Ellas kai Xenoi*, p. 177.
31. Kitsikis, *Istoria tou*, p. 137.
32. RAP (30 10 171 185 20).
33. *Cumhuriyet*, 21 January 1942.
34. *Cumhuriyet, Vatan* and *Tan*, 22 January 1942.
35. Ironically, Dumlupınar was the name of the place where the Turkish army won its last battle against the Greek army in the Turkish War of Liberation, in August 1922.
36. *Vatan*, 9 March 1942.
37. Pantazidis, *I Istoria*, p. 300.
38. Kitsikis, *Ellas kai Xenoi*, p. 147.
39. Ibid., pp. 169 and 179.
40. Dimitri Kitsikis, 'La Famine en Grèce (1941–1942): Les Conséquences Politiques', *Revue d'Histoire de la Deuxième Guerre Mondiale*, 74 (April 1969): 38.
41. Ibid., p. 30.
42. *Vatan*, 7 April 1942.
43. *Vatan*, 24 April 1942.
44. Kitsikis, 'La Famine en Grèce', p. 39.
45. Ibid., p. 32.
46. *Vatan*, 21 February 1942.
47. RAP (30 10 178 227 11).
48. *Cumhuriyet*, 6 March 1942.
49. *Cumhuriyet*, 23 April 1942.
50. RAP (30 10 179 235 20).
51. RAP (30 10 178 227 11).
52. RAP (30 10 169 177 2).
53. Esra Danacıoğlu, 'Yunanistan'a Uzanan Yardım Eli', *Popüler Tarih*, 9 (February 2001): 43.
54. RAP (30 18 01 107 90 8).

6

Inter Arma Caritas: the Swedish Red Cross in Greece in the 1940s

Marie Mauzy

When, in the early 1980s, I arrived in Athens from my native Sweden and started work at the American School of Classical Studies in Athens (ASCSA), I was intrigued to learn that the school was situated on *Odos Souidias*, or Sweden Street. The street, located in the Kolonaki district of central Athens, had originally been called Spefsipou but was renamed in the late 1940s in recognition of the humanitarian work of the Swedish Red Cross in Greece during the Second World War. But why had Spefsipou Street been so renamed? I soon learned that the headquarters of the Swedish Red Cross in Greece in the 1940s had been established at the Marasleion School, adjacent to the British School (sometimes referred to as the British School of Archaeology) and a short distance from the American School of Classical Studies which shares a campus with the British School. But it was even more surprising to discover that from the summer of 1942 until the end of the war in 1945 the buildings of the ASCSA were occupied by the staff of the Swedish Red Cross Commission. The personnel of the Swiss Red Cross, which was likewise involved in relief work in Greece, were billeted in the British School and also used parts of the dormitories of the ASCSA. The Marasleion School, and the American and British Schools occupy a city block and it was one side of this block that was renamed *Odos Souidias*. The road running parallel to it was renamed *Odos Elvetias*, in honour of the Swiss Red Cross mission, although this name has fallen out of use.

In 1941, as the German invasion of Greece became imminent, most of the personnel of the ASCSA had been advised to leave Greece and the buildings were declared American property. The American Red Cross had already asked for an option on the buildings as they would have made an excellent headquarters building or hospital. The American School's buildings had large signs in four languages making clear that the buildings were under the protection of the United States government. The windows had been reinforced with paper strips as a precautionary measure against bomb blast. The letters USA had been painted on the roofs, to alert enemy bombers. But, as someone pointed out, if America entered the war these would have to be removed in short order.[1]

With the entry of the United States into the war in December 1941 the Swiss Legation undertook the protection of American interests in Greece, as it had already done with British, interests. These included the property of both archaeological schools. The deeply loyal Greek legal consultant of the ASCSA, Anastasios Adossides,[2] was left to care for the administration of the ASCSA. He felt that even though the premises were under Swiss protection 'such large well appointed buildings were a great temptation to the Germans and Italians. Officials would often pass by looking longingly at the buildings.'[3] He feared that some loophole or excuse would be found for their takeover by the Axis occupying powers. Adossides' wife was a nurse working for the Greek Red Cross and, through their many connections, he invited the Swiss and Swedish Red Cross delegates in Greece to utilise the buildings. Their presence rendered the buildings and the library of the ASCSA safe from the occupation forces. This is but one of many instances where the name of the Red Cross would command great respect among Germans, Italians, resistance partisans and civilians alike.

Illustration 6.1 shows the renaming ceremony in 1945. The ceremony is taking place on the corner of Souidias Street and Marasli Street. A Greek minister, to the left, is shaking hands with Knut Thyberg, chargé d'affaires at the Swedish Embassy in Athens and the Swedish government's representative on the Red Cross Commission in Athens. To the right stands Gottfrid Walldén, who worked for the Swedish Red Cross delegation as a financial officer. He was originally a bank employee from a small town in Sweden and had joined the Swedish team in Greece in 1942. He is characteristic of the majority of the Swedes working for the Red Cross. Without any background in humanitarian work he had decided to accept the invitation and challenge of coming to Greece to help ameliorate the effects of the famine.

But how did Sweden become a key part of the largest humanitarian aid initiative in occupied Europe during World War II? Sweden's neutrality during the war enabled her to initiate and to participate in a number of such humanitarian projects. Besides providing aid to Greece, Sweden also assisted her Nordic neighbours, Norway, Denmark and Finland. In monetary terms, the largest amounts of Swedish aid went to Finland and Norway. The state allocated only 250,000 kronor in financial aid to Greece in 1942/43 and 450,000 kronor the following year. This compared to the millions of kronor made available to the Nordic countries in the form of direct aid or credit.[4]

Sweden's contributions to Greece for the most part did not consist of economic aid, but the country's neutral position was crucial both in initiating negotiations, in organising the logistics of delivering relief, in supplying the large vessels required and in establishing a neutral commission in Greece to oversee the distribution of relief. As the British concluded, Sweden was especially suited for the mission not only on account of her neutrality but also on account of the 'honourable position which her practical sympathy with humanitarian causes has won for her'.[5]

The complex political manoeuvring and negotiations between the different actors that eventually resulted in the Red Cross relief plan for Greece are addressed elsewhere in this volume in Chapters 3 and 4. The discussions were conducted at a high level between the Allies and the occupiers, sometimes with Sweden acting as a mediator. On another level, negotiations continued between the International, Swedish and Greek Red Cross. But it should be stressed how important were the efforts of a number of individuals and private organisations in informing the governments and people in the US and in Europe of how terrible the situation in Greece was.

The suggestion that neutral ships should be used to deliver supplies to otherwise inaccessible ports in Europe was made by Marcel Junod, a Swiss doctor who worked for the International Red Cross, visiting prison camps and organising relief operations during the Second World War.[6] He was troubled by the fact that supplies from the British Red Cross to British prisoners of war in Germany had not reached the detainees. Thousands of parcels had piled up in Lisbon, the only open port in Europe. He travelled to London to persuade the British authorities to allow Red Cross ships to sail in contested waters, following strictly agreed routes and times. The ships, a number of them Swedish, were to be painted white with a red cross on their sides and were to be clearly illuminated at night. Agreement was reached and within months several large white ships flying the flag of the International Committee of the Red Cross delivered food, clothes and medical supplies in the Mediterranean. The timetables and exact routes of each ship were carefully agreed in advance and unloading was strictly overseen by members of the Red Cross.

In the autumn of the same year, 1941, while Junod was in Turkey on Red Cross business, he received an urgent telegram from Robert Brunel, the Red Cross representative in Athens. The telegram read as follows: 'Food situation in Greece extremely grave. Mortality increased sixfold in last two months. Catastrophe inevitable unless outside help arrives quickly.'[7] Brunel added that he thought that sending food supplies through Turkey, which was subject to the blockade, would afford the quickest solution. Through negotiations with the different parties involved in the arrangement, a cargo boat named *Kurtuluş* loaded with foodstuffs, painted with a bright red crescent instead of a red cross, sailed to Piraeus in October of 1941. The cargo had been organised and paid for by American private organisations, in particular by the Greek War Relief Association. The ship made six voyages between Turkey and Greece before being shipwrecked and sinking in the sea of Marmara in January 1942 (see Chapter 5). Deliveries continued for a short while afterwards with another ship, the *Dumlupınar* (Illustration 6.2). In the memories of many older Athenians the sinking of the *Kurtuluş* was a great loss. The ship, stocked with the most basic foodstuffs, is still very much remembered as *the* ship that brought food to the Greeks. One woman recalls how as a child she might forget her school bag, but never her spoon and tin for the meals the children would be served from the soup-kitchens (Illustration 6.3). With the arrival of the *Kurtuluş* suddenly the air smelled like pea soup with meat.[8] The crew of the *Kurtuluş* were shocked by what they saw in Piraeus: 'no written account can describe what we see, it is like entering hell'.[9]

Junod himself travelled to Athens and described how the streets were full of beggars and corpses. It was obvious that the Turkish shipments alone would not be enough to help the starving Greek people. Their stores were empty. It was clear that the Red Cross would have to find further assistance and a different system of bringing in food. But how would they be able to make the different governments realise the scale and urgency of the tragedy that was so quickly developing before them?

As Junod was about to leave Athens, a Greek nurse called Amalia Lykourezos came to see him. Among other things she was responsible for milk distribution for infants. She handed him a folder and asked him to take it to Switzerland so that people there could see for themselves the plight of the Greek children. It contained numerous images of starving and suffering children (Illustrations 6.4a–4c). She added that if nothing was done before the coming winter no one would be left alive.[10] People around the world became aware of the starvation in Greece through photographs, written accounts and eyewitness reports and this awareness acted as catalyst for the different agencies and governments that would eventually take part in humanitarian aid to Greece. Junod returned to Switzerland where he showed the contents of Amalia Lykourezos' folder to members of the International Committee of the Red Cross and to foreign diplomats.

At the same time, a Swede named Gunnar Cederschiöld alerted the Swedish government and public to the situation in Greece. Cederschiöld, a journalist and businessman, predicted that the famine in Europe was going to be worse than that which had followed the First World War.

In a number of European countries people were undernourished, but what he witnessed in Greece was starvation. He reported:

> I thought I had seen the most ghastly things in life. I have seen executions where the condemned screamed in agony, the battlefields of the Somme, Verdun and Kemmel where the injured begged for help and water and corpses lay rotting in the fields. In Venezuela, I saw the victims of leprosy with decaying limbs. In west African villages I watched victims of sleeping sickness slumped next to corpses which were being eaten by vultures. But never have I seen anything that shocked me as much as what I saw in Athens during the summer months of 1941; children dying of starvation, without understanding why. Like Dante in the Inferno, I walked from children's clinics, to orphanages and to soup kitchens. Everywhere I saw starving children. In the clinics, mothers were waiting with their hungry and sick children. The babies tried to suckle their mothers' breasts that were unable to produce any milk. One orphanage had 1,200 children. Those that were still able to, screamed continuously with hunger. The rest were apathetic, unable to utter a word.[11]

He went on to say that the daily ration of 180 grams of black bread was not enough to survive on, but that fortunately the black market saved lives (Illustration 6.5). The scenes which Cederschiöld witnessed must have been very similar to some of those illustrated in Chapter 7.

Cederschiöld's eyewitness report in the daily *Stockholms-Tidningen* had an immediate effect. He contacted the Swedish Red Cross and the government suggesting that Swedish ships could transport supplies to Greece. The Red Cross started preparations by ensuring that the Swedish Maritime Administration would supply the ships and that the boats would sail under the Red Cross flag. Much of Sweden's mercantile marine fleet was laid up because of the war. Sixty per cent of the ships lay inside the Skagerrak blockade while the rest had been caught outside.[12] The ships outside the blockade were inaccessible to Sweden and instead were put into service by Great Britain and the US. Some of these ships were to be used by the International Red Cross to bring grain from North America to Greece. However, although Sweden was prepared to dispatch ships and supply personnel, it was not until March of 1942 that the first ships and delegates reached Greece.

Negotiations between the parties involved were complex and slow. One condition stipulated by the Allies was that the relief should not benefit the occupiers. They asked Sweden to oversee the distribution.

While Germany did not seem to object, Italy protested. The Italians wanted the International Red Cross, which was already established in Greece, to be in charge. A compromise, acceptable to all parties, was eventually reached. A commission, using the name of the International Red Cross and consisting of eight Swedish and seven Swiss delegates, would be responsible for overseeing the distribution. It was agreed that the chairman of the commission should be a Swede. Its official title was Commission de Gestion de la Délégation du Comité International de la Croix-Rouge en Grèce.[13] The Swiss Red Cross delegates were to deal mainly with medical issues and the distribution of medicines. Contact with the occupation forces was assigned to a committee consisting of representatives of the German, Italian and Greek Red Cross and the Turkish Red Crescent.

The chairman, who was appointed by the Swedish government, was in charge of the entire organisation, overseeing the distribution and control of relief supplies. He also had responsibility for contacts concerning practical matters with the occupying forces and the Greek authorities. The Swedish delegates, 29 in total, have been described as a slightly odd bunch of individuals that had been hastily assembled and sent to Greece. Many of them were academics, without any previous experience in relief work, but recruited primarily because of their knowledge of Greek and familiarity with the country. Classicists and archaeologists were naturally one of the groups that were targeted. Others had special skills in finance, milling, logistics, statistics or seafaring. But most importantly they were all united in their desire to participate in a unique humanitarian mission.[14] The Swedish Red Cross selected the delegates, with the exception of the chairman, through word of mouth recommendations. Illustration 6.6 depicts one of the groups leaving for Greece in January 1944 and clearly illustrates the diversity of their background. From the left these are: the Reverend Arvid Wikerstål; Professor Stig Wikander, a specialist in Sanskrit; Karl Borg, an engineer with the Swedish Match Company; Einar Gjerstad, a professor of classics; Prince Carl, chairman of the Swedish Red Cross; Jean Lieberg, a customs official; Hans Ehrenstråle, a student; and Dag Bergman, a lawyer.

The primary task for the Swedes in Greece was to receive and distribute the supplies that arrived by sea from North America. In reality, the mission had to solve a variety of problems, social, financial, industrial, maritime, psychological and so on that had not been mentioned in the short briefing paper that they had been handed in Sweden. The commission was charged with distributing supplies where they were most needed. They were not to make a profit, but only to cover such costs as would be incurred. Food supplies were not be diverted for political or military purposes.

Illustration 6.1   The renaming in 1945 of Odos Souidias (Sweden Street) to mark the Swedish contribution to relief operations during the occupation

Illustration 6.2   The Turkish Red Crescent ship *Dumlupınar* which brought the first emergency supplies to Greece in the winter of 1941–42

Illustration 6.3   Starvation in Athens, 1944/45

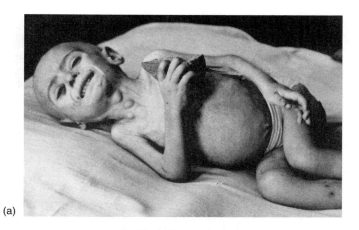

(a)

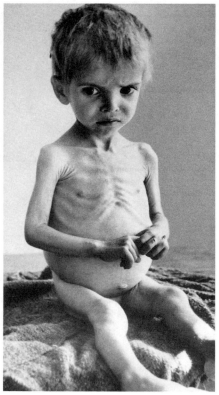

(b)

Illustration 6.4 Victims of famine in Greece, 1941/42

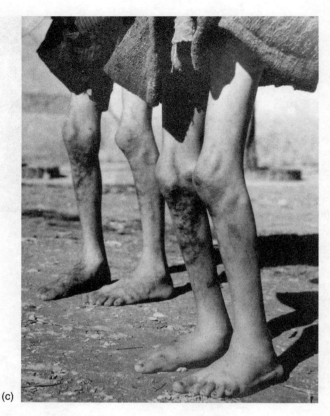

(c)

Illustration 6.4   (Continued)

Illustration 6.5   The black market functioning openly in Athens, 1944/45

Illustration 6.6   Swedish volunteers about to leave for work with the Swedish Red Cross in Greece. The elderly figure in the centre is Prince Carl, the Chairman of the Swedish Red Cross

(a)

(b)

Illustration 6.7   The unloading of Red Cross supplies in Piraeus. Note the guards standing on the lorries

(c)

Illustration 6.7 (*Continued*)

Illustration 6.8 A soup-kitchen overseen by a well-dressed Athenian woman, 1944/45

Illustration 6.9   Dangerously overcrowded public transport

Illustration 6.10   The Swedish Red Cross ship *Wiril* ablaze in Chios harbour in February 1944 after being bombed by mistake by the RAF

Illustration 6.11   A caique with Red Cross insignia used for the local distribution of supplies, Thessaloniki, 1944

Illustration 6.12 A Red Cross nurse, Sister Lenio, travelling by donkey on her way to Souli

Illustration 6.13 Swedish Red Cross workers in Greece. Axel W. Persson and his team. Persson, front left, with his wife Elsa Segerdahl, front right

Illustration 6.14   Minas Geramas, a teenage worker for the Red Cross in Athens

Three-quarters of the foodstuffs supplied consisted of grain. The remainder was made up of dried fruit and vegetables, sugar, canned milk, medicine and so on. The supplies mainly originated from Canada and the US, although Argentina was also a source. The supplies were paid for by private organisations such as the Greek War Relief Association in the United States and the Greek War Relief Fund in Canada (see Chapter 4). National Red Cross committees also contributed financially. It was agreed that eight Swedish ships were to be given safe conduct across the Atlantic, supplying 15,000 tons of wheat per month. One unexpected drawback was that in the heavy seas of the winter months of 1942–43, ships ended up carrying fewer supplies because the larger boats could not travel back across the Atlantic without any cargo. To compensate for the absence of cargo on the return journey from Greece to Canada, some 400 tons of ballast had to be taken on board in Canada before the ship was loaded with supplies.[15] As a consequence, less wheat was shipped, but the practice proved time-saving in the long run since loading the ballast in Greece and unloading it in Canada would have been difficult and time consuming.

The ships, belonging to different Swedish shipping companies, were chartered by the Swedish Red Cross, painted white with a large red cross and *Sverige* (Sweden) in bold letters on the sides of the boats (see cover illustration). The cargo was loaded in Montreal and the ships had to follow a carefully laid out route to Greece. In principal it was not safe for ships even from neutral countries to cross the northern Atlantic on account of the danger from German submarines. It was eventually agreed that the ships would traverse the eastern seaboard of the United States and then cross to Gibraltar, pass south of Crete, head towards Kastellorizo and then turn northwards towards Piraeus. The ships travelled in pairs and were clearly illuminated at night. The fact that two ships would arrive together at crowded harbours more than once created problems.

During the journeys, the ships had to report their positions three times a day to the Swedish authorities. Before leaving Piraeus, the Swedish Ministry of Foreign Affairs had to obtain the necessary clearance for the ships from the occupying forces. This communication was carried out via dispatches channelled through the German authorities and the Swedish Legation in Berlin.[16]

Each ship needed approximately three months to sail to North America, load the cargo, cross the Atlantic, pass through strict security checks at various points in the Mediterranean and unload. Initially, only the ports of Piraeus and Thessaloniki were allowed to be used, but from 1943 it was agreed that Iraklion on Crete and Izmir [Smyrna] in Turkey could also be used. Izmir was used as a port for storing and distributing the relief to the nearby Greek islands of Samos, Chios and Mytilini.

When the much-awaited ships arrived at the designated ports the goods had to be unloaded. Distribution was initially concentrated on the inhabitants of Athens, Piraeus and Thessaloniki where the need was the greatest. Some time later it was agreed that cities in other parts of the country would also be permitted to receive consignments of aid (Illustrations 6.7a–c).

The grain that was shipped had to be milled into flour and this was done in the large flour mills in Piraeus. One mill was located right at the harbour, complete with a device that sucked the grain straight into the mill from the holds of the ships, but this could only process a part of the daily need and other mills in the area had to be found. Most motorised vehicles had been confiscated for the war effort but every available truck, whatever state it was in, was used to transport and distribute the supplies. The Red Cross had set up heavily guarded storage areas around Athens where the goods were stored before final distribution.

The mills in Piraeus employed a thousand workers who were paid by the Greek Ministry of Food, but the Red Cross had to employ an additional 100 people to guard the shipments during unloading, transport, weighing and milling. In such desperate times every gram of flour had to be guarded. When workers left for the day they were all carefully searched. Threats of strikes and work stoppages among the workers constituted another problem. One day's delay could mean starvation for many people.

It would have been easier to import flour that had already been milled, but unfortunately only white flour could be supplied. This lacked the nutritional content, the minerals and vitamins, that were necessary for the undernourished people. Since their diet consisted mainly of bread, with little meat, vegetables or milk it was crucial that the most nutritious flour be used. Also, dark, coarse bread had long been part of the Greek diet.

The Red Cross was not permitted to sell the flour to the Greek Ministry of Food, but only directly to bakeries, of which there were more than 700 in Athens. Bread requires yeast, salt and water as well as flour, and since flour was a valuable commodity on the black market, it was a great temptation for the bakers to add more water to their dough and save on the flour. In order to establish the ratio of flour and water Red Cross personnel had to carry out numerous baking tests and it was established that 100 kilos of flour should make 141.3 kilos of bread. To make sure that the bakers adhered to the regulations it proved necessary to set up a bread control agency. Another important task was to establish the daily bread quota. Initially it was fixed at 50 *dramia* (160 gr) per person a day. In order to feed the inhabitants of Athens with that amount 5000 tons of bread was required a month.[17] The Red Cross had planned to feed three million people, one million of whom lived in the capital.

Another major problem that the Red Cross had to contend with was the existing ration card system. There were more cards in circulation than actual people. Many of these cards had been illegally obtained in the chaos that followed the German invasion. Moreover, many families failed to report the death of family members to the authorities in order to keep hold of their cards. The suggestion that a census be held had to be cancelled amid protests both from the Greek side and the occupation authorities. Instead, new rules were applied whereby each person had to pick up his or her new cards in person. Through this process, more than 200,000 false cards were removed from circulation.[18]

By marking the fingertips of babies that were brought to the milk distribution centres it was soon discovered that some babies were used by many different mothers to visit the centres and acquire milk rations. At hospitals, institutions, orphanages and prisons there were special distribution centres to which the Red Cross delivered supplies. But there were also a number of soup-kitchens in existence, run by private philanthropic organisations and by the Greek authorities (Illustration 6.8).[19] One of the earliest soup-kitchens in Athens had been established by an American couple in the suburb of Melissia as early as the end of 1940. Eugene Vanderpool was an archaeologist working for the American School of Classical Studies, where the Red Cross delegates were billeted during the war. His wife, Joan, was caring for their small children on the outbreak of the war. Despite the difficulties and dangers of the war the Vanderpools decided to stay in Greece.

In Joan Vanderpool's diary and letters one comes across passages such as these:

> We love Greece, and we are now suddenly proud to see that other people have grown to respect her and feel her vitality and greatness. And then that morning when, after months of tension and seeing the clouds gathering, the skies burst, and were black with enemy planes. I am not ashamed to say that that morning as I carried the babies from where they had been playing in the sun, to the darkness of the dreaded air shelter, I felt as close to utter misery and terror as a human being can feel. I learned in that hour I am no heroine.[20]

She and her husband erected a small building on their property to feed the children in their neighbourhood, to be called 'The Children's House'. At the same time, the American School of Classical Studies started collecting money among archaeologists and classicists in the US for the purchase of an ambulance, which Vanderpool and other members of the school took turns driving to and from the Albanian border with injured soldiers.[21] The ambulance was eventually turned over to the Greek Red Cross when the Americans were obliged to leave. But the Vanderpools remained in Greece throughout the war years, although Gene Vanderpool was sent to a detention camp in Germany in November 1942 and was not released until February 1944. Joan Vanderpool, as did a number of other foreigners, undertook the work of organising relief. For many months the work was privately funded until it was no longer possible to receive money from America, and the Near East Foundation took over.

As Joan Vanderpool writes:

It began gaily. The war was going to be a short one and meanwhile there were everyday astonishing advances. Good humor and good will was everywhere.

We discussed which foods contained the most vitamins and how many calories we could supply. We weighed things out and planned menus. Food was plentiful then and money was sufficient.

We bought books in which to keep records of the history of each child and scales upon which to weigh them regularly. We little suspected then that after a short time the weight charts, in spite of all our efforts, would show a steady downward curve.

From having in the beginning fifty children we later had over three hundred. There is no doubt that for many months we kept these children alive. But then starvation began throughout Greece and in spite of the fullest help of the Red Cross and the already mentioned support of the Near East [Foundation], we found ourselves no longer able to supply an adequate meal to an already undernourished child, and we often found children fallen by the roadside while trying to fight their way through the wind and rain to get to us. The tragedies of that winter [1941–42] are still unbelievable. Transportation had become nearly impossible [Illustration 6.9] and my husband used to bicycle up from Athens laden with what food he could find. It was little enough and obviously not sufficient enough for a starving child. We had then to consider what could be done. The first thing, we thought, was to re-organise the Children's House and feed only children who lived close to us – thus not subjecting them to long exposures for the sake of a meagre meal. I was myself expecting our fourth baby in a few months.

People urged me not to spend so many hours doing strenuous physical work, especially as our own diet then consisted chiefly of water boiled vegetables, rotten eggs and once in a long while donkey. If they knew of the insignificance of the physical work compared to the strain of having, in those days and later, to make decisions, which, while helping some children, literally condemned others to death.

The silence of the days and especially the early mornings is unforgettable. No dog remained to bark, one never heard a cock crow and rats overran even the streets of Athens because cats had long since been eaten. Only the tramp of feet, one heard, and the dull rumble of cart wheels on the road. This rumble was to become the symbol of starvation. It represented the only means of survival for some. In the carts one saw usually wood and charcoal, but sometimes only pine-cones and acorns, which, hand drawn to Athens, were sold in the streets or exchanged for a piece of bread. The forests are stripped now and the mountain seems to have been visited by human locusts.[22]

Before the arrival of the Red Cross, the soup-kitchens had to supply the food themselves, but subsequently the Red Cross was the source of supplies. Nine hundred thousand people were registered at the soup-kitchens in Athens, 300,000 of them children.[23] The Red Cross found many of the soup-kitchens ineffective and demoralizing for those seeking help. At mealtimes people would queue endlessly waiting for some thin soup and a piece of bread. There were rumours that some of the soup-kitchens were being run by dubious characters and organisations. Paul Mohn of the Swiss Red Cross felt that a major reorganisation was needed. At this stage in the mission's history the Red Cross were able to distribute dried vegetables and other foodstuffs in addition to grain. Mohn's idea was to let people get their rations from the local grocer instead of having it prepared by the soup-kitchens. By preparing the food at home a sense of family life and normality would be restored. An announcement was placed in the papers informing Athenians about the alternative to the soup-kitchens. A vote took place and the new system was soon brought into being. Seven hundred grocers handled the distribution without encountering the problems experienced with the bakers.[24]

The commission in Athens employed some 2000 administrators and 2900 workers and drivers. The administration was divided into numerous departments and sub-units. In the rest of the country there were approximately 1000 administrators, of which 400 were stationed in Thessaloniki.[25] It is estimated that there were about 5000 people working for local committees in the provinces. Given the severe shortages of motor vehicles the transportation of relief supplies was inevitably a major problem. On the mainland the Germans allowed the Red Cross to use empty train carriages going north, after they had transported their own supplies south. When the Gorgopotamos viaduct carrying the railway line from Athens to Thessaloniki was blown up in November 1942 alternative ways had to be found for some weeks. Land transport was facilitated with the arrival of fifteen Volvo trucks from Sweden, together with cars from the US. In the Peloponnese the bulk of the relief supplies were transported on the trains that the Germans allowed them to use, while in the region of Corinth and the Argolid most aid was transported by truck. Caiques were also used to a certain extent in the coastal areas of the Peloponnese (see Illustration 6.11).

Swedish ships delivered shipments directly to Crete, Corfu, Samos, Chios and Mytilini. In the Cyclades, goods would be transhipped and delivered by smaller boats. Transportation always carried with it an element of danger, with caiques on occasion being bombed by the Allies. On the roads the trucks were attacked or hit mines. In areas where resistance forces were active, the trucks were frequently given a military escort by the occupiers. One ship, the *Wiril*, was bombed by British planes in Chios harbour in February 1944.[26] As a result of miscommunication with the Swedish authorities, the *Wiril* sailed from Samos without proper clearance. The British believed the ship to be carrying weapons to the Germans and attacked it (Illustration 6.10). Two Swedes died. One of these was Nils Erik Nilsson, who worked for the Red Cross, and was due to marry a girl from Chios the following day.[27] The other was the ship's engineer Sven Brant. In addition, 14 Greek crew members died. A marble plaque on the harbour of Chios now marks the bombing of the *Wiril*. Three other ships were also lost. The *Fenja* hit a mine near Kalymnos, while the *Stureborg* was struck by an Italian torpedo near Cyprus, with only one Greek surviving from the entire crew. The *Eros* ran aground near Milos but the crew was saved.[28]

Besides Athens, Swedish Red Cross delegates were also stationed on Crete, Corfu, Chios, Mytilini, Samos, in the Cyclades, in Patras, Tripolis, Trikkala, Volos, Lamia and Thessaloniki. One of these delegates, a former customs official, Jean Lieberg, who was stationed in Thessaloniki during 1944, recalls that he was very honoured by the appointment to Greece, but before arriving in the country had only a very vague idea what the work entailed. 'I thought I would drive a van and hand out bread to hungry hordes', he said.[29] He was astonished to find out that he was to handle a food distribution organisation the size of a government department. Many refugees poured in from Bulgarian-occupied Eastern Macedonia and Thrace; areas that had not been included in the Red Cross's planning. Before Lieberg arrived in Thessaloniki, he visited the village of Kastraki, which had just been destroyed by Germans. He describes ghastly scenes. Despite the cold and wet snow, no one was wearing shoes. Barefoot in mud, with rags around their feet, their faces pasty and afflicted by scabies and parasites, the villagers were only able to survive on the provisions supplied by the Red Cross.

Sture Linnér, a 28-year-old student of classics from the University of Uppsala, was the youngest of the Swedish Red Cross delegates. While he was posted in Thessaly the intense fighting between the occupation forces and the Greek partisans in the area often meant that it was impossible to receive supplies. Linnér remarks in despair 'We are cut off from all supplies from the Red Cross in Athens and the local reserve food warehouses are depleted. Even the medicine is gone, so are the clothes. The border between life and death is fragile in these times, many succumbing to death without having the strength to resist. What is the use of leaving the house – I can't help anyway.'[30] Shortly after the massacre by the Germans in Distomo on 10 June 1944 Sture Linnér reached the village. What he witnessed was horrendous. 'In every tree, lining the road leading into Distomo, for hundreds of meters, there were bodies, some still alive, nailed [to the trees] by bayonets. This was the way the villagers had been punished.'[31]

In the Peloponnese, the work of the Red Cross delegates was very different from that in the cities, due in great measure to continuing fighting between the occupiers and the resistance guerrillas. Hans Ehrenstråle,[32] taking up his post in Patras in early 1944, received instructions from his superiors that his first priority was to help the mountain community of Kalavryta, isolated in sheer misery after its destruction in late 1943 and the shooting of some 500 of its male inhabitants by the Germans in reprisal for guerrilla activity. After the massacre the village was cut off and was in great need of supplies. This would be only the first of many burnt and destroyed villages he would have to try to reach with food, clothing and medicine. Many times it was not possible to use cars to travel, and he and his assistants had to walk or use donkeys (Illustration 6.12).[33]

In Tripolis, Professor Axel W. Persson, in peacetime an archaeologist, worked together with his wife Elsa Segerdahl, a medical doctor and one of the two female delegates of the Swedish Red Cross (Illustration 6.13).[34] Persson had been instrumental in selecting the delegates for the Swedish Red Cross. With many years experience of excavations and a passion for Greece and its people, he and his wife worked tirelessly in the distribution of food, in soup-kitchens and children's welfare. The couple were profoundly committed to the Red Cross mission and would remain for two years in Tripolis.[35] Another archaeologist, Einar Gjerstad, found that his ability to classify systematically ancient sherds could be applied to huge shipments of clothes and shoes. With his expertise and the subsequent help of the bone specialist Nils Gejvall, people were equipped with perfectly matched shoes in the right size. Martin Nordenström, an officer in the reserve and a physical education teacher, was stationed in the Cyclades for almost three years. During his mission he had been exposed to danger many times, but ironically it was on his last journey from Piraeus to Syros that the overloaded passenger ship he was travelling on capsized outside Hydra and killed him and a hundred others.[36]

For many of the delegates the time spent in Greece shaped the rest of their lives in different ways. Both Sture Linnér and Hans Ehrenstråle would be offered positions in the newly-established United Nations. Several of them married, or planned to marry, Greek women. One such was Dag Bergman (the brother of the Swedish film director Ingmar Bergman) who married the daughter of Anastasios Adossidis, who had facilitated the use by the Red Cross delegates of the American School in Athens. Gottfrid Walldén also married a Greek woman and settled in Athens. Both Bergman and Walldén are buried in the First Cemetery in Athens.

Between September 1942, when the first Swedish ships arrived, to March 1945, when UNRRA took over, the Red Cross supplied 623,000 tons of foodstuffs.[37] They also brought medicine and large quantities of clothes and shoes. It is impossible to estimate how many lives were saved because of their action.

Minas Geramas, shown in Illustration 6.14, will serve as a symbol for the survivors. As a teenager he worked for the Red Cross in Athens, living with 50 other workers at the headquarters on Marasli Street, delivering food around Athens. He poses in a jacket with a zucchini flower in his pocket, holding a bouquet of garlic bulbs. This photo fixes a moment in time when fresh vegetables were as precious as roses.

Notes

1. American School of Classical Studies Archives, Administrative Records, Series 800, Box 804/2, folder 7.
2. Adossides was a Greek diplomat who had served as Governor of Macedonia during and after World War I, and later as Governor of the Cyclades and Samos. He was also appointed Secretary of the Refugee Settlement Commission supervising the exchange of populations between Greece and Turkey. Lucy Shoe Meritt, *History of the American School of Classical Studies at Athens 1939–1980* (Princeton, 1984), p. 16.
3. Lucy Shoe Meritt, p. 17.

4. A.E. Bjelle et al. (eds), *Sveriges internationella Hjälpverksamhet 1939–1950 / en redogörelse från Svenska Kommittén för Internationell Hjälpverksamhet och Svenska Europahjälpen* (Stockholm, 1957), p. 19.

5. Quoted in Jonas Collsiöö, *Greklandshjälpen I- Förberedelse, tillblivelse mars 1942–mars 1943*, p. 23, unpublished seminar paper at Department of History, Stockholm University 1993 (C-uppsats framlagd vid Historiska Institutionen våren, 1993).

6. For an account of Marcel Junod's experiences as a delegate of the International Committee of the Red Cross see Marcel Junod, *Warrior without Weapons* (Oxford, 1951). The chapter 'Unhappy Arcadia' deals with Greece in particular.

7. Marcel Junod, pp. 184–5.

8. Kostas Chatzipateras and Maria Fafaliou-Dragona, *Martyries 40–44: I Athina tis Katokhis*, vol. I (Athens, 2002), p. 210.

9. Kostas Chatzipateras and Maria Fafaliou-Dragona, p. 182.

10. Marcel Junod, p. 204.

11. Gunnar Cederschiöld, *Sviker Sverige?* (Stockholm, 1943), pp. 30–2.

12. The Skagerrak blockade was established in April 1940 by the Germans to prevent British-French naval forces attacking German shipments passing through the Kattegatt on their way to Oslo. The blockade, which ran between the south coast of Norway and the north coast of Denmark, also cut off the eastern supply route for Great Britain. (See M. Fritz et al., *En (o)moralisk Handel? Sveriges ekonomiska Relationer med Nazityskland* (Stockholm, 2006), Skriftserie. Forum för Levande Historia, 2006:2, pp. 19–21.)

13. Jonas Collsiöö, p. 33.

14. For a more in-depth description of the individual Swedish delegates see Hans Ehrenstråle, 'Svenskarna i Greklandskommissionen', *Hellenika*, 67 (1994): 4–17; Anders Sundberg, 'Biografiska Notiser till Svenskarna i Greklandskommissionen', *Hellenika*, 67 (1994): 18–19, and the same author's, 'Svenska Gravar i Grekland', *Hellenika*, 67 (1994): 20.

15. Paul Mohn, *Krumelurer i Tidens Marginal* (Stockholm, 1951), p. 142.

16. Bengt Helger, *Ravitaillement de la Grèce pendant l'Occupation 1941–1944 et pendant les premiers cinq mois après la Liberation. Rapport final de la Commission de Gestion pour les Secours en Grèce sous auspices du Comité International de la Croix-Rouge* (Athens, 1949), p. 172, Uppsala University dissertation 1949.

17. Bengt Helger, pp. 54–5.

18. Paul Mohn, pp. 150–3.

19. Bengt Helger, pp. 39–44.

20. Letter dated Christmas Day 1940 in the unpublished archive (diaries, letters and journals) of Joan Vanderpool. I wish to thank Joan Vanderpool's descendants for the permission to consult and publish material from the collection.

21. Lucy Shoe Meritt, p. 7.

22. Joan Vanderpool Archive, *The Children's House*, chapter III (journal written shortly after World War II), pp. 21–6.

23. Bengt Helger, pp. 138–9.

24. Paul Mohn, pp. 152–5.

25. Bengt Helger, pp. 164–6.

26. For a full account of the *Wiril* tragedy see *O Vombardismos tou Ploiou tou Erythrou Stavrou Wiril sto Limani tis Chiou stis 7 Fevrouariou 1944*, Andreadio Gymnasio Vrondadou Chiou, *Topiki Istoria*, Number 1 (Chios, 1993).

112   *Bearing Gifts to Greeks*

27. *O Vombardismos tou Ploiou Erythrou Stavrou Wiril*, pp. 30–8
28. For more information about the Swedish ships see Bengt Helger, pp. 168–84; Ivan Dovren, 'Medelhavsseglare med Humanitär Insats', *Odyssé*, 2/2003 (Svenska Kryssarklubbens Medelhavsseglare): 2–3.
29. Mats Lieberg, *Thessaloniki 1944 – Photographic Documents by Jean Lieberg* (Thessaloniki, 1999), Agnostes Ikones kai Piges 2, p. 66.
30. Sture Linnér, *Min Odyssé* (Stockholm 1982), p. 201
31. Sture Linnér, p. 208
32. www.hansehrenstrale.co.uk (accessed 24 September 2006).
33. Hans Ehrenstråle, *Fredsmäklare i Grekland- med Röda Korset bland Partisaner, Patrioter, Patrasiter* (Stockholm 1945), pp. 34–47. Interview in his home in Rugby, England, 24–26 March 2005.
34. The other female delegate was Karin Pettersson-Giavassi. She was a physical education teacher from Sweden, who had married a Greek. For many years she worked for the Greek royal family as a teacher. She was the only delegate who was not handpicked from Sweden, but appointed on an ad hoc basis in Athens. She worked in the Corinth area for the Red Cross mission in 1943–44. Hans Ehrenstråle, 'Svenskarna i Greklandskommissionen', *Hellenika*, 67 (1994): 15; Anders Sundberg, 'Biografiska notiser till Svenskarna i Greklandskommissionen', *Hellenika*, 67 (1994): 18; interview with her nephew Minas Geramas, Athens, 21 September 2004.
35. For supplementary information about Axel W. Persson and his work as a Red Cross delegate see, Hans Ehrenstråle, 'Axel W Persson-Rödakorsdelegaten', *Hellenika*, 44 (1988): 7–9; Kostis Papakongos, *Arkheio Persson – Katokhika Dokoumenta tou D.E.S. Peloponnesou* (Athens, 1977).
36. www.svefor.levandehistoria.se/1_0_1.php?id=3002 (accessed 15 November 2005), 'Röda kors-man död i Grekland, fartygskatastrof', *Dagens Nyheter*, 8 May 1945, 'Äreminnet på Tinos: Svensk kapten Cykladernas hjälte', *Svenska Dagbladet*, 20 February 1948.
37. Bengt Helger, p. 236.

7

'Ce que j'ai vu dans la Grèce d'aujourd'hui': Alexandros D. Zannas and the Greek Red Cross

Alexandros P. Zannas

This chapter focuses on Alexandros (Alekos) D. Zannas' association with the Red Cross, his contribution in providing relief to the starving population of Athens, and his attempt to raise international awareness of the Greek famine during the German occupation before his arrest by the German occupation authorities in late April 1942.

Alekos D. Zannas, a Vlach by descent, was born in 1892 in Thessaloniki. He studied political science at Strasbourg (1909–12), but no sooner had he completed his studies than the Balkan Wars broke out and he hastened back to Greece to enlist as a volunteer in the guerrilla force of Mikhail Anagnostakos (Kapetan Matapas) in the Olympus-Pieria region. During the First World War he was an aviator on the Macedonian front. His plane crashed and he suffered serious wounds, subsequently developing Parkinson's disease which afflicted him for the rest of his life. In 1916 he became actively involved in *Dimokratiki Amyna* (National Defence), the pro-Venizelos movement which in 1916 established a rival government in Thessaloniki in opposition to the royalist government in Athens. He worked closely with Eleftherios Venizelos, taking part in operations on the Macedonian front during the First World War as well as in the Asia Minor campaign between 1919 and 1922, where he commanded a squadron of fighter aircraft. He also took part in the 1922 coup against the royalist government held responsible for the disastrous defeat in Asia Minor. He spent the better part of the Pangalos dictatorship (1925–26) in exile on the island of Santorini.

Zannas played a significant role in establishing civil aviation in Greece as a result of his membership of the Venizelos government of 1928–32 when the Ministry of Aviation was created. He was initially a deputy minister, becoming Minister of Aviation from 1930. His involvement in politics continued, for he was elected a Liberal Party deputy for

Thessaloniki in 1933, 1936 and again in 1950. Due to his involvement in the attempted Venizelist coup of 1935 he was again arrested, but was granted a pardon by King George II, newly restored to the throne, a few months later.

During the German occupation of Greece – the period that is the focus of this book – Zannas was Chairman of the Food Distribution Committee and the representative in Greece of the International Committee of the Red Cross (ICRC). However, he was at the same time engaged in significant resistance activities: according to papers in the British Public Record Office and Zannas' own memoirs, he was involved with the British counter-espionage services, helping British military personnel escape from Greece. It was as a result of these activities that he was eventually arrested in 1942 by the occupation authorities and sentenced to eighteen years imprisonment. His rapidly deteriorating health meant that he was given permission to serve out his sentence under surveillance in a hospital in Italy. After Greece was liberated, Zannas served as President of the Greek Red Cross from 1945–46.

The primary source for this chapter is the Alexandros and Virginia Zannas Archive in the Benaki Museum, Athens. In working in the Zannas archive I encountered a particular difficulty which should be mentioned here, since it determines both the scope and limits of my presentation. The Alexandros and Virginia Zannas Archive consists of private records covering mainly the first half of the twentieth century. They contain a great deal of material related to the activities of Alekos D. Zannas, but there are some serious gaps. For example, very little information has survived regarding Zannas' pre-war business and political activities in Thessaloniki. But more importantly for the subject which interests us, the records dealing with Zannas' involvement in the administrative affairs of the Red Cross prior to the occupation are missing. We can only assume that they were burnt – for the Zannas family house in Thessaloniki had been requisitioned by the occupation forces, who deemed the library, together with all the papers in it, good fuel for their winter fires.

As regards the period with which we are concerned, the Zannas archive has three discrete sections: (1) Prisoners of War Bureau; (2) Return of demobilized soldiers to their home towns and villages; (3) Famine and international agencies.[1] The first section does not concern us here. My reference to the second section will be brief since I shall only highlight the role this played in the famine. My main focus will be on the third section, where I shall be presenting original material, which will provide scope for questions and further research.

Return of demobilised soldiers

A major problem confronting Greece during the Axis occupation was that of feeding its people. Before the war, Greece needed to import approximately one-third of its food. With the outbreak of the war, these imports abruptly ceased and due to mobilisation the essentially productive segment of the population no longer worked in production. Added to this there was the long dry autumn in 1940 which proved disastrous for the agricultural yield, and the fact that a large part of the food reserves was used to cover the needs of the army. Means of transport – pack animals, vehicles and so on – had been requisitioned by the military, which further contributed to reducing the quantities of food reaching the urban centres and made it increasingly difficult to keep up a steady supply. As a temporary solution to this problem – during the war and prior to the occupation – ration coupons were issued by the government in an effort to control the distribution of some foodstuffs to the market. This system was relatively successful until the early days of the occupation when shortages of staple foods had just begun to be apparent, although the lack of food had not yet become acute.

When Greece was invaded by the Axis forces the situation rapidly deteriorated. Agricultural activity declined because seeds, fertilisers, fuel and so on were all lacking. Weather conditions were unfavourable, farmers had been mobilised en masse, and livestock, agricultural implements and machinery had been seized by the occupation forces. Industrial production – mainly in the manufacturing sector – had virtually ceased owing to the lack of raw materials and fuel. Some factories were in fact requisitioned by the invaders and were operating exclusively for them. No fishing was allowed since sailing had been banned for military reasons. Most means of transport, both on land and on sea, had been requisitioned by the invaders. Fuel was hard to find, if available at all. Any road and railway networks that were still operational were used, almost exclusively, to meet the needs of the occupation forces. This lack of transport meant that many soldiers were unable to return home once the front had collapsed, posing a problem particularly for those wanting to return to their islands. The fact that demobilised soldiers were unable to return home precipitated a substantial increase in the population of urban centres and thereby further intensified the need for food in the cities.

A special committee under A.D. Zannas, G. Pazis and Loukia Kountourioti was set up for the care of soldiers returning home from the front. They cooperated with Alexandros Svolos, who had established the Committee for Assistance to Macedonians and Thracians. The American

Greek War Relief Association financed the effort to provide for these refugees, even though it appeared as if the funding had come from the Comité International de la Croix Rouge (CICR).[2]

This influx of soldiers waiting to return home put unprecedented pressure on the already scant food supplies available in the urban centres. The population was suddenly 25–30 per cent higher in the cities than it had been before the war – a fact that cannot be explained by social, political or other population changes which might have occurred during peacetime. In the autumn of 1941, Zannas estimated the population of Athens as being 1,100,000, a huge number, compared with the pre-war population.[3]

It is also relevant that the occupation forces did not abide by international agreements requiring them to organise a commissariat for their troops. On the contrary, Greece's agricultural produce was requisitioned to feed not only the occupation troops in Greece but those on the North African front as well. Needless to say, the Greek population, especially in the urban centres, found itself in a terrible plight.

A few weeks after the occupation became fully entrenched, the food supply problem was already very evident. Previous distribution systems fell apart and efforts by the Agricultural Bank to collect agricultural products and distribute them among the population did not have the desired results. Here one should perhaps emphasise the passive resistance of the population to the quisling occupation government. Most of the government's efforts to collect food failed because farmers either refused to hand over their harvest on some vague pretext, or simply hid it. For many farmers, the black market was clearly a more lucrative outlet.

In August 1941, the President of the Hellenic Red Cross (HRC), the elderly Ioannis Athanasakis, then eighty-eight years old, appealed to the Comité International de la Croix Rouge for help with the food supply problem. Due to Athanasakis' contacts with his German colleagues in the Red Cross and to the catalytic presence of the CICR's Swiss representative, Robert Brunel, a branch of the International Committee of the Red Cross was set up in Greece. Members of this Committee included representatives of the Greek Red Cross, the CICR and the occupation authorities. Robert Brunel, the permanent representative in Greece of the CICR, was appointed chairman. After negotiations between the CICR, the Greek Red Cross, the British Red Cross, and the Turkish Red Crescent and the occupation authorities, a 'CICR Committee to Manage Food Shipment' was formed – better known as the 'Red Cross Distribution Committee'. The director of this committee was Zannas. He played an important part in all these relief efforts – with the soldiers and prisoners of war, as well as the distribution of food – not only because of his position in the Red Cross Distribution Committee, but also because he often replaced the aged chairman of the Greek Red Cross, Athanasakis, at meetings and contacts with the occupation authorities.

In October 1941, shipments of food gradually began to arrive through Turkey, on the legendary steamship the *Kurtuluş* which was then 60 years old.[4] The shipments had been purchased with funds coming mainly from Greek-American organisations, such as the Greek War Relief Association. After its sixth voyage, the *Kurtuluş* sank in the Sea of Marmara and it was some time before an alternative vessel was found to transport food. This delay had disastrous effects on the country's food supplies. It was only after considerable pressure from the Allies, through the CICR, that the Swedish Red Cross was able to resume shipments of food to Greece.[5]

The problems encountered at this stage were not just that the *Kurtuluş'* cargoes were insufficient to feed the population of Athens, but there were also serious problems regarding the safe transport of food to the warehouses and to the soup-kitchens. Alekos D. Zannas wrote a memorandum that provides a valuable insight into these problems:

> The situation could not possibly have been addressed solely with the few cargoes shipped with the *Kurtuluş*. The Germans always promised that they would not confiscate our produce – particularly the raisins, or the wheat which came from the northern provinces, or the olive oil which they in fact converted to fat and sent to Germany. They never kept their promise and what is more, they always watched us closely and constantly raised objections.
>
> The first and second voyage of the *Kurtuluş* went relatively well. The German guard kept order and prevented the Piraeus port workers from stealing the food. Naturally there was some pilfering, mainly of the 'personal packages' [sent by members of the Greek community in Istanbul to relatives and others].
>
> But when the *Kurtuluş* docked for the third time, things did not go at all well because the German guard had conspired with the Piraeus port workers and many sacks of beans, chickpeas etc. were stolen.
>
> Fortunately, the Distribution Committee representative in Piraeus at that time was the Colonel of the Commissariat – Emmanouil Phradellos – a man of merit, tireless and conscientious. He kept track of everything and he kept me informed down to the last detail. It was an advantage for the Committee to have Phradellos in the tough position of Piraeus. Phradellos described the situation to me as tragic, which it certainly was, because if the conspiracy between the German

guard and the port workers continued, a large part of the cargo would have been channelled into the black market.

I considered it my duty to keep the Italian and German representatives informed and Brunel supported me in this. I requested D. Dziobek (the representative of the German Red Cross in Greece) to ask the German harbour master to replace the guard, ostensibly because the guard felt sorry for the workers whom they knew, and were therefore allowing them to take substantial quantities of food home. Dziobek did not give me a reply. Gulielmo Arno (the representative of the Italian Red Cross in Greece) agreed with my observation, because he, too, had been informed that on the third voyage much of the food had been stolen. He advised me, however, to proceed carefully because the Germans were very touchy about people accusing their troops. Their classic reply was that 'Germans never steal'. And Arno was actually right.

The next morning Dziobek informed me that, at precisely nine o'clock, a Flag Captain, whose name I do not remember, would come to the Distribution Committee offices and escort me to the German Harbour Master's office in Piraeus – then housed in the premises of the Athens-Piraeus Electric Railway.

On the way there, the Captain and I exchanged no more than five or ten words and when we arrived at Captain Kremer's office, I found myself confronted with ten officers who did not even greet me. The Flag Captain sat me on his right with Dziobek on the other side. The introduction was made by the Flag Captain in an angry tone, and he addressed the officers roughly as follows: 'Mr. Zannas has made several complaints to Mr. Dziobek regarding the forces in Piraeus and he said that the guard must be replaced because the soldiers stationed there, in collaboration with the sailors, steal and rob the food arriving from Turkey'.

I interrupted him, saying that I had never uttered such a charge and I asked Mr. Dziobek to confirm this. Dziobek in fact, made a good statement – with a bit of humming and hawing – but not daring to compromise himself since he held a lower rank than the Captain. I then told the Captain that I had asked to come here in order to co-operate with the German authorities – in particular with Captain Kremer – whom I wanted first of all to thank for the genuine interest he had showed during the unloading and transporting of food to the Committee's storerooms.

I had been informed by Brunel that Kremer was a first class man and a very brave officer who had been decorated for valour three times and had been given this post because of his wounds.

Kremer, who was not afraid of his superiors, said: 'Mr Zannas is right, the guard must be changed; I, too, had noticed the incidents Mr Zannas mentions and, in fact, I even punished a few guards'. After Kremer's words, the ice was broken and we had an objective discussion, resulting in my achieving what I had set out to gain. . .

However it was not only theft by the Germans that we had to look out for. We also had to take measures against the 'jumpers' [*oi saltadoroi*]. Every lorry had to be accompanied by a policeman or a gendarme. As soon as the trucks left the port, twelve- to fifteen-year-old children would be waiting at the exit to jump onto the truck if they could, pull down a whole sack and throw it onto the road where it would be picked up by their pals. If they couldn't jump onto the truck, then they would quickly slash the bags with their penknives and the others would pick up the beans and other foodstuffs that spilled onto the road. . .

Together with Mr Aristotelis Koutsoumaris, former director of the Athens General Security, who had undertaken the distribution of food to the children's soup kitchens, hospitals, charitable institutions, prisons, etc., we organised a special police force which saved us from these 'jumpers'.[6]

Food was initially distributed through soup-kitchens and later, when the number of servings of food exceeded 800,000 per day in the Athens region, food coupons were reinstated through general food supply shops. Initially, the collaborationist government wanted to undertake the organisation of food distribution. But the dissolution of the state machinery, the serious reservations of the Greek and International Red Cross with regard to the collaborationist governments, and the organisational inability of the Ministry of Food Supplies, eventually made it necessary for the food to be distributed through the Distribution Committee, mentioned above. After a systematic study of the situation in the provinces, food distribution began there as well. This distribution of food continued until August 1942 when the worst of the famine was over but also perhaps market forces, as we would say today, brought pressure to bear so that they too could have a slice of the food supply pie! What did continue, however, were the soup-kitchens for children and for the war handicapped.

The famine

We see, therefore, that the greatest problems with the food supply occurred in the winter of 1941–42, a particularly harsh winter by Greek standards. Bad weather combined with food shortages to cause a devastating famine.

In a letter to Raphail Raphail, the Greek ambassador in Ankara, Zannas noted: 'hunger is now knocking at the doors of the bourgeoisie. The stores are all finished; whatever gold there was in every house has now been sold; the only way out is the soup kitchen, which is where all your acquaintances find refuge: generals, admirals, ambassadors, councillors of state, bankers etc.'

In his letter, Zannas also mentioned the fact that 530,000 servings of food were handed out every day in the capital, pointing out that food shortages affected not only Athens, but the entire country, even rural areas. This letter was not, of course, sent by post since it would have been censored, but was carried by the CICR emissary, Dr Junod.[7]

The last part of my contribution touches on an issue of great importance – an issue which has not yet received the attention it deserves: namely the alerting of international agencies to the realities of the famine in Greece. There were two main obstacles in the way of the shipment of food to Greece faced by the Allied governments. The first was their own lack of conviction that there was a genuine need. If one takes the view that the occupation forces should have assumed the responsibility of dealing with this problem, then one can say that the Allied governments were justified, up to a point, in maintaining this position. The other obstacle of course, was the British blockade of Greece. British planning was essentially aimed at the military defeat of the Axis forces, so the humanitarian aspect of the issue was secondary. The problem of drawing the attention of international public opinion to the food supply problem in Greece was a very difficult issue. Zannas took the initiative in creating a photograph album that would depict the tragic living conditions in Athens during the winter of 1941–42. The album was intended to be used as a propaganda tool to exert pressure on governments and to convince them of the immediate need to ship food to Greece, irrespective of the political or strategic expediencies of the Allies at the time.

The task of obtaining the material, was undertaken by Aristotelis Koutsoumaris, a former director of the Athens General Security. Koutsoumaris agreed to locate and photograph all the characteristic aspects of daily life in Athens, but above all else to provide images of the famine. He cooperated with Police Sergeant Nikolaos Papadimitriou, who was director of the Criminal Investigation Service. The photographs were taken by Sergeant Papanikolaou with a camera hidden in his hat which was activated by a shutter-release in his pocket. The negatives were developed in the workshops of the Criminal Investigation Service. In his memoirs, Koutsoumaris mentions that Zannas arranged things in such a way that the entire cost of this undertaking was included in the CICR expenditures.[8]

Thus an incontrovertible historic record was created, and three hand-made photograph albums were secretly sent abroad. One was for the International Red Cross, one for the British Ambassador in Switzerland and one for the Greek government-in-exile. Two of the albums were sent via the Swiss Embassy to the International Red Cross in Switzerland, with the help of Junod and Brunel. A small anecdote that Zannas mentions is that these albums were delayed in reaching their final destinations. The secretary of the president of the CICR had placed them in her office drawer and there they lay forgotten until Robert Brunel went to Geneva three months later, when they were found and finally forwarded to those to whom they had been addressed.[9] The third album was dispatched through the Turkish representatives of the Red Crescent who had accompanied the *Kurtuluş* shipments. This one found its way to the Greek ambassador in Ankara, Raphail Raphail, who we assume forwarded it to the Greek government-in-exile, at that time based in London.

The work that was carried out by the Criminal Investigation Service in compiling and producing these photographs is referred to in a letter written by the director of the Criminal Investigation Service in March 1945 to the Prime Minister, Nikolaos Plastiras. In this letter, there is also a brief reference to what happened to these albums and to the impact the photographs had. We are told that the government-in-exile had some of these photographs printed in book form and then arranged for them to be circulated in large numbers. (Even though I have not been able to locate one, I believe it is more probable that they were in leaflet form.) This publication was distributed mainly in Britain and the United States. The writer of the letter, furthermore, informs us that the British government forbade its circulation because of the horrendous content of the photographs. The London Greeks, however, found ways around this by leaving the leaflet in popular public places, in buses and trains, pubs and the like, and by posting copies to friends, acquaintances and public figures.[10]

According to assurances made by the Swiss, British and Americans to Zannas after the war, these photographs had a tremendous impact, and the ensuing public outcry contributed greatly to obliging the Allied governments to lift the blockade. Until this material was published, the British government had refused to consent to shipping food to Greece, claiming that, according to international law and the treaties pertaining to war, the occupation authorities were responsible for feeding the Greek population. When these albums were circulated, however, public opinion in the Allied countries brought great pressure to bear on their governments to send aid. The Oxford Committee for Famine Relief, the precursor of Oxfam, was established precisely because prominent members of British society had became aware of the dire situation facing Greece (see Chapter 10). Public pressure played a major role in forcing the British government to overcome its objections and, ultimately, partially to lift the blockade, thus allowing humanitarian aid to be dispatched to Greece.

In the Zannas archives in the Benaki Museum, we found two albums: not two copies of the same album, but two different collections of photographs accompanied by text. The first, written in French, consists of 58 A4 pages. It is entitled: 'Ce que j'ai vu dans la Grèce d'aujourd'hui' ('What I saw in today's Greece').[11] This was the album that was sent abroad. Short typewritten captions accompany the photographs taken by Papadimitriou and Koutsoumaris. The photographs are obviously of far greater significance than the text, which is simply explanatory.

The book can be divided into the following sections:

1. The centre of Athens – queues for food
2. The absence of the means of transport
3. The garbage problem – searching through the rubbish for food
4. The winter of 1941–42
5. Beggars
6. Images of the starving population – soup-kitchens
7. Death by starvation
8. Transferring bodies to the mortuary – mass graves

The second album[12] has the same external features and roughly the same structure. It has no title and consists of 52 pages with photographs and Greek typewritten text. In this instance the text is more substantial. The album portrays mainly the children of the occupation, their destitution, starvation and death. These two albums were obviously put together with the sole aim of evoking horror and to shock the reader so as to achieve the ultimate goal.

In the same archive I found a third, handwritten, photograph album. It had been created by the Piraeus branch of the IKA Social Security Fund.[13] What is of interest here is that this album had been created for a different reason. It covers the specific period from November 1941 to November 1942, the peak of the famine – and it depicts the results of the aid efforts. In particular we are shown the effects that the soup-kitchens had on children. The album begins with photos of starving children and adults, taken during the winter of 1941–42. It shows the queues at the soup-kitchens a year later, depicting how well they were organised. And finally it ends by showing the undoubtedly beneficial results that the soup-kitchens had.[14]

Although the photographs of Athens in the album that was sent abroad were taken in September 1941, we cannot say precisely when these albums left Greece. Nor do we know whether in fact these were the first such documents to reach foreign officials and how much they contributed to the change in government policies. It is highly probable that other photographs portraying the tragedy of 1941–42 famine had been sent abroad. Certainly much had been written about the famine at that time in the form of reports by representatives of the CICR, as well as in personal memoirs and diaries. However, we do not know whether during that time, publications similar to the one found in the Zannas archive had circulated outside Greece with the intention of arousing public opinion and exerting pressure on the Allies. We are therefore unable to say to what extent, if at all, the CICR's neutrality was affected by the publication of these photos.

The photographs which follow are from the first album in the Zannas archive. They are reproduced together with the original captions in French. An English translation of these has been added.

Ce que j'ai vu dans la Grèce d'aujourd'hui

What I saw in today's Greece

On ne voit plus que des piétons squelettiques en quête de nourriture quotidienne, là où naguère encore la vie palpitait et les véhicules circulaient par milliers. [We see only emaciated pedestrians searching for their daily food (in the centre of Athens), which, not long since, was throbbing with life and the streets full of cars.]

Illustration 7.1 Pedestrians searching for food in Athens

Une sorte de caisses carrées en bois sont les seuls moyens de transport qui restent encore au service du public. A la place 'Omonia', aux sorties de la gare du chemin de fer électrique on voit plusieurs de ces brouettes qui attendent en file la clientèle. [Wooden crates on wheels are the only means of public transport still in use. We can see many of these vehicles waiting to be hired at the exits of the suburban train station in Omonia Square.]

Illustration 7.2 Crates on wheels: transport for hire in Omonia Square

Des camions découverts et délabrés sont utilisés pour le transport de la population, qui s'y entasse comme sardines en boîte. Sur ces véhicules, qui font le trajet entre la capitale et les environs, on y voit parfois des voyageurs accrochés ou suspendus, debout sur les marchepieds, ou couchés sur les garde-boues et sur le capot. [Open and dilapidated lorries are used to transport people packed in like sardines in a tin. These trucks are used for public transport between the centre of the capital and the suburbs. Sometimes you see people standing on the running boards or lying on the bonnet and bumpers.]

Illustration 7.3   An open truck used as public transport

Les ordures s'entassent aux coins de rues, car la Mairie n'a pas d'essence pour ses voitures. A l'entrée de la clinique 'Hippocrate' on peut voir un gros tas d'ordures. [Rubbish piles up in the streets because the municipality has no fuel for its lorries. At the entrance to the Hippocrates Clinic we can see a big pile of rubbish.]

Illustration 7.4   Uncollected rubbish in front of the Hippocrates Clinic

La poubelle est vidée. Alors les enfants se plongent littéralement dans les ordures pour trouver, fût-ce une pelure de citron au fond du récipient. [The rubbish bin is empty. The children literally dive into the rubbish hoping to find something to eat, even if it is just a piece of lemon peel at the bottom of the bin.]

Illustration 7.5   Children scavenging for food

Devant l'immeuble Spyraki, au Pirée, où sont logées des troupes d'occupation, des groupes d'enfants se rassemblent dans l'espoir qu'on va leur jeter par la fenêtre quelque chose à manger. [Outside the Spyraki building in Piraeus, used by the occupation forces, children gather in the hope that someone will throw something for them to eat from one of the windows.]

Illustration 7.6   Children waiting for scraps to be thrown to them by occupation forces in the Spyraki building in Piraeus

Quelque chose a dû tomber. Tous se précipitent pour s'en emparer. Ils se battent jusqu'au sang pour un morceau de pain coriace, pour un fruit pourri. [Something must have fallen. Everyone rushes to get it. They fight one another viciously for a piece of stale bread or rotten fruit.]

Illustration 7.7   Children fighting over scraps of food

Cet hiver le froid est intense. Il n'y a plus d'anthracite. Le mois précédent on le vendait à 80,000 drachmes la tonne, ce qui faisait 100,000 drachmes avec les frais de transport. Le lignite de qualité détestable coûtait 25,000 drachmes la tonne. Tout le monde grelotte chez soi faute de chauffage.

A la place 'OMONIA' aux abords de la gare du chemin de fer, la bouche d'un tuyau d'échappement dégage un air tiède mais vicié. Des groupes d'enfants s'allongent sur la grille, heureux de trouver un peu de chaleur. [This winter is very cold. There is no more coal. Last month it sold for 80,000 drachmas per ton, 100,000 drachmas including transport. Appalling quality lignite used to cost 25,000 drachmas per ton. Everybody shivers at home because of a lack of heating. In Omonia Square, near the suburban train station, the ventilation fan yields hot but dirty air. Children gather round the grille, happy to have found a little heat.]

Illustration 7.8   Children trying to keep warm over a ventilation grille in Omonia Square

Plus loin, une mère avec ses quatre enfants devant un hôtel particulier de l'avenue Kifissia demande l'aumône. Elle en a honte et a couvert son visage d'un fichu noir pour qu'on ne la reconnaisse pas. Son mari a été écrasé par une auto militaire. On voit sur le mur le '<u>V</u>' et la croix gammée du vainqueur. [A bit further, a mother with four children stands in front of a private home in Kifisia Avenue asking for charity. Feeling ashamed, she has covered her face with a black veil so as not to be recognized. Her husband died after being hit by a military vehicle. On the wall we can see the 'V' sign and the swastika of the conqueror. (Virginia Zannas has added that the photograph was taken in the main entrance to the Benaki Museum.)]

Illustration 7.9   Begging on Kifisia Avenue, Athens

Derrière la devanture d'un magasin, où il ne reste que des écriteaux, les vendeuses de la maison regardent un homme mort la nuit de faim et de froid. Il gît là depuis des heures car il n'y a personne pour le transporter au cimetière. [Behind the shop window, where there are only placards, the employees stare at a man who died the night before from cold and famine. The dead body lies there for hours because there is no one to transport it to the cemetery.]

Illustration 7.10   The body of a famine victim lies on the pavement outside a shop

Après la constatation de la cause du décès, les cadavres sont de nouveau chargés pêle-mêle sur les camions et transportés au cimetiere où ils sont déchargés comme des ordures. [After establishing the cause of death, dead bodies are thrown haphazardly into lorries and transported to the cemetery, where they are unloaded like garbage.]

Illustration 7.11 Bodies transported on open trucks to the cemetery

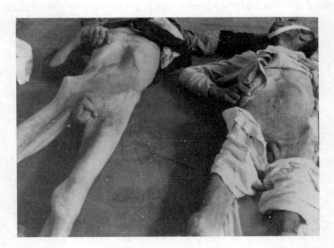

Dégraissage complet de l'organisme. [Total emaciation of the human body.]

Illustration 7.12 Emaciated bodies of famine victims

El l'on creuse les fosses de plus en plus profondément pour y entasser les cadavres, vieillards, jeunes gens, enfants, tous pêle-mêle. [The graves are dug deeper and deeper, so that the bodies of the old, the young and children, can all be packed in together.]

Illustration 7.13   A mass grave for victims of the famine

Notes

1. The Zannas papers are deposited in the Historical Archives Department of the Benaki Museum (Numbers 542 and 562).
2. Xenophon Pantazidis (ed.), *I Istoria tou Ellinikou Erythrou Stavrou*, vol. 1 (Athens, 1987), pp. 262–3.
3. Alexandros Zannas, *I Katokhi: Anamniseis – Epistoles* (Athens, 1964), p. 18.
4. For more details on the story of the *Kurtuluş* see Chapter 5. The *Kurtuluş* acquired legendary status in Greece for it proved to be the only hope at that time for the relief of the starving population. The ship was, as a consequence, always greeted with great joy and excitement on her arrival. I thank Mrs Irene J. Papaioannou for remembering the following verse from a popular poem of the time:

    Στα πόδια σου θα πέσω   At your feet I shall fall
    και ύμνον θα συνθέσω   And a hymn I shall compose
    Ω! Θείον Κουρτουλούς!   O! Holy Kurtuluş!
5. On the activities of the Swedish Red Cross in Greece during the occupation, see Chapter 6.
6. Zannas, *I Katokhi*, pp. 23–6.
7. The Zannas archive at the Benaki Museum-Historical Archives Department, Document No. 562/594. Letter dated 6 February 1942.
8. Zannas, *I Katokhi*, p. 27.
9. Zannas, *I Katokhi*, p. 27.
10. The Nikolaos Plastiras papers in the Benaki Museum-Historical Archives Department. Photographic Archive, Document No. 372, File No. 9.
11. The Zannas archive at the Benaki Museum-Historical Archives Department, Document No. 562/2226.
12. The Zannas archive at the Benaki Museum-Historical Archives Department, Document No. 562/2227.
13. According to the widow of the late Mikhail Goutos, who was director at this IKA branch, the photographs were taken by the well-known photographer Dimitris Harissiadis. For information on Harissiadis, refer to the Benaki Museum website, http://www.benaki.gr/archives/photographic/harissiadis/en/thumbs.htm.
14. The Zannas archive at the Benaki Museum-Historical Archives Department, Document No. 562/2224.

8
Ethniki Allilengyi (National Solidarity): Resistance and Welfare

Rolandos Katsiaounis

Ethniki Allilengyi (EA), or National Solidarity, was an offshoot of the coalition of parties and political formations that constituted the National Liberation Front (EAM), the major resistance organisation in Axis-occupied Greece. The roots of EA can be traced in the early efforts of the Communist Party of Greece (KKE) to withstand government repression by offering solidarity in money, kind and legal counsel to imprisoned comrades and their families. During the dictatorship of General Theodoros Pangalos (1924–25) these efforts led to the formation of an organisation called *Laiki Voithia* (People's Aid). The policy of Eleftherios Venizelos, the Liberal Party leader, of seeking to contain communism not only by judicial means but also by executive authority, through the so-called *Idionymo* law of 1929, obliged the KKE to develop a larger organisation, *Ergatiki Voithia* (Workers' Aid – EV).[1] The dictatorship of General Ioannis Metaxas, established on 4 August 1936, made repression of the labour movement official state policy and persecuted not only trade unionists but also their relief organisations. Members of EV, along with other left-wingers, were now detained in the regime's jails and islands of exile.[2]

Cutting off the inmates' sources of outside support was deemed essential by a regime which sought not only to detain communists but also to break them in spirit. Konstantinos Maniadakis, the minister responsible for domestic security, widely utilised the practice of *dilosi* (statement of repentance), by which pressure was exerted on the inmate to barter his release by publicly denouncing his political ideas and his party.[3] Given that this was a trial of soul as well as of body, pressure upon the prisoner was not limited to crude physical violence. It was also augmented by methodical psychological blackmail, such as inducements to the interned breadwinner by his own family, themselves under pressure from the police, pleading the most difficult circumstances and urging him to sign and return home.[4]

By 1939, practically the entire leadership of the KKE and most of its membership had been rounded up and sent to jails and islands of exile, where they experienced the severity of the regime's system. During the Greco-Italian war, between October 1940 and April 1941, there was no change to their status. Most of the prisoners held out despite the ill-treatment, thus gaining in experience and commitment. These were valuable attributes when, following the Nazi occupation of Greece, in April and May 1941, they undertook the immensely more substantial and complicated task of providing relief for the victims of the burgeoning national liberation movement, as well as assuming the leading role in this movement.[5]

King George II and his government, on fleeing Athens for Crete at the end of April 1941, left instructions for the release of political prisoners, with the exception of those convicted for their communist beliefs. The gendarmerie, as a rule, stood fast until the Germans arrived, and prevented around 2000 communist inmates from escaping. This was arguably the first act of collaboration, the policy of the government of General Georgios Tsolakoglou, installed in power by the German occupation authorities. The collaborationist government's line, that the only hope for the defeated Greeks was to convince the Axis of their willingness to seek a place in the Nazi New Order, was, in practice, scarcely distinguishable from that of the traditional bourgeois parties, monarchist and Venizelist, who preached caution, patience and prudence.[6]

The beginnings of resistance in an organised form can be traced in the activities of approximately 200 members of the KKE, most of whom managed to escape from the exile islands of Kimolos and Folegandros in the confusion of the occupation during the third week of May. These escapees formed the nucleus around which the party was reorganised during the summer of 1941. The KKE Central Committee's Sixth Plenum, the first in conditions of fascist occupation, was held on 1–3 July. EAM itself, in which KKE was the major participant, was founded on 23 September 1941.[7]

Ethniki Allilengyi, however, was formed as early as 28 May 1941, while fighting continued on Crete. The founders were five escapees from Folegandros, the most prominent of whom was Pantelis Simos-Karagitsis, an alternate member of KKE's Central Committee and former leader of EV.[8] Their recent and painful experience of imprisonment and exile was the reason for this haste, which reflected their concern for the welfare of comrades still in jail in a country now occupied by fascist powers.

Although the five pioneers, who convened their clandestine meeting in the forest behind the *Sotiria* hospital, did not have the documents relating to the KKE's Plenum or to the foundation of EAM, they formulated their purpose, namely to assist prisoners and victims of the war, within the framework of popular front anti-fascism, aiming at national liberation. Article 2 of EA's first charter noted:

(a) EA considers the struggle of the Greek people for their national liberation . . . as the struggle of progress against barbarism and medievalism, a struggle for the existence of civilised society, and therefore worthy of every support.

(b) It believes that all human beings, irrespective of race or religion, have the same rights to life and culture. It opposes and condemns every theory which acknowledges so-called superior races or nationalities, destined to govern, oppress and exploit other, supposedly inferior races and nationalities.

(c) It opposes and condemns any action aiming to curb the sovereign rights of the Greek people with regard to the administration of their country and to impose a dictatorial and tyrannical system of government. It also considers worthy of all support the struggle of the people of Greece to restore their sovereign rights and freedoms and to raise their living and cultural standards.[9]

This was a highly subversive message in the political atmosphere of May 1941, which was one poisoned by resignation and defeatism. Having harnessed the promotion of welfare issues to the primary purpose of freeing the country from foreign occupation, EA was in accord with the mass associations in the formation of which the KKE had taken the initiative. EEAM (Workers' EAM) established on 16 July 1941, seven weeks after EA, although still ten weeks before the foundation of EAM, likewise espoused not a narrow trade union programme but a broader and deeper political commitment to end the occupation.[10]

At the beginning of the occupation, according to most accounts, the Greeks, although stunned, were still undaunted. What affected their morale, more than the experience of military defeat, was the misery which accompanied it. Pillage and requisitioning by the occupation forces coupled with the dislocation of internal communications led, as early as July, to hunger for the poorest districts, particularly amongst the victims of the war and orphaned families. By the beginning of autumn famine had spread to the working classes, public employees, professionals, students, and petty merchants. Between November 1941 and March

1942 Athens and Piraeus experienced famine, in the true sense of the word, so severe as to have become enshrined in the national memory. No capital in occupied Europe, not even Warsaw, lost such a proportion of its people from sheer want.

The collaborationist government's attempts to deal with the situation had little effect. It was hampered by its very low credibility and by its inability to formulate policies outside the framework of collaborationism. Having shouldered the enormous responsibility of accepting office at the hands of the occupation powers, its most devout wish was that the occupied would accept their lot. Those who could afford it sought refuge in the black market, the financial aspect of collaborationism. A number succumbed, worked for and even established social relations with the occupiers. From among the new poor, a few thousand were induced to seek employment in the industries of the Reich. Others ended up in the collaborationist detachments in return for regular pay and three meals a day.[11] It was this state of affairs that was particularly targeted by the resistance. In the classic statement of resistance, *What is EAM and what does it want?* Dimitris Glinos, an intellectual and member of the KKE's Political Bureau, listed as the national liberation struggle's first objective:

(a)   The daily struggle to ensure that the people are not crushed by hunger, sickness and material deprivation. When you allow people to die on the streets, to be abused in body and soul and then say that you will conduct a people's liberation struggle 'at the appropriate time', you are a conscious deceiver and collaborator with the enemy. Because it is as if you were to say that you will use a corpse to fight with.

The national liberation struggle, then, begins with the daily struggle for bread, for soup kitchens, for wages, for medicines, against the degradation and starvation to death of the people.[12]

EAM's arguments captured the mood of the population, whose anger turned to wrath at the sight of bare shelves, amidst reports of recent wagonloads of goods leaving for Germany. The traditional political parties, for their part, offered no guidance or evidence of effectively caring for the people, who became increasingly aware that they had nothing to lose and more to gain by disobedience and resistance.[13]

Quickly, the desperate food situation led to a crime wave and phenomena of blind revolt, such as gangs of youths (*saltadoroi*) who, at enormous risk, grabbed food from moving Italian and German lorries.[14] However, the protests and actions of individuals gradually began to give way to organised group activity. Widespread misery and unrest had prepared the ground for policies such as those advocated by the KKE:

People of Greece
The lowering of the bread ration to 30 drams is the consequence of the plunder of our wheat by our foreign tyrants. Only the all-national rising with strikes, demonstrations, work stoppages and other means of struggle will ensure for us more bread and other foodstuffs. This will stop the murderous plans of the foreign occupiers.[15]

EAM's programme likewise called for mobilisation against the requisitioning of food by the occupation authorities, for extending the *syssitia* (soup-kitchens) to all the neighbourhoods of Athens and Piraeus, and for organising consumer cooperatives in places of work.[16] In fact, the earliest resistance activity can be traced in the early efforts of professionals and employees to bypass black marketeers, form their own consumer cooperatives, obtain food directly from the rural areas or the Red Cross, and prepare meals at their work places (*esties*).[17] The members of EA, with experience of trade union activity and a clear political commitment, were in the forefront, offering the alternatives of organised struggle, clear objectives and hope.[18]

The *syssitia* movement culminated, through the initiative of the lawyers' *estia*, in the formation of a central coordinating body (*Panestiaki*), which sought to target the government and the Red Cross.[19] This development in particular threatened to render irrelevant the upper class philanthropic organisations, which were proven to be incompetent as well as corrupt.[20] The fact that private charity, which had traditionally absorbed pressure for state-provided relief, proved demonstrably inadequate, forced the government to call upon the assistance of the church. Archbishop Damaskinos and the collaborationist prime minister were already indebted to each other given that Tsolakoglou had replaced Archbishop Khrysanthos, who had remained loyal to the government of King George, and installed Damaskinos in his place. The new archbishop in turn swore in Tsolakoglou and his cabinet.[21] In November 1941 the Minister of Relief and Health, Konstantinos Logothetopoulos, promoted the formation and financing of EOXA (National Organisation of Christian Solidarity), under the chairmanship of Damaskinos, which was meant to assist the ministry's duties, albeit bypassing the bureaucracy.[22]

The ongoing negotiations for food, from Turkey, Sweden and Canada, had involved highly political questions in the diplomacy between the International Red Cross (IRC) and the belligerent powers (see Chapters 3,

4 and 5). By the same token, for the collaborationist government, the handling and distribution of food and welfare amongst Greeks was not unrelated to agitation in the *esties*. This was viewed with suspicion, if not, as yet, with alarm. The archbishop's biographer admits that EOXA was concerned not only with people's welfare but also with their ideas. In several *syssitia* the children were overseen and taught by specially qualified teachers, on such topics as fatherland and freedom.[23] During the occupation, however, more than in any other period in the modern history of Greece, such concepts meant different things to different people. In EOXA's structure, a section as neutral as that of distribution in children's soup-kitchens, hospitals, philanthropic organisations and prisons was overseen by a former chief of general security.[24] These overtones became more pronounced with the sharpening of political confrontation in occupied Greece. According to EAM sources, EOXA, having initially offered some assistance to the relatives of those executed by the Germans, later reserved their support for the families of the collaborationist Security Battalions[25] (see Chapter 9).

In the context of the occupation, therefore, issues regarding welfare, wages and the distribution of food were laden with political overtones. Guided by EAM, transport workers, civil servants, even policemen, staged strikes for higher wages. Though each march and each contingent met with hostility and even brutality on the part of the occupation authorities, it also expanded the movement's popular base. Competition between the government and EAM intensified with the arrival of the first shipments of wheat by the IRC in the spring of 1942. EA activists carried out their work in the *esties* and *syssitia* with great success (Illustration 8.1). An agent of the British Special Operations Executive noted in a dispatch (circa January 1944) from Greece that, of the ninety-six original soup-kitchens organised by the Archbishop of Athens, ninety-one ended up under the political control of EAM.[26]

A perpetual tug of war was in fact being waged between EAM, which favoured distribution through soup-kitchens, and the government, which preferred the private sector. The latter solution was, of course, unpopular because groceries were largely controlled by wholesalers, who engaged in black marketeering. The government's first effort to limit the soup-kitchens led to widespread unrest. EAM simply asked those dependent on the soup kitchens to take to the streets, attaching openly political slogans to the issue: 'Bread and soup kitchens', 'Down with terrorism', 'We demand soup kitchens and grocery stores' and 'Freedom to those in prison'.[27]

The Finance Minister, Sotirios Gotzamanis, in a letter to the prime minister of 16 July 1942, laid the unrest at the door of trouble-makers

Illustration 8.1 Distribution of food by *Ethniki Allilengyi* in the village of Petrilia, Evrytania, in the Agrapha mountains. Note the barefoot children, the priest on the left and the ELAS partisans looking on. The food is being handed out by Lena Zappa, a member of a prominent Athenian bourgeois family (information from Ms Nina Kassianou)

who followed the strategy urged in communist leaflets. What worried him was its political message: 'the misery of the people is such that, despite the presence of a dictatorial government and an army of occupation, they ignore everything, owing to their hunger, and take to the streets in a show of protest'.[28] But in his reply, Tsolakoglou found it impossible to defend Gotzamanis' views in public. The government, having lifted restrictions on price controls, had in effect legalized the black market. Public opinion had become suspicious of the government's intentions 'seeing no action toward the creation of new food sources, postponements, rigidity and inability to adapt in the prevailing circumstances'.[29]

On the issue of food distribution EA and EAM had Gotzamanis where they wanted him. Their agitation was typical of their general tactics, in the sense that it was rooted in the prevailing consensus. Without it, not only EA but the entire EAM edifice could have been met by repression alone. Agitation regarding provision of relief in fact kept the government permanently on the defensive. EA militants stressing that the solution to the people's misery was the end of occupation, while at the same time catering for the people's needs, had convincing arguments. The extent of their public support enabled EA, in September 1942, to convene a conference of delegates from the *esties*, cooperatives and trade unions. This led to the founding of the *Panathinaiki Laiki Epitropi* (Athens People's Committee) (PLE).[30] Similar committees followed in Piraeus, Thessaly and Thessaloniki. By March 1943 delegates from these areas held a first joint conference. A year later, like the rest of the offshoots of EAM, EA was fully active all over Greece.[31]

The organisation of *syssitia* brought EA into contact with a very large segment of the population, of which political prisoners were the most important. As in the days of EV the primary need was to assist those interned to survive with dignity. The experience of the Metaxas dictatorship had demonstrated the significance of helping internees maintain not only their physical well-being but also their morale while they survived in camps whose every device was designed to break them down. Under intense pressure, inmates might agree to become informants and collaborators. Others might be utterly broken and their condition when released might undermine the general will to resist.[32]

From the outset of the occupation, EA found common cause with the state of public opinion, which during 1941 was concerned with the plight of another group of prisoners, the members of the British Expeditionary Force – including many Australians, New Zealanders and Cypriots – now held in camps at Larisa, Athens and Crete.[33] Political prisoners were, of course, much more vulnerable than ordinary POWs, a fact only too familiar to the founders of EA. In Akronafplia, from the beginning of the occupation until the intervention of the IRC, in January 1942, the prisoners were tormented by hunger. During this period aid sent from EA kept casualties to a minimum.[34] The significance of this contribution is demonstrated in those cases where it could not be delivered in time. In the remote exile island of Ayios Efstratios, in the north-eastern Aegean, the prison governor exploited the prisoners' isolation in order to starve them into signing declarations of repentance. The consequences were deadly. Despite EA's representations to the Red Cross, the government and the church, the first load of food arrived only on 28 February 1942. Out of approximately 108 who refused to submit, thirty-three perished and another eleven were in the final stages of tuberculosis.[35]

The tasks of EA multiplied as the number of political prisoners grew. Approximately half a million Greeks, 7 per cent of the population, were incarcerated in jails and camps of various kinds during the occupation years. The delivery of parcels and messages was secured using members of the inmates' families, clergy, doctors, nurses, contacts in the Red Cross and even guards sympathising with EA. According to figures provided by EA, during the occupation, in the camps and prisons of the Athens area, that is, Haidari, Averoff, Kallithea, Embirikio and Tatoi, EA delivered something like 540,000 parcels. According to the same sources, during the occupation up to August 1943, prior, that is, to the Italian collapse, EA introduced into the camps 1,161,000 portions of food. The task must have been enormous considering that this was not a politically neutral organisation, regarded as harmless by the occupation authorities. Writing to his wife, Kostas Tsirkas, an inmate of Akronafplia, freely mentioned the food parcels he received from the Red Cross, but concealed EA behind grateful references to his cousin.[36]

Food for the prisoners was obtained from the Red Cross, although an equally significant amount came from the population, itself living on the borderline between hunger and starvation. This food had to be prepared in safe houses, passed on, taking care to avoid discovery, to several hundred pre-arranged spots in the city, and then transported, past road blocks and guards, into the prisons and to the final recipients.[37] Access to prisoners involved boldness and ingenuity. K.A., an EAM member, recalled how, in 1942, while a prisoner in Patras, he was visited by an unknown lady, who gave him food and money. Although in the presence of guards, she reminded him that she was his old friend, Mrs Ea; he later realised that she had been hinting at her organisation's acronym.[38] These complicated operations took place in an occupied Athens that was rife with spies, informers and dangers of all sorts. The situation was even more difficult in Thessaloniki, which was heavily patrolled. Food supplies were imported from all quarters and redistributed to the concentration camps and prisons of the district. As in Athens, EA enlisted support from traditional philanthropic organisations and also from a number of sympathetic members of EOXA.[39]

Influential people in high places facilitated the work of EA in prisons and concentration camps. They were as a rule genuine philanthropists with no particular political convictions, who considered EAM members to be decent individuals and were prepared to cooperate with them. One such was Sister Eleni Capari, a Belgian Uniate nun and friend of the Italian royal family. This patrician, having visited Akronafplia as a Red Cross representative, witnessed the drive and efficiency with which the inmate community utilised their meagre resources. She later contrasted her experience at Akronafplia with the situation in Larisa concentration camp, where the Italian guards, in league with a group of prisoners, stole the miserable rations. Sister Capari used her influence to establish a committee of prisoners responsible for administering the rations, whose head had been transferred to Larisa from Akronafplia.[40]

After the political prisoners, those most vulnerable were the members of their families. The death or internment of the breadwinner in the circumstances of the occupation could spell ruin for his dependants, whose position became more difficult and complicated due to political circumstances. The Red Cross initially gave very little to very few. This was not only due to their limited means. There was no way the members of an avowedly neutral organisation could be allowed to function if they were even suspected of indirectly assisting subversion. Nor could there be any question of a prisoner's or partisan's family presenting a welfare claim to the collaborationist government. The burden, therefore, of granting relief to the resistance fell on EA. Support was in kind, approximately seven kilograms of food every month, though in urban centers money was also provided. The awarding of this assistance kept pace with the intensification of the conflict between EAM and the occupation authorities. According to EA figures, in 1943 1000 families were assisted in Athens alone. By the first six months of 1944 the figure had reached 1500 and, by the end of the occupation, 2500. In Piraeus 500 families were assisted and another 1100 in Thessaloniki.[41]

Victims of atrocities comprised another category that received aid. The German application of the principle of collective responsibility meant that reprisals were not only directed against those who actually resisted but were often indiscriminate. Following the first mass executions of hostages in early January 1943, EA issued an announcement that it had decided to take under its wing the families of those executed and called upon the EA branches of Athens and Piraeus to find their addresses in order to offer them a regular pension.[42]

Apart from those taken hostage, reprisals could also strike rural communities thought to harbour partisans, such as Kalavryta and Distomo. In these circumstances entire communities were left without food or shelter. The task of supporting them was particularly difficult because the timing of reprisals could not be predicted. Even after the raid had become known assistance was not always readily available because many villages were in remote regions. The IRC, receiving supplies from abroad, possessing mechanised transport and supported by international conventions, could not always offer effective relief to victims of punitive expeditions. In this kind of emergency, the immediate aim was to prevent mass deaths from hunger and exposure. As a rule the task fell upon the nearest EA committee of putting together such assistance in food and clothing as was available from nearby villages and establishing a makeshift medical centre. After that, efforts were made to collect raw materials for repairing houses, to establish, where possible, tile-making workshops, and to utilise the labour of the inhabitants and the limited provision of wages for craftsmen. It also involved a communal spirit of reconstruction witnessed, in September 1944, by a British non-commissioned officer on a mission to Karpenisi, a hotbed of partisan activity:

This soup kitchen was at the time furnishing one meal a day to about 800 children in the town of Karpenisi. The lumber gangs, although very poorly equipped, comprised one of the few efforts at providing some shelter for the population of this badly devastated area. The hospital, together with its outpatient clinics at Megalokhorion and Karpenisi, was doing excellent work on a large scale – about 2,300 patients having been handled in the last week of August and the month of September.

A hospital was organised with excellent co-operation from the civilians of Marathia who contributed fifteen beds, complete with bedding, to begin with, and promised to increase this number as required.

A Dr. Dhrandhakis had been entrusted with the purchase and distribution of wheat and the employment of doctors to cover the burned villages of the Agrinion area. He seemed to be doing an excellent job.[43]

In the cities, the code of collective responsibility was epitomised by the *blocco*, that is, the rounding up of the population of entire quarters in order to arrest suspects, hostages and workers for the labour camps in the Reich. With the growth of ELAS (the Greek People's Liberation Army), the Germans and their collaborators were increasingly and effectively squeezed out of the working-class quarters of Athens and Piraeus. By summer 1944, a 'red' belt was formed, effectively making EAM a state within a state.[44] This defiance meant constant and bitter clashes. *Bloccos*, if successful, were truly deadly. In these cases, Red Cross personnel were able to offer little or no aid. Comfort to the families of the hostages and the dead was essentially the task of EA.[45]

As ever-wider areas of the country, comprising what came to be known as Free Greece, came under the control of EAM, services such as medical care reached remote villages hitherto ignored by the Athens government. In these areas, EA set up five teacher-training colleges and a very large number of schools, with textbooks and meals for the pupils. In April 1944 the Panhellenic Committee of National Liberation (PEEA), which administered areas under EAM control, with portfolios and secretariats for health, welfare, education and culture, in effect ratified the functioning of institutions that had in many cases largely been set up by EA.

Naturally the level of support and collective involvement generated by EAM was also channelled to the units of ELAS, a partisan army which lacked mechanised transport and was exposed to the elements of nature. The degree of wear and tear in shoes and clothing was very high. Cooking and washing as well as the transport of ammunition and equipment was, therefore, often the task of the population, directed by EA. The organisation also provided ELAS military hospitals with medical supplies, equipment and personnel. Some support was also given to the families of the guerrillas in the countryside. In fact this was the sole comfort provided to the dependants until, in early 1944, EAM established a separate service termed *Epimeliteia tou Andarti* (Guerrilla Commissariat).[46]

Looking after the enemies of the state necessarily meant that EA was at the receiving end of violence and repression. The Nea Smyrni quarter in Athens was a case in point. In early 1943, the doctor directing EA activities was murdered by the occupation authorities. Despite this warning, EA's activities expanded and membership increased. In Nea Smyrni almost all families had a member who was in some way associated with EA, actively participating or giving donations. They expressed their support openly, surrounded as they were by a population which shared their loyalties and their complete confidence in Germany's eventual defeat. In Pharos, Nea Smyrni's poorest neighbourhood, on 1 January 1944 the populace welcomed the New Year in the café of Spyros Alevizos, local EA activist, singing EAM songs and awaiting liberation. The catastrophic consequences of this recklessness were demonstrated four days later, when the Germans and the Security Battalion staged a *blocco*. Alevizos resisted and died fighting. Fifty members of EAM, mostly from EA were arrested, out of whom only fifteen were still alive at the time of liberation.[47]

Indeed, EA's work, particularly for the leaders, could be as perilous as any of the other activities of EAM. Giorgos Kotsiras, secretary of the Athens Committee, was caught by the Special Security and tortured to death in July 1944. Another member of the Central Committee, Alex Kousopoulos, while on a mission to the Peloponnese, was caught and hanged in Patras. Not surprisingly, the dead included a large proportion of women. Sophia Topali, a botanist, and her mother, were caught and hanged by EASAD (a collaborationist detachment) in Pilion in August 1944. Athina Mavrou, leader of the organisation in the working-class quarter of Kokkinia, was executed in the notorious *blocco* of 17 August 1944. Ariadne Dalari, a dentist and secretary of the organisation's branch in Larisa, was shot by the Germans. The list could go on.[48]

In addition to the contribution of loyal activists, relief for the victims of famine and repression all over Greece also required resources on a very considerable scale. EA personnel, in fact, were able to conduct their welfare activities because EAM was growing into an organisation which commanded not only men but also means, funds and weapons. In rural areas, most of which were by 1943 under EAM's effective control, a tax in kind was paid by peasants, which went to feed the partisans and to enable EA to offer support where necessary. The sheer size of the organisation, whose activities extended practically everywhere, was used to advantage. In the German supply depots in Piraeus, the largest in Greece, the majority of Greek employees worked on behalf of EAM. This resulted in large quantities of food being smuggled out for the use of ELAS or EA, by all kinds of means, including on fire engines and garbage trucks.[49]

EAM's military capacity was also very significant in the competition for scarce resources. This capacity increased considerably in September 1943 when, following the Italian collapse, EAM managed to disarm an entire division in Thessaly. Thereafter, the region's produce was largely denied to the Germans. It was not unusual for peasants to collect the harvest with a rifle on their back. Horses from the former Aosta regiment formed the basis of ELAS cavalry units, which patrolled outlying wheatfields.[50] In Athens, the increase in ELAS's authority enabled it to inaugurate, in October 1943, a new policy against black marketeers. As a rule, a local committee gathered the local population outside a store known to stock food supplies. The owner would be forced to open the store and its contents were distributed at low prices, or for nothing if he were known to be a collaborator.[51] A Special Security report noted that members of EAM went round the streets warning merchants to stop overcharging for their goods and making illegal profits to the detriment of the people. The report also contained an implicit admission that EAM was more effective than the state in controlling the black market:

> In one case members of the anti-national organisations forced, by violence, a merchant dealer in olive oil to distribute a considerable quantity of his stock to the public for 34,000 drachmas an *oke* [2 1/2lbs]. They also shouted abuse at policemen who were present, because of their inactivity.[52]

The point to be made was that the black market would not go on unpunished and that the perpetrators should be made aware of what was in store for them. In actual fact, prices fell.[53] The Special Security noted that the merchants of Athens and Piraeus presented themselves to the quisling prime minister Ioannis Rallis, requesting protection of their merchandise from the anarchists. The merchants also promised that they would thereafter sell to the public at a price 50 per cent lower than the prevailing one.[54]

EA's resources were also supplemented by collections of money. On 19 November 1943, the Central Committee of EA announced a 'Collection for the Victims' aiming to raise three billion drachmas. The sum would be collected through the issuing of coupons, ranging in value from 1000 to 100,000 drachmas. The committee, confident of EA's influence in the population of a country under Nazi occupation, noted:

> The collection must be carried out openly, from street to street, from shop to shop, from house to house. The groups conducting the collection should ask for the thousand of the poor and the million of the rich for the victims of the national liberation struggle . . . For the same purpose it is necessary and possible to organise events and theatrical performances.[55]

In areas where the presence of Germans and collaborationist detachments was significant, members of EA did not use coupons, which would be damning evidence if they were caught. A Special Security report noted that people entered shops and restaurants, spoke against Rallis and then produced a piece of cloth with the word 'Allilengyi' on it.[56]

EA agitation increasingly engaged sections of society which had until then not been active in politics or had only been involved in peripheral ways. Women were particularly targeted for enrolment. An EAM booklet explaining their role in the resistance touched on all capacities in which they were active in society: worker, peasant, teacher, clerk, housewife, mother and student. The booklet dealt with the particular tasks arising out of each capacity, but also allocated to each one of them the general tasks of EA.[57] A high percentage of women were nurses and social workers caring for children and the elderly. Although other sectors of the resistance movement were joined by the most active and militant members of the female population, in which some of them held responsible posts, they were everywhere in a minority. EA was the only EAM offshoot in which women, especially at the lower level, were in the majority. In EA's Athens branch they made up 55 per cent of the membership, a figure which rose to 60 per cent in rural areas. This, perhaps, was the reason why EAM, despite having a military wing (ELAS), a youth section (EPON) and a labour branch (EEAM), never developed a separate women's organisation.

While remaining primarily concerned with welfare, EA increasingly moved to the forefront as EAM's confrontation with the occupation authorities became more bitter and bloody. Participating in EAM's mass political protests, EA utilised its considerable support in the cities and asserted itself as a resistance organisation. In 1943, the strikes against recruitment for work in the Reich and against the threat of Bulgarian occupation of Western Macedonia were not strikes in the traditional sense of the term, but rather national mobilisations. EA members had a dual task. The first was to be there, in their sheer numbers, even though at the head of the phalanx marched the experienced members of EEAM or the militants of EPON. Second, they were the ones who, after the clashes with occupation or collaborationist forces, cared for the wounded, taking them to hospital or to places where they could be treated in relative safety.[58]

EA also organised its own demonstrations, made up exclusively of women, in their hundreds. Wearing local dress or black kerchiefs, they demanded the release of hostages, protested against their execution or rained down curses upon the occupation forces and their local collaborators. In a country where ritual lament was rooted in popular culture, these processions had a formidable impact. Orestis Makris, *kapetanios* (politico-military commander) of the ELAS First Regiment in Athens, describes in his memoirs a procession by the women of Kaisariani, a working-class quarter and EAM stronghold, once it became known that seven local youths had been killed in battle defending the neighbourhood. The hardened commander was moved by the rhyme and verse, which he traced to the heritage of ancient Greek drama: 'Housewives wiped their tears, youths clenched their fists, like a wave they joined the sea of people marching toward the square.'[59]

In fulfilling its tasks EA had to earn the confidence and cooperation of broad sections and strata within society. The backbone of the organisation, its local branches, were generally led by teachers, doctors and people with qualifications and training in administration and accounting, such as the staff of local cooperatives and branches of the Agricultural Bank of Greece. These were the elements of the intelligentsia who were in close contact with the local population and shared their hardships.[60] Wider still was the network of solid citizens, who sympathised with the aims of EA and assisted with donations. A record from the EA branch in Crete notes contributions from ninety-five merchants in money and kind (soap, oil, stationery, cloth, food and cigarettes), fourteen building contractors in money and seven tanners in money and leather for shoes.[61]

Given its acceptance among professionals, EA also recruited a number of lawyers, whose task was to defend members of the resistance. The mission was fraught with danger and some of these lawyers paid with their lives, during the occupation as well as during the civil war. Amongst the best known were Minos Galeos, defence lawyer of Nikos Beloyianis, a member of the KKE Central Committee, who was executed in 1952; Nikiforos Mandilaras, who was murdered while in police custody during the military dictatorship of 1967–74; and Ilias Iliou, who later became leader of the Unified Democratic Left (EDA), the political expression of EAM's heritage in the 1950s and 1960s.[62]

Like other EAM offshoots, EA developed a press section. The first newspaper, bearing the name of the organisation, *Ethniki Allilengyi*, came out in November 1941. EA committees responsible for the Peloponnese, Thessaly, Macedonia, Epirus and Sterea Ellada produced their own newspapers, as did several other districts. They combined the features of an EAM paper with more specialised items relating to welfare, health and the region in which they were printed. Kleon Papaloizos, the organisation's secretary, has calculated a total of fifty-three printed newspapers and another 105 mimeographed publications.[63] One of these was *I Phoni ton Thymaton* (The Voice of the Victims) which came out in May 1942, by which time executions had become a regular feature of the occupation. Its contents were meant to stigmatise the culprits, stimulate public opinion and diminish the possibility of further executions. Toward the same end, EA issued *Deltia Tromokratias* (Bulletins on Terrorism), giving details of raids and executions.[64]

The other important social group associated with EA was the clergy. A considerable number of priests were able to identify with the more humanitarian and philanthropic aspects of the resistance. Although the senior clergy were more reserved, EAM enjoyed the support of a number of metropolitans, the best known of whom were Joachim, Bishop of Kozani, and Antonios, Bishop of Ileia.[65] The lower clergy, however, who were closer to the suffering of their flock, were more forthcoming. According to EA's own figures, in Central Greece 60 per cent of all priests were members or active supporters of EA. In Epirus and Macedonia the figure rose to 70 per cent and in Thessaly – a breeding ground of partisan activity – to 80 per cent. The highest figure, 90 per cent, was recorded in Evia, despite the considerable presence of collaborationist groups on the island.[66] These figures are not exaggerated. An operative of the Special Operations Executive reported on the situation in Evia during the last month of the occupation:

> There are 120 priests and 23 monks in north and central Evia, all of whom, with two exceptions, support and work in the resistance movement. The Bishop of Khalkis and the priests of Limni and Skiloyianni have been arrested by the German-Rallis forces because of their outspoken support.

The church not only lends its prestige to the organisation but actively participates in the collection and distribution of relief supplies, in educating the children and in giving medical assistance. One monastery houses both a children's camp and the *andarte* (guerrilla) hospital.[67]

Finally EA, perhaps more than other EAM offshoots, was able to draw on the support of public figures within Greek society at large. From the early efforts to coordinate the soup-kitchens, the Athens Popular Committee, through which EA members implemented its policies, was headed by the well-known Athens University professor, Konstantinos Amantos.[68] The effort to ensure support from such figures was deemed essential, given that the organisation's activities were more public than those of any other branch of EAM. Following the formation of EA's Central Committee, its second plenum in June 1943, held in occupied Athens, elected as president Athanasios Rousopoulos, a professor at the Athens Polytechnic. Rousopoulos had, from the early stages of EA's existence, aided the cause of political prisoners through his prestige and respectability. In fact, the association of public figures with EA reflected the group's growing influence. By the time of the third plenum, in September 1943, the honorary president was Bishop Joachim of Kozani, spiritual father of the EAM movement.[69]

Given its size and the welfare nature of its activities, EA was more acceptable to the leaders of organisations outside EAM. Hence, the September 1943 plenum, was attended by delegates from a number of centrist political formations, such as the Agrarian Democrats, the Progressive Liberals and even Giorgos Papandreou's Socialist Democrats, all of whom had already declined to cooperate with EAM. Such relations, however, did not develop further owing to the growing polarisation of Greece's internal politics.[70]

Political considerations, in fact, seem also to have influenced EA's relations with the International Red Cross. EAM sources, while acknowledging the contribution of the IRC, are critical of the fact that its leadership went along with the Germans and denied relief to the areas under EAM control. Petros Kokkalis gave special credit to EA for the fact that there were no deaths from hunger in these areas and castigates the IRC for having cooperated with the German strategy of isolating communities.[71] Some members of the IRC such as Axel Persson, secretary of the Peloponnese branch, were sympathetic to EA. There was, however, little he could do to assist EAM even if he had wanted to, given that the Germans and Security Battalions only allowed access to the towns but not to the villages in EAM-controlled territory. In this way, IRC food, Persson noted, was used by the Germans as a bribe for well-behaved communities.[72] Persson, of course, operated within the framework set by the IRC authorities. On the other hand, some leading members of the Security Battalions expected the IRC to feed their troops. General Demetrios Liakos, the collaborationist prefect in Evia, submitted such a demand in writing to the IRC in Athens, asking for food for his 1200 men.[73]

An interesting dispatch on the IRC's policy, dated 19 October 1944, was submitted by C.G. Yavis, a member of the US Office of Strategic Services in Greece, to OSS's Middle East Headquarters in Cairo. Yavis based his dispatch on EAM reports dated 30 April and 3 June 1944, which contained several complaints against Emil Sandström, the director of the IRC in Greece. According to the reports, which were in Yavis' opinion not far from the truth, Sandstrom strongly favoured the Germans and the collaborationist administrations. What is more, according to Yavis' personal experience from the areas he had visited, the people had received little or no help at all from the IRC. Yavis recorded his amazement at what he had witnessed at Karpenisi, in EAM controlled territory, namely that Sandstrom had travelled to the town for the purpose of asking the partisans to set free the collaborationist prefect of Lamia if they wanted to get Red Cross help for the district.[74]

At the time of liberation EA enjoyed immense prestige. Apart from the contribution to Greeks, suffering or resisting, EA had also succeeded in instilling in broad popular strata a moral uplift which it would not be possible to envisage in ordinary political circumstances. During the Metaxas dictatorship, informing and spying upon one's circle and even family was elevated into a duty. This mentality had been supplemented by the ruthless spirit of black marketeering which flourished during the occupation. Within a climate of amoral individualism EA put forward an alternative value system, the system after which it was named, that is to say 'national solidarity'. The fact that EA members were the first to visit the homes of those who lost a loved one or to care for the victims of the resistance left a lasting impression on Greek society.[75] The significance of EA's work was such as to have been acknowledged even by enemies of EAM. One such was Nikolaos Anagnostopoulos, an avowed supporter of the Security Battalions. Anagnostopoulos noted about EA:

> The solidarity which developed during the occupation among the supporters of EAM was great. In fact it was so great that we can say, without hesitation, that one member of EAM or ELAS lived for the other. This solidarity was strengthened even more when, as a result of

the action and reaction of Nationalist Greeks and especially of the Security Battalionists, in the form of reprisals, EAM suffered casualties and grave material damage. For its part EAM – KKE set up ... an important organisation, whose activity was, it must be admitted, very serious and useful and whose name was *Ethniki Allilengyi*.[76]

During the events of December 1944 in Athens, EA, not surprisingly, supported ELAS in their clash with the British troops and those under the control of the returning government of National Unity, headed by Giorgos Papandreou. Though most of its personnel, along with the rest of EAM, abandoned Athens, its branches continued their activities throughout the rest of Greece. In fact the administration set up by EAM functioned for months in several localities, until the arrival of the right-wing National Guard. Thereafter, its branches were methodically dissolved. By June 1945, out of something like 4000 establishments, nurseries, medical centres and hospitals only about ten were still functioning. The rest had been destroyed, even though the perpetrators of the destruction had nothing to put in their place.[77]

Throughout the period of White Terror which followed the December events and preceded the civil war, EA attempted to continue the well-tried system of relief to the several thousand members of EAM interned by the government.[78] However, as with the rest of EAM organisations, EA could not survive the civil war. In early 1947 it was dissolved by a court order, on the ground that it had deviated from its stated aims. On 8 January 1948, in accordance with law 509/47, for the protection of the social order, EA, together with EAM and KKE, was declared illegal. The leadership was sent to Makronisos, a Dachau-like island prison camp, to receive 'national re-education'. A few members of EA who managed to evade capture continued to function clandestinely until the remnants of the organisation were completely eliminated by the end of the civil war in 1949.

Thereafter, the members of EA suffered their share of the repression and discrimination which marked the political life of Greece. The passions generated during the turbulent years of occupation and civil war were not laid to rest, nor was the significance of morally subduing the opponents of the regime, the essence of *'dilosi'* forgotten by Greek governments up to 1974. Applicants for all kinds of public posts and even for some certificates, had to complete notorious forms, stating whether they or members of their family had ever belonged to the organisations listed on the questionnaires, all of which related to EAM. In correct alphabetical order *Ethniki Allilengyi* was listed first.

Notes

1. See, generally, Vasilis Bartzotas, *Stis Phylakes kai tis Exories* (Athens, 1978), pp. 43, 45, 98, 101 and 112. Bartzotas had been in prison continuously between 1932–43. He later became secretary of the Athens branch of the KKE in occupied Athens. See also the involvement of communist youths in EV activities in Avra Partsalidou, *Anamniseis apo ti zoi tis OKNE* (Athens, 1983), pp. 15 and 22.
2. The murder of an EV leader in police custody is recorded by Antonis Phlountzis, a medical doctor who was in prison for several years between the 1930s and the 1970s, in *Akronafplia kai Akronafpliotes 1937–1943* (Athens, 1979). Akronafplia prison held the largest number of communists (around 600) between 1937 and 1943.
3. Richard Clogg, *A Short History of Modern Greece* (Cambridge, 1986), pp. 134–5.
4. A collection of heartbreaking letters from the families of inmates is cited in Vasilis Bartzotas, *Ki astrapse fos i Akronafplia* (Athens, 1981), pp. 47–9.
5. Clogg, *History*, p. 139.
6. Mark Mazower, *Inside Hitler's Greece* (London, 1993), pp. 99–100.
7. Petros Rousos, *I Megali Pentaetia*, vol. 1 (Athens, 1982), pp. 101 and 152–7.
8. The others were Spyros Antypas, Kleon Papaloizos, Georgios Vasilopoulos and Dionysia Konstadopoulou-Papadomikhelaki. See Kleon Papaloizos, *Istorioviographika Simiomata – Kypros, Aigyptos, Ellada* (Athens, 1977), p. 65.
9. *Ethniki Allilengyi – Mia Prospatheia kai enas Athlos* (Athens, 1945), p. 15.
10. Angelos Avgoustidis, *To Elliniko Syndikalistiko Kinima kata ti Dekaetia tou 40* (Athens, 1999), pp. 89–90.
11. For the impact of the famine see Chapter 2 in the present volume and Mazower, *Inside Hitler's Greece*, pp. 41 and 325.
12. Cited in Richard Clogg (ed.), *Greece 1940–1949: Occupation, Resistance, Civil War* (London, 2002), p. 85.
13. Mazower, *Inside Hitler's Greece*, pp. 108–11.
14. Giannis Kairophylas, *I Athina tou '40 kai tis Katokhis* (Athens, 1985), p. 282.
15. See the articles in *Kommounistiki Epitheorisi – tis Epokhis tis Fasistikis Katokhis 1941–1944*, 'To Drama tis Laikis Diatrophis', 1, October 1941: pp. 13–17. See also 'Resolution of the 7th Plenum of the Central Committee of the KKE', early September 1941, cited in *KKE, Episima Keimena*, vol. 5 (Athens, 1981), pp. 50–1.
16. Thanasis Khatzis, *I Nikiphora Epanastasi pou khathike*, vol. 1 (Athens, 1983), pp. 245–6.
17. Spyros Kotsakis, *Eisphora sto Khroniko tis Katokhis kai tis Ethnikis Antistasis stin Athina* (Athens, 1986), p. 69.
18. Giorgos Margaritis, *Apo tin Itta stin Exegersi* (Athens, 1993), pp. 102–5 and 191–2.
19. Petros Kokkalis, 'I Symvoli tou Ethnikoapeleftherotikou Agona stin Epiviosi tou Laou', *Ethniki Antistasi*, July–September 2001: 55. Kokkalis was Secretary for Health and Welfare in PEEA, the administration established in 1944 in EAM-controlled territory (Free Greece).
20. On the state of philanthropic associations see Alexandros Zannas, *I Katokhi* (Athens, 1964), p. 18.
21. Georgios Tsolakoglou, *Apomnimonevmata* (Athens, 1959), pp. 206 and 227. Damaskinos also swore in the other two collaborationist premiers who succeeded Tsolakoglou.
22. K. Logothetopoulos, *Idou i Alitheia* (Athens, 1948), p. 151.

23. Ilias Venezis, *Arkhiepiskopos Damaskinos: Oi Khronoi tis Douleias* (Athens, 1981), p. 169.
24. Zannas, *Katokhi*, p. 26.
25. *Ethniki Allilengyi*, pp. 34–5.
26. HS5/231, 'EAM in Athens', undated, circa January 1944.
27. Giannis Kyriakidis, *Ethnikoapeleftherotikos Agonas, Nea Smyrni-Phaliro 1941–1945* (Athens, 1983), p. 302.
28. Historical Archive of the Foreign Ministry (IAYE), Occupation Government, File 1942 II/1, Prime Minister's Office, Sotirios Gotzamanis, Minister of Finance, to General G. Tsolakoglou, Prime Minister, 16 July 1942.
29. Ibid., Tsolakoglou to Gotzamanis, 22 July 1942.
30. Kokkalis, *Symvoli*, p. 55.
31. *Ethniki Allilengyi*, p. 20.
32. On the pressures exerted on political prisoners, see Vasilis Bartzotas, *60 Khronia Kommounistis* (Athens, 1986), p. 178.
33. By January 1942, two organisations in Thessaly, which had been founded for the welfare of these prisoners, were absorbed by EA, *Ethniki Allilengyi*, p. 17.
34. Three died and some of them became deranged. There were no statements of repentance, Bartzotas, *Akronafplia*, pp. 122–4.
35. Kostas Bosis, *Ai Stratis: I Makhi tis Peinas ton Politikon Exoriston sta 1941* (Athens, 1995). The chief of police in the nearby island of Lemnos, having visited the prison and the wing of the so-called unrepentants, reported that he witnessed yellow faces on skeletons, inspiring emotions akin to those of Dante's inferno, IAYE, 1942 File IV/8, Inspector E. Papoutsakis to Ministry of Public Security, 25 February 1942.
36. Phlountzis, *Akronafplia*, pp. 370–1.
37. For the use of EA youths to transport items see Janet Hart, *New Voices in the Nation: Women and the Greek Resistance, 1941–1944* (Ithaca, NY 1996), p. 171.
38. Ilias Papasteriopoulos, *O Morias sta Opla*, vol. IV (Athens, 1975), pp. 372–3.
39. See generally, *Tessera Khronia Agones kai Drasi tis EA Thessalonikis* (Salonica, 1945).
40. Antonis Phlountzis, *Stratopeda Larissas – Trikalon 1941–1944* (Athens, 1977), p. 369. He was the lawyer Zisis Zographos, later member of the Political Bureau of the KKE.
41. *Ethniki Allilengyi*, p. 37.
42. 'Anakoinosi tis K.E. tis Ethnikis Allilengyis' (Athens, 15 January, 1943). Cited in *Keimena tis Ethnikis Antistasis* (Athens, 1981), p. 495.
43. HS5/707, Secret, 'Report of Activities in Greece by Sgt. Paul A. Phillips', circa October 1944.
44. Vasilis Bartzotas, *I Ethniki Antistasi stin Adouloti Athina* (Athens, 1984), p. 239.
45. Nikandros Kepesis, *O Pireas stin Ethniki Antistasi* (Athens, 1988), p. 414.
46. A detailed account of the support offered by EA to ELAS units is given in Tasoula Vervenioti, *I Gynaika tis Antistasis* (Athens, 1994), pp. 243–52.
47. Kyriakides, *Nea Smyrni*, p. 60.
48. *Ethniki Allilengyi*, pp. 98–100.
49. Gianni Petropoulos, 'I Pyrosvestiki Ypiresia Pirea ton Kairo tis Katokhis', *Ethniki Antistasi*, 48 (December 1985): p. 42.
50. Alexis Sevastakis, *Kapetan Boukouvalas: To Antartiko Ippiko tis Thessalias* (Athens, 1991), pp. 171 and 178–9.

51. Bartzotas, *Athina*, pp. 114–15.
52. General State Archives, ABE 730/163, Special Security Directorate, 'Information Bulletin', 12 October 1943.
53. Kokkalis, 'Symvoli', p. 55. Opening stores by force was applied by EAM again in January 1944, when black marketeers raised their prices.
54. General State Archives, ABE 730/163, Special Security Directorate, 'Information Bulletin', 18 October 1943.
55. *Ethniki Allilengyi*, 'Eranos ton Thymaton', No 20, 24 December 1943.
56. General State Archives, ABE 730/163, Special Security Directorate, 'Information Bulletin', 5 October, 1943.
57. *Pos prepei na doulevei i Gynaika sto Ethniko Apeleftherotiko Metopo* (Athens, 1943), pp. 9–10, 14, 20, 24, 31 and 37.
58. Bartzotas gives several descriptions of such confrontations between unarmed demonstrators and the occupation forces, Bartzotas, *Athens*, pp. 127, 135–8 and 318–19.
59. The *kapetanios* noted the name of the girl leading the procession. She was Aspassia Papathanassiou, KKE secretary in the nearby quarter of Kouponia, Papathanassiou later became Greece's leading performer of ancient Greek tragedy, Orestis Makris, *O ELAS tis Athinas* (Athens, 1985), pp. 38 and 101. For the processions in Karditsa by women in traditional *karagouni* uniforms, see Apostolos Strongilis, *I Protevousa tis Eleftheris Elladas* (Athens, 1988), p. 172. The ritual use of the black kerchief is mentioned in Lazaros Arseniou, *I Thessalia stin Antistasi*, vol. 2 (Larisa, 1990), p. 140.
60. For the social composition of EA committees see, for instance, Thanasis Kakoyiannis, *Mnimes kai Selides tis Ethnikis Antistasis: Agrinio – Dytiki Sterea Ellada* (Athens, 1997), pp. 134–5 and Kostas Vouyiouklakis, *I Ethniki Antistasi sti Lakonia* (Athens, 1987), p. 138.
61. D. Vlysidi and L. Eliaki, *Ta Prota Vimata tou EAM stin Kriti* (Khania, 1997), pp. 35–6.
62. See a list of EA lawyers in Papaloizos, *Istorioviographika*, pp. 111–12.
63. Ibid., p. 107.
64. *Ethniki Allilengyi*, p. 93.
65. See generally Dimitris Kailas, *O Kliros stin Antistasi* (Athens, 1981).
66. *Ethniki Allilengyi*, p. 21.
67. HS5/235, 'Greece: Political–Religious Position of the Church in Evia', 13 September 1944.
68. Antonis Phlountzis, *Khaidari, Kastro kai Vomos tis Ethnikis Antistasis* (Athens, 1986), p. 599. Amantos is reported to have joined EA after he had been assured that it was not a communist organisation.
69. *Ethniki Allilengyi*, p. 18.
70. Mikhalis Lyberatos, *Sta Prothyra tou Emphyliou Polemou* (Athens, 2006), p. 37.
71. Kokkalis, 'Symvoli', p. 56.
72. Kostis Papakongos, *Arkheio Perrson: Katokhika Dokoumenta tou DES Peloponisou* (Athens, 1977), p. 86.
73. Giannis Douatzis Archive: Dimitrios Liakos, Commissioner of the District of Evia, Security Detachments Camp, to the Central Committee of the IRC, 2 February 1944. I am grateful to Giorgos Douatzis for having allowed me access to his father's archive on the occupation in Evia. The records contain no evidence of the IRC's response.

74. RG 226/19/24, 'EAM Report on International Red Cross', C.G. Yavis, to William Langer, Chief of the Research and Analysis Branch, Office of Strategic Services, 19 October 1944. Some articles in the report, as summarised by Yavis, are worth quoting:

2. During the period May–September 1943, when the shipment of food to Epirus was forbidden, he did nothing to have the embargo lifted. With an insignificant exception in September 1943, Epirus was given no aid until March 1944. 3. Although in February the Germans had given permission for distribution of food in the *nomos* (district) of Evrytania under IRC supervision, by 20 April no representative had been sent. 4. For the past eight months nothing had been sent to the Northern Sporades Islands. The excuse given by the President was a German prohibition, which however the Germans denied. 5. The Kyklades Islands received their first food shipment in 17 months in April 1944. 8. In April the president loaned 500 tons of wheat to the Germans, without any understanding as to the time of repayment. 9. On all questions discussed with Minister Tsironikos, the President and his Deputy are always in agreement with the Minister's views. 10. The Italian community receives regular food allotments from the IRC, but the IRC claims that 'the agreements' prevent it from sending food to the Serbian hostages. 11. Whereas the IRC makes every effort to prevent the shipment of food to *andarte*-held districts, and to prevent food from falling into the hands of the *andartes*, the Rallist forces receive their bread from the IRC regularly. 12. The President has collected about him the most reactionary elements of Greece, and those most willing to collaborate with the Germans.

75. Interview with Klio Ioannidou, member of the committee of EA in Piraeus. Ioannidou was the sister of Kostas Khristodoulidis, General Secretary of the Communist Party of Cyprus, and Khristodoulos Khristodoulidis (Alexis), member of the KKE Political Bureau. She moved to Greece in 1927 and remained a member of the KKE till her death in 1990.
76. Nikolaos Anagnostopoulos, *Paranomos Typos – Katokhi 1941–1944* (Athens, 1960), p. 95.
77. *Ethniki Allilengyi*, pp. 101–2.
78. Polymeris Voglis, *I Empeiria tis Phylakis kai tis Exorias: Oi Politikoi Kratoumenoi ston Emphylio Polemo* (Athens, 2004), pp. 221 and 265. For the English language version of this book, see *Becoming a Subject: Political Prisoners during Greek Civil War* (Oxford, 2002).

9
The Greek Orthodox Church and Social Welfare during the Second World War

Vasilios N. Makrides

I

I have discussed elsewhere the involvement of the Greek Orthodox Church in welfare activities during the 1940s. That paper focused on the role of the religious organisation *Zoi* during the civil war (1946–49) that wracked Greece in the aftermath of the Second World War.[1] Brief mention was made of the fact that this organisation as a whole played a vital role in welfare activities during the Second World War, ranging from famine relief to the material and spiritual support of war-afflicted families. In the present chapter my intention is to focus more systematically on this issue, firstly by presenting and discussing the welfare activities of the Orthodox Church of Greece during this period of general turmoil, and, secondly, those of *Zoi*.

Before addressing the main subject, it should be noted that the Church of Greece had faced a deep internal crisis before the country's involvement in the Second World War. This had erupted after the death of Archbishop Khrysostomos (Papadopoulos) in October 1938. Throughout the modern history of Greece the Church has been subject, to a greater or lesser degree, to political influence and has often experienced political turbulence. This was the case in this particular ecclesiastical crisis. The death of Archbishop Khrysostomos (1868–1938) took place during the dictatorship of General Ioannis Metaxas (1936–41), which, though not in the strict sense fascist, nonetheless demonstrated marked fascist tendencies. It was no surprise that politics were involved in the election of a successor to Khrysostomos. There were two strong candidates. The first was Damaskinos (Papandreou). Born in 1891, he had been Metropolitan of Corinth since 1922 and was considered a supporter of the late Prime Minister Eleftherios Venizelos and his foreign policy, as opposed to that of the royalists. At the time he was also in charge of church finances and his candidature was backed, among others, by the Minister of Education, Konstantinos Georgakopoulos.[2] The other candidate was Khrysanthos (Philippidis), born in 1881, the former Metropolitan of Trebizond in Asia Minor, who, after the Asia Minor disaster of 1922, had settled in Athens. An influential figure, he undertook important missions for the Patriarchate of Constantinople.[3] He had royalist leanings that were influenced by the Byzantine tradition, although he had given his backing to Venizelos at the time of the short-lived Peace Treaty of Sèvres (1920). The dictator Metaxas, though he adopted a neutral stance regarding the electoral procedure, was much closer to Khrysanthos, who was also clearly favoured by the King, George II.

On the day of the election (5 November 1938) Damaskinos received a total of thirty-one votes in the Holy Synod, while Khrysanthos had just one vote less, that is to say thirty. As the voting was so close, this opened the way to outside interference. Following intervention by Metaxas, an intra-governmental crisis and an appeal to the Council of State, Damaskinos' election was annulled (28 November 1938). Under the provisions of a new law (no. 1493 of 1938), the election of the new archbishop was transferred from the full assembly of bishops to the thirteen members of the Permanent Synod of the Church of Greece. This eventually elected Khrysanthos as the new archbishop on 11 December 1938. However, after the occupation of Greece by the Axis powers in April 1941, Khrysanthos refused, inter alia, to swear in the cabinet of the collaborationist occupation government of General Georgios Tsolakoglou or to collaborate with the Germans. He was then forced to resign and Damaskinos, who had been exiled to the island of Salamis, was reinstated. Damaskinos, however, did not become the tool of the occupation forces, but sought to keep good relations with all sides, from the Germans to the leftist EAM (*Ethniko Apeleftherotiko Metopo* – National Liberation Front) and its guerrilla army ELAS (*Ellinikos Laikos Apeleftherotikos Stratos* – Greek People's Liberation Army). He exhibited both strong leadership skills and political ambitions, and dominated the period through his extraordinary personality. After the liberation he also became regent for a short time, thus preventing a dangerous vacuum in political leadership.

The deposed Khrysanthos, for his part, did not disappear altogether from the scene, but retained considerable influence, albeit mostly in the background. This was due to the strong support he enjoyed in the ecclesiastical, political and military world (including that of the exiled King George II, the royal family, and the government-in-exile). Acting as the king's representative in Greece, Khrysanthos in 1943 initiated with others a widespread Orthodox liberation movement. Its aim was not only the liberation of Greece from the Germans and the return of the king, but also defence against the communists, who had emerged as a very powerful force in the resistance, and against Soviet designs on Greece. After the liberation, Khrysanthos was reinstated by the Holy Synod, but only in a symbolic fashion. Yet after the death of Damaskinos (20 May 1949) there was an attempt by his supporters to bring him back to the archbishopric. The plan did not materialize, because he died soon afterwards (28 September 1949). It is no exaggeration to claim that the 1940s were ecclesiastically, socially and politically influenced by these two eminent hierarchs, who, despite their differences, left an indelible imprint and legacy in many areas.[4]

Despite these problems, it is no surprise that the Church showed from the very beginning of Greece's involvement in the Second World War a determined interest in defending the interests of the nation in a number of ways. This is due above all to previous tradition and practice. More specifically, the Church had shown since the late nineteenth century a keen interest in supporting the national cause of the Greek people and had presented itself as the principal bastion of Greek national identity in previous centuries and particularly during the period of Ottoman rule. In the traditional view, the national role of the Church always became more apparent at critical moments in the country's history. The period of the Second World War was certainly one of those. Such a perspective led the Church to bestow a particular religious legitimacy upon the just, defensive war of the Greeks, who had been attacked by the Axis powers without provocation.

Within this discourse the role of the Mother of God (*Theotokos*) in protecting the Greek nation and leading it to victory and liberation was given a very prominent place. This element can be readily observed in official and other texts as well as in expressions of popular piety during the period under consideration and subsequently.[5] It is no accident that the Holy Synod of the Church of Greece decided in 1952 to celebrate the feast of the 'Protecting Veil' (*Agia Skepi*) of the Mother of God every 28th October, which coincides with the national celebrations of the Greek victory over the forces of Fascist Italy. This simultaneous celebration of a national and religious feast, which is not the only one in the Greek calendar, demonstrates the strong bonds between Orthodoxy and Greek national identity. The Greek victory against Italy on the Albanian front was hailed as being in accordance with the will of God and as demonstrating God's protection of the Greek nation over the centuries.[6]

The fact that the Church showed a clear interest in welfare activities on behalf of the war-stricken Greek population should occasion no surprise. It is well known and amply documented that philanthropic activities in a variety of forms and ways have been at the heart of the Church's practices not only in the past (in the early church, in Byzantine times and later under

Ottoman domination), but also in the present day.[7] This is demonstrated by the large number of charitable institutions and other related organisations operating under the auspices of the Church (for example, orphanages and homes for the poor, needy schoolchildren/students and the aged, hospitals, summer camps, relief funds and distribution of food and clothing for the poor). Historically speaking, the Church had always exhibited a strong social consciousness and concern for social problems, albeit in its own particular way, based on specific theological premises. But this does not mean that the Church was in a position to satisfy fully the strata that profited from its welfare activities or that its own views on social welfare and justice were generally accepted by other socio-political actors. Nonetheless, through welfare activities the Church tried to demonstrate its usefulness to the Greek nation, to remain socially present and active, and finally, to enhance its influential position within Greek society. The reason for this attitude should be sought in the fact that since the foundation of the modern Greek state the Church had been socially marginalised to a large extent and remained dependent on the political establishment of the country. Therefore, its dream was always to overcome the social marginalisation induced by the state and to acquire greater responsibilities.

Aside from this, which constitutes the historical and traditional framework for the Church's welfare activities, it is also useful to look at the immediate context of the Church's strong social involvement during the Second World War. This must be understood against the background of the ever-increasing influence of communism in the country, which represented a clear challenge to the Church's influence and authority. Since their first appearance in the nineteenth century, socialist and communist ideas and currents came into conflict with Christian views and institutions in Western Europe. Their expansion and manifestation in the form of Marxism-Leninism in the Soviet Union after 1917 appeared as a serious threat to the liberal West and its Christian heritage. Related ideas, through a variety of channels, also entered the Greek world at an early stage. Exhibiting at times an anti-religious and anti-Christian spirit,[8] Greek Marxism acquired a considerable influence among the population at large, especially among the small working class, and soon gained a foothold within society and the political establishment. In the January 1936 elections, the Greek Communist Party (KKE) managed to elect 15 deputies. This alarmed bourgeois political and religious forces for the KKE now held the balance of power in parliament. Throughout the interwar period there was thus a constant tension between the Church's activities and those of the communists. This opposition was not only evident at the ideological level, when both sides tried to refute one another using different lines of argument. It was also manifested in their continuous attempts to develop extensive social networks throughout the country by helping Greek citizens in need. These practical initiatives were vital for both sides, albeit for different reasons. The Church, on the one hand, sought to demonstrate its social responsibility by undertaking extensive charitable work. The communists, for their part, sought to demonstrate that they alone were trustworthy and efficient in dealing with social issues and that all other actors, including the Church, were hypocrites who refrained from addressing social problems and inequalities effectively. Behind this criticism was the Marxist idea that religions, and in particularly Christianity, are too otherworldly-oriented to undertake any meaningful and productive social action.

Admittedly, the Church was at odds with communist ideology, but its position towards the communists during the Second World War was far from uniform. The need to resist the Axis conquerors had in fact led many Orthodox clerics to join the broad resistance movement, including those powerful groups controlled by the communists. It is thus no surprise that several metropolitans (Ioakheim of Kozani, Antonios of Ileia, Ioakheim of Chios) as well as monks and clerics of all ranks were linked to the resistance organized by EAM.[9] The question is, however, how one should understand this rather unlikely affiliation. In my view, this has to be done from the broader scope of the overall resistance of the Greek people and not as indicating full identification with communist ideology and party. It is also worth mentioning that, initially, Archbishop Damaskinos declined officially to condemn EAM during the Axis occupation. Yet inevitably the whole situation changed dramatically after the events of December 1944 (the so-called *Dekemvriana*), when the communists appeared to be launching a bid to overthrow the government. The Church wholeheartedly supported the anti-communist struggle at all levels, while clerics previously associated with EAM faced disciplinary measures and, at times, even persecution. Archbishop Damaskinos thus now took a much more critical stance towards the communists, while the latter accused him of being a British pawn. As was to be expected, it became difficult for the Church to refrain from opposing the communists, a phenomenon that became even more pronounced during the ensuing civil war.[10]

II

To turn now to an examination of the activities, including those related to welfare, undertaken by the Church of Greece during the Second World War. After Italy had declared war on Greece in October 1940, Metaxas immediately contacted Archbishop Khrysanthos, who issued an appeal asking for God's assistance for the Greek army in those difficult times. Khrysanthos also provided the Greek army with an icon of the Mother of God, made according to Byzantine style by the painter Aginor Asteriadis. This was also reproduced in printed form and distributed to soldiers at the front. He also sent twenty crosses to provide moral support to army officers at the front. This attests clearly to the religious legitimation given to the Greek defensive war. In addition, Khrysanthos sent a letter to the Christian churches in Western Europe denouncing the unjust attack by Italy against Greece,[11] while in encyclicals he urged local metropolitans to support the defence of Greece and of its fighting soldiers.[12]

Aside from the moral and psychological help offered to the Greek army by the Church, considerable attention was also paid to the material support of the army and to relief measures for war-stricken families. More specifically, Khrysanthos set up a number of organisations in the capital to undertake social welfare and charitable activities. In this he was particularly helped by *Zoi*, with its extensive networks and powers of mobilisation. Among these organisations, the 'Support for the Family of the Fighting Soldier' (*Eniskhysis tis Oikogeneias tou Agonistou*) should take pride of place. This operated over 150 branches in the greater Athens area. About 2500 women from this organisation cared (with each looking after approximately twenty to twenty-five families) for the families of soldiers from the greater Athens area (about 60,000 soldiers in all). Due to the increased needs of the day the whole organisation expanded its structure shortly afterwards and was renamed the 'Welfare of the Soldiers' (*Pronoia ton Stratevomenon*). It operated 156 offices in the Athens area (six of them in central parts of the capital and 150 in the suburbs) and its budget in April 1941 exceeded fifteen million drachmae. Another organisation set up by Khrysanthos was the 'Company of the Fighting Soldier' (*Syntrophia tou Agonistou*), which was focused on assistance to the soldiers and their support with religious literature. Social welfare was to be combined with appropriate religious enlightenment.

The main person behind this official church network was the Archimandrite Ieronymos Kotsonis (1905–88), the secretary of the Holy Synod of the Church of Greece and the right-hand man of Khrysanthos.[13] He also happened to be a close affiliate of *Zoi* and of the 'Christian Union of Academics', a fact demonstrating the close relations of these organisations with the official Church at the time. It should be remembered that Khrysanthos himself had close ties with the powerful *Zoi* organisation and its extensive networks and was well aware of its power. All in all, it is estimated that 61,235 families received help in this way: 10,178 families received food supplies, 15,753 families received clothes, 9983 received tinned food, while 14,245 found work to support themselves.[14] Khrysanthos also donated valuable objects from various churches in Athens for the support of the Greek air force and presided over the committee established to provide soup-kitchens for the poor and needy. In addition, he visited wounded soldiers, gave support to troops at the front through correspondence and through the pamphlet *Ena Gramma pros tous Stratiotes mas* (A letter to our soldiers), published in some 75,000 copies, and undertook many other activities aimed at strengthening the morale of the Greek people in those harsh times.[15]

After the deposition of Khrysanthos in 1941, Archbishop Damaskinos continued the previous welfare work of the official Church under Axis occupation, albeit in a somewhat different way. Among other things, he founded the more centralised 'National Organisation of Christian Solidarity' (*Ethnikos Organismos Khristianikis Allilengyis*), focusing on the needs of the Greeks under foreign occupation. This depended less on volunteer work and was organised along the lines of state organisations as legal entities of public law. In Athens and Piraeus this organisation was staffed with approximately 200 higher public, bank, municipal and private officials together with 4698 workers, mostly women. It ranged beyond the capital and reached the provinces with a total of 3000 branches. Four hundred thousand children, 4000 pregnant women, 14,000 nursing mothers and 23,000 destitute people attended the soup-kitchens provided by this organisation. In 1942 it distributed 480,834 rations of milk and nourishment for children, while these portions were substantially increased in both 1943 (2,888,947) and 1944 (3,403,964). In addition, it provided needy Greeks with all kinds of useful goods and cared especially for their health problems. For example, 153 doctors in Athens examined sick people free of charge, and in the years 1942–43 a total of 277,769 persons received medical treatment in this way. Two other social welfare organisations founded by Damaskinos were the 'Support Service for Poor Prisoners' (*Ypiresia Prostasias Aporon Kratoumenon*) and the 'Support Service for the Orphaned Families of Executed Greeks' (*Ypiresia Prostasias Aporphanistheison Oikogeneion Ekteloumenon*), the latter founded in April 1943: 1854 families in various areas of the country received the support of this organisation in a number of ways before December 1943. These organisations provided help to numerous Greeks, especially during the winter of 1941–42, when widespread food shortages in Athens and other cities led to thousands of deaths. From September 1942 onwards they also played a role in distributing foreign aid, provided mainly by the International Red Cross.[16] Equally important was the role of individual clergymen in supporting prisoners and hostages during this period, including those who were to be executed.[17]

All these activities bestowed upon the Church some 'privileges' and enhanced its importance as a social actor and intermediary between the population and the foreign conquerors. Damaskinos thus intervened with the Germans on behalf of the Greeks living in north-eastern Greece in the Bulgarian occupation zone, because they were subjected to harsh measures, including systematic de-Hellenisation.[18] It was in this context that Damaskinos intervened in March 1943 on behalf of the Greek Jews. In a meeting with the German plenipotentiary for Greece, Günther Altenburg, he asked that they should not be deported. Damaskinos' intervention was ineffective at the official level, although he did issue two declarations (23 and 24 March 1943), one addressed to the prime minister of the collaborationist government in Athens, Konstantinos Logothetopoulos, and the other to Altenburg, condemning the deportation of Greek Jews to Poland. In early spring 1944, Damaskinos helped Athenian Jews to avoid arrest by issuing 560 backdated false baptism certificates, which were used by the Greek administration (for example, police) to provide Jews with false papers.[19] Other efforts to help the Jewish population were undertaken locally by a number of metropolitans in their dioceses.[20]

Material support of the Greek army, their families and other war-stricken persons was also undertaken in the provinces throughout the war years. This applied both to the higher and to the lower echelons of the Church. The governing board of the Holy Establishment of the Mother of God on the island of Tinos (1 December 1940) donated precious objects, offerings and jewellery from this famous place of pilgrimage (at an estimated value of 5 million drachmae) to the needs of the Greek army, an act that drew the thanks of Prime Minister Metaxas.[21] Extensive welfare activities, combined with spiritual ones, were also undertaken by numerous metropolitans in their respective dioceses.[22] The same holds true for many priests throughout the country.[23] The late Archbishop of Athens and All Greece, Serapheim (Tikas) (1913–98), who served as a deacon in the Athens area, was later active in the Greek resistance in the Epirus region.[24] Documents describe the activities of chaplains serving with the army at the front, in military hospitals and aiding in numerous other ways,[25] as well as the role of the monasteries during this period.[26]

Needless to say, there were many victims from the ranks of the clergy during the Greek-Italian war and during the Axis occupation.[27] There was large-scale destruction of church buildings and other precious sacred objects by Axis soldiers.[28] The Greek Orthodox clergy also played a significant role in the areas of Greece under Bulgarian occupation (that is, Eastern Macedonia and Thrace), where the Greek population fell victim to Bulgarian nationalism.[29] Finally, substantial spiritual and material help for the Greek army and people came from Greeks abroad; for example, from the USA where the Archbishop of North and South America, Athenagoras (1886–1972), who subsequently became Ecumenical Patriarch of Constantinople, was one of those who sent food, medicine, clothing and other supplies to a value exceeding twenty million US dollars during the period 1940–47[30] (see Chapter 4).

III

Parallel to the activities of the official Church, an organisation that played a vital role during this period was the brotherhood of theologians known as *Zoi* (Life).[31] This was a new phenomenon in the religious life of the country, dating from the beginning of the twentieth century. A basic reason for *Zoi*'s emergence and subsequent influence should be sought in the inability of the official Church to satisfy the religious needs of the Greek people at that time. *Zoi* was the best known and most influential religious organisation of this kind. It was founded as an Orthodox, semi-monastic brotherhood in 1907 by the Archimandrite Evsevios Matthopoulos (1849–1929), and consisted initially of a few celibate lay theologians and other men. From 1911 onwards, the brotherhood regularly published a periodical with the same name. *Zoi* gradually became an organisation with significant influence and solid social support as well as international recognition, especially after the Archimandrite Serapheim Papakostas (1892–1954) undertook its leadership in 1927.[32] The range of activities and the social appeal of *Zoi* were further enhanced by many affiliated sisterhoods, such as *Evseveia* (Piety), founded in November 1938, and other associations, such as *O Apostolos Pavlos* (The Apostle Paul), founded in 1929 for the purpose of Orthodox domestic mission. All these bodies were destined to serve specific social strata such as academics, parents, workers and students. *Zoi* developed extensive networks through its representatives throughout the country and thus managed to extend its influence beyond the Athens area. This sometimes caused tensions either with the official Church or with local metropolitans, although *Zoi*'s overall policy was careful and diplomatic and the organisation usually managed to avoid conflicts.

Through strategic alliances in the 1930s – such as with the circle of academics around the professor of law, Alexandros Tsirindanis (1903–77), who was the president of the *Khristianiki Enosis Epistimonon* (Christian Union of Academics) – *Zoi* acquired a strong presence in the academic-scholarly world of the country. The main aim was the defence of the Christian faith against the irreligious currents of the day, including Marxism and communism, and the development of a thorough Christian apologetics.[33] Furthermore, *Zoi* managed to infiltrate many areas of religious, political (as a result of the support of the Metaxas dictatorship) and social life and even extended its influence to the royal court. In 1940, *Zoi* controlled 494 Sunday schools in the greater Athens area and in the provinces, which were attended by approximately 60,000 male and female students, while the weekly circulation of the periodical *Zoi* was about 110,000 copies.[34] It is thus small wonder that *Zoi* played a considerable role in the politics of the official Church or that Archbishop Khrysanthos was closely associated with the movement. Apart from the laudatory comments about him found in the official bulletin of the brotherhood, it is noteworthy that the special prayer composed by Khrysanthos for the support of the Greek nation and army during the war, which was recited on Sundays during the divine liturgy in Athens cathedral and in which the role of the King George II was particularly extolled, was reprinted in the periodical *Zoi*.[35]

For this reason, the welfare activities of *Zoi* during the Second World War should be examined alongside those of the official Church, because such issues, as well as missionary objectives, had been at the heart of *Zoi*'s interests at least since the early 1930s.[36] Moreover, due to the tension between the official Church and religious organisations such as *Zoi* – a tension which is still manifest – their welfare activities during this period are often treated in the relevant literature separately from one another, with the intention of downplaying the significance of their mutual influence and collaboration. For example, the Khrysanthos era is often portrayed with no explicit reference to his close links with the *Zoi* organisation.

As was to be expected, *Zoi* from the outset wholeheartedly supported Greece's defensive war against the Italian attack, legitimised it religiously and drew moral implications from the war. This is evident from many sources,[37] including the articles written in the official bulletin of the brotherhood.[38] Members of *Zoi* fought at the front, while *Zoi* clerics served as military chaplains, assisting the troops spiritually and morally and providing them with the publications of the brotherhood.[39] Apart from this, the *Zoi* movement mobilised to meet the needs of the war-afflicted population and participated actively in welfare activities. According to Ioannis Th. Kolitsaras, a member of *Zoi*, the welfare activities promoted by Archbishop Khrysanthos were to a large extent due to the initiatives of the leadership of *Zoi* and its affiliates. They were also carried out mostly through *Zoi*'s extensive networks. Kolitsaras mentions that during the first week of the Greek-Italian war Serapheim Papakostas, Alexandros Tsirindanis and Ieronymos Kotsonis met regularly and outlined a concrete programme of welfare action. This was shortly afterwards submitted to Archbishop Khrysanthos and, with his approval, led to the foundation of the aforementioned organisations, directed by Kotsonis and entrusted with handling the relief and welfare programme. Kolitsaras also makes clear that without the active involvement of the *Zoi* networks the realisation of this welfare programme would have been very difficult. This argument, albeit somewhat exaggerated, is nonetheless not far from the reality, given the fact that the early welfare programme during the Khrysanthos era was largely based on volunteer work and that only a movement like *Zoi* was in a position to mobilise such a large number of volunteers.

In addition, numerous meetings for the coordination of all these efforts and the persons involved in them took place in a building owned by *Zoi* (Karytsi 14), the base of the association for the Orthodox domestic mission *O Apostolos Pavlos*. Various bodies took part in this common endeavour under the general title 'Missionary Union of Co-operating Christian Associations *The Apostle Paul*', including the Brotherhood of Theologians *Zoi*, the Sisterhood *Evseveia*, the Christian Union of Academics, the Panhellenic Union of Parents *I Khristianiki Agogi* (Christian Education), and other groups. The activities of these cooperating bodies included the spiritual and material support of wounded soldiers through correspondence and religious literature (distribution of some 100,000 books and periodicals); care for the families of combatants and wounded soldiers; collection of all kinds of goods, food, medicines and money to be distributed to individuals and families in need; housing facilities for the homeless; medical care supplied by nurses and volunteer doctors (approximately 325 doctors who undertook some 12,000 medical visits without charge); specialised services for various categories of people, such as the underwriting of costs for those who had legal disputes; and the organisation of soup-kitchens for the poor, refugees and others suffering from the consequences of bombing. In addition, *Zoi* collaborated with other foundations that operated in the country in support of the fighting soldiers, such as the organisation *Phanella tou Stratiotou* (Comforts (literally Flannel) for the Soldier). Volunteer women managed to knit 53,984 pairs of socks, 14,509 pairs of gloves, 7803 scarfs and 1046 woollies.[40]

The same policy continued under Axis occupation as the needs of the population for welfare became even more acute.[41] On 29 June 1941, the coordinating network *O Apostolos Pavlos*, operating under the auspices of *Zoi*, decided to initiate a systematic philanthropic effort through the collection of money and goods for the needy, similar to the one suggested by the Apostle Paul to the Christians of Corinth (1 *Corinthians* 16: 1–4).[42] This effort was given a Christian legitimation in a leader in the periodical *Zoi* entitled 'Without Delay'. There the need to apply the principle of *diakonia* out of Christian love was emphasised and readers were admonished always to keep in mind the immense needs of the poor.[43] Another strategy used was that of the so-called 'holy portion' (*agia meris*). In other words, people were admonished to save from their daily food a small portion and collect it separately for their brothers and sisters in need.[44] In this way, a substantial amount of food as well as money was collected and distributed. Further, in the official bulletin of the brotherhood a number of articles (editorials, features, reports and so on) dealt with this pressing issue of the day and criticised wrongdoing, including the black market.[45] The famine in the Athens area was addressed by *Zoi* in other ways as well, for example through the cultivation of vegetables and fruit on its private estate in Agia Paraskevi as well as through livestock breeding. Various means of transport were bought by *Zoi* to assist in the rapid distribution of goods.[46] Members of the organisation were active in transferring food supplies and other goods from the provinces to the Athens area, a hazardous undertaking given the turbulence of the times. Without taking money from selling its publications, the brotherhood chose instead to receive various goods and food supplies and distribute them later to the needy.[47] There was also a special service named *Estia Asthenon* (Centre for the Sick), in which, among other things, eleven doctors with different specialities offered medical help free of charge to sick people between July 1941 and the end of the Axis occupation in October 1944.[48]

Another well-known contribution of the *Zoi* movement related to the organisation of soup-kitchens to address the lack of food for thousands of poor people. In addition, these soup-kitchens for the needy were hailed in the official bulletin of the brotherhood as demonstrating Christian love and self-sacrifice.[49] After an appeal by the brotherhood's leadership, people brought to Karytsi 14 all kinds of personal belongings, which were subsequently sold in order to buy food. From March 1942 soup-kitchens were systematically organised in Athens and Piraeus – initially for 700 people – before any other state or private body undertook such an initiative. This was facilitated to a considerable extent by the volunteer work of *Zoi* members and affiliates. The whole scheme was later given a legal, viable framework through the foundation of the special non-profit organisation, *Pistotikos Synetairismos* (Credit Cooperative). Care was also demonstrated for poor university students who were provided with clothing. Another philanthropic organisation was founded specifically for the victims of bombing.[50]

The philanthropic activities of *Zoi* members and affiliates in the provinces should also be mentioned. These included, inter alia, the support of prisoners and hostages and attempts to secure their release; care for their families; mediation between the occupation forces and the resistance; and care for the dead or executed. Efforts were also made to provide a number of cities in the provinces (Thessaloniki, Patra, Larisa, Agrinio, Kalamata, Lamia, Volos, Karditsa, Katerini, Kavala, Edessa, Ioannina, Mytilini, Chios, Samos, and so on) with food supplies and soup-kitchens.[51] These various activities drew recognition from the International Red Cross.[52] Needless to say, such efforts were complemented by similar ones in the domain of the religious and spiritual enlightenment of the Greek people, especially in the light of the widespread anti-religious currents of the day.[53]

Zoi published a number of books dealing with this period and with the activities of the organisation. Among them were *Iroon Gi: Anamniseis apo to Alvanikon Epos* (Land of Heroes: Reminiscences from the Epic in Albania), published in Athens in 1950, which included various stories, based on real events and reported by *Zoi* members, from the Greek-Italian front, in which the transforming power of Christianity was emphasised; *Apo to Pikro Glyky. Douleia kai Erga Agapis* (From Bitterness, Sweetness: Slavery and Works of Love), published in Athens in 1947, which described the various welfare activities of the organisation under Axis occupation; *Oi Neoi ston Pono kai sti Drasi* (Young People under Stress and in Action), published in Athens in 1946, which reported on the activities of the 'Christian Union of University Students' under Axis occupation; *Xanazontanema* (Reawakening) (Fourth edition Athens, 1969), which included eighteen short stories relating to the role of Christianity under Axis occupation and the philanthropic work to which it gave rise; and *I Megali Kataktisis* (The Great Achievement) (Second edition Athens 1960) which described the welfare activities of the *Evseveia* sisterhood, for example their work in military hospitals.

The welfare activities of *Zoi* were highly influential in the Thessaloniki region. The most interesting account of these comes from a man of letters, Giorgos Ioannou (1927–85), who as a child became closely involved with the *Zoi* movement in the city. His personal *Diary of the Occupation Period* includes numerous entries regarding the Sunday schools and soup-kitchens organised by *Zoi*, and his own relations with *Zoi* members in the area, such as with the Archimandrite Leonidas Paraskevopoulos (1904–84) and the lay theologian Athanasios Phrangopoulos. Both played an important role in coordinating soup-kitchens in the area.[54] Ioannou gives a full account of this period and his involvement with *Zoi* from 1943 until 1948 elsewhere. Although he was critical of some aspects of the organisation, he also recognised that the role of *Zoi* in social welfare was vital for the survival of large numbers of people. In particular, he praised the personality and talents of Paraskevopoulos.[55] Admittedly, Paraskevopoulos was the individual who left an indelible mark on the population of Thessaloniki. His extensive welfare activities under Axis occupation were not forgotten, for he was considered responsible for saving the lives of thousands of children and adults in the famine. The soup-kitchens that he sponsored started in Thessaloniki in February 1942, initially for children attending Sunday school, but later for others.[56] It was as a result of his uncontested popularity that Paraskevopoulos later became Metropolitan of Thessaloniki (1968–74), during the period of the Colonels' dictatorship. Even after his dethronement he had numerous supporters and continued to work in the area until his death.[57]

The activities of *Zoi* in Thessaloniki during this period are also discussed in the diary of Leonidas Yiasimakopoulos (1884–1968), a prisoner in the Nazi concentration camp *Pavlos Melas* between April 1943 and the liberation. He reports regularly reading books published by *Zoi* that had been distributed by *Zoi* clerics Photios Stamatopoulos and Leonidas Paraskevopoulos.[58] He also talks positively about their role in supporting prisoners spiritually, and admired Paraskevopoulos for his eloquence. In addition, he makes clear that *Zoi*'s activities included supplying prisoners with food and other goods.[59] The role of *Zoi* members during this period has also been attested by others, among them by the Archimandrite Dionysios Kharalambous.[60] He was initially imprisoned in the *Pavlos Melas* camp in Thessaloniki, was later sent to a concentration camp in Germany, and after the liberation became Metropolitan of Trikkis and Stagon.

The difficulties and adversities of the war and the occupation period led to a strengthening of religious feelings and sensitivities among the population. Religion was seen as a means of alleviating personal anxieties and problems, and it is no wonder that we observe a rise in religiously-inspired mass phenomena during this period. The well-known poet and man of letters in Thessaloniki, Dinos Khristianopoulos (*b.* 1931), gives us a vivid account of the religious climate of the day and of the 'miracles' that were observed, as well as his involvement in relief activities (for example, with the *Phanella tou Stratiotou* organisation). He describes, inter alia, apparitions of the Virgin Mary in the windows of various stores in Thessaloniki, which attracted public wonder. On the one hand, these 'icons' aroused controversy, but on the other they led to various devotional phenomena and symbolic interpretations regarding the war and its future course.[61] This was, of course, not unrelated to the association, discussed above, of the Mother of God with the fighting Greek soldiers, which was officially promulgated during the war. Inevitably this climate of religious fervour particularly favoured not only the activities of the official Church, but also those of organisations such as *Zoi*.

It was clearly important for *Zoi* to show that it paid equal attention to the material as to the spiritual welfare of the people. The ultimate aim was to demonstrate that Christianity did not neglect the problems of everyday life but, on the contrary, that it was deeply involved in them. In this way, the old communist claim that Christianity was too focused on the life to come and showed no interest in the concerns of everyday life could be rebutted. This frequently resulted in antagonism, and at times open confrontation, between *Zoi* and the communists, not only as a result of the irreconcilable nature of their respective ideologies, but also on account of various practical matters. The clear opposition between the activities of *Zoi* and its allies and those of the communists is a matter of record.[62] The communists generally feared the extensive charitable activities of *Zoi*, because they demonstrated an unprecedented sensitivity to social issues and might undermine the communists' own claim to be the sole promoters of social equality and justice (see Chapter 8 for an analysis of the charitable activities of *Ethniki Allilengyi*, the welfare arm of EAM/ELAS). Thus, the communists often tried to disrupt *Zoi*'s work.[63] But the members of *Zoi* in general sought to act as mediators between the occupation forces, the communist-led guerrillas and the right-wing nationalists for the sake of the whole population.[64] They offered help to communists and in some cases this assistance was reciprocated.[65]

In some instances, members of *Zoi* contacted communist guerrillas in the mountains in an attempt to persuade them to refrain from attacking the Germans and causing minor damage, for which vicious reprisals could be expected.[66] It is worth mentioning here a member of *Zoi*, Father Konstantios Khronis (1906–91), who left a strong legacy in Kavala from which he had been expelled by the Bulgarian occupation forces.[67] In late 1944, while in the area of Aigialeia, he met with Aris Veloukhiotis, the ELAS leader, near Tropaia in Gortynia, and managed to persuade him not to destroy the railway connection to Diakophto, because this would have grave consequences for the greater Kalavryta area, especially after the massive reprisal executions of December 1943 in the town.[68] Father Khronis' activities in Kalavryta were praised by the Swedish Red Cross delegate in Greece, Hans Ehrenstråle, as well as by the mayor of Kalavryta, Alexios Bres, in a letter of 15 October 1947 sent to the Holy Synod of the Church of Greece.[69] Khronis later became Metropolitan of Alexandroupolis (1967–74).[70] Furthermore, in Agrinio, a number of communists were treated in hospital through the intervention of local adherents of *Zoi*, a fact that led some of them to being 'converted'.[71] In 1944, two communists managed in turn to free a member of *Zoi* from prison.[72] Some communist guerrillas from Chios publicly thanked (in the newspaper *Proodevtiki*, 5 January 1945) members and adherents of *Zoi* for their support and help when they were in prison in Thessaloniki.[73] Nevertheless, the 'impartiality' of *Zoi*'s activities did not prevent it from demonstrating its clear opposition to communist ideology and criticising it as anti-Christian and anti-Greek.[74] Indeed, there had often been open competition between communist ideology and traditional Christian worldviews, promoted by itinerant members of *Zoi*, with mixed results.[75] In addition, those opposed to communism in Greece were often supported by *Zoi*,[76] a fact that placed some *Zoi* members in the provinces under serious threat from the communist side. Some even received death threats.[77] It is interesting to note that from 1943 onwards communist hostility meant that there were no *Zoi* members at all to be found in some parts of the country.[78] After all, the communists intended to render redundant not only *Zoi*, which was accused of being an ally of the rich, but also the official Church.[79]

It is against this background that the mobilisation of the *Zoi* movement and its active role in welfare activities, not only during the early 1940s but also during the period of the civil war, should be understood. As Demetrios Constantelos, who had been associated with *Zoi*, remarked:

> During the war and postwar years, between 1940 and 1947, the young people of Greece were sought after by Communist youth organizations and religious youth societies, and most joined one or the other. Young men and women, perplexed and confused as a result of the decadence, injustices, and brutality introduced by the 'civilized barbarians' of the twentieth century, desperately needed guidance and structure in their lives. Several young men I knew would undoubtedly have joined the Communist movement had a vigorous Church and vital religious organizations not attracted them away from communism. The Christian organizations worked though various channels and reached every class of people. The simple peasant as well as the university professor, the young laborer as well as the university student, the parent as well as the young girl could find in the Church a place of love and solace.[80]

IV

The role of the Greek Orthodox Church during this period of upheaval in Europe has in the past given rise to controversy. There are those who claim that the Church played – as always – a negative, indeed disastrous, role in the life of the Greek nation,[81] whereas others portray the Church as its perennial supporter and saviour in times of adversity.[82] This is a question that is seldom considered from a neutral perspective. Certainly, the Church, as any other institution in the country, is not free from blame. Yet historically speaking, it has been a fundamental pillar of the modern Greek nation-state with a multifaceted role. It thus remains inextricably intertwined with politics, society and culture. No doubt, during the 1940s the Church acted in the light of its own principles and for the sake of its own objectives. As in the past, and indeed the present, it also sought to legitimise its presence and privileges within Greek society. But this does not diminish its positive role during this period for the Greek population. Even persons who later distanced themselves from the official church or religious organisations like *Zoi* and were critical of them, recognised that surviving the famine was in many cases largely due to their help.[83] In this way, regardless of whether or not one agrees with the Church's premises and policies, one cannot overlook its fundamental presence within Greek society; something that unfortunately still happens as a consequence of the continuing absence of a religious (not ecclesiastical) history of modern Greece.[84] From this perspective, without engaging in polemics against or apologetics for the Church, this chapter has sought to present and to assess its role during the critical period of the Second World War by focusing mainly on its extensive welfare activities.

Notes

1. See Vasilios N. Makrides, 'Orthodoxy in the Service of Anticommunism: the Religious Organization Zoë during the Greek Civil War', in Philip Carabott and Thanasis D. Sfikas (eds), *The Greek Civil War: Essays on a Conflict of Exceptionalism and Silences* (Aldershot, 2004), pp. 159–74.
2. On Damaskinos, see Elias Venezis, *Arkhiepiskopos Damaskinos*, 2nd edn (Athens, 1981); Sifis Kollias, *Arkhiepiskopos-Antivasilefs Damaskinos o apo Korinthias*, 3rd edn (Athens, 1975); Kharalambos D. Kharalambopoulos, *Arkhiepiskopos Athinon kai Pasis Ellados Damaskinos Papandreou Antivasilefs – Prothypourgos (1891–1949)* (Athens, 1990).
3. On Khrysanthos, see Georgios N. Tasoudis, *O Arkhiepiskopos Athinon Khrysanthos o apo Trapezountos. I Ethniki kai Ekklisiastiki Drasis tou (1926–1949)*, vol. 2 (Athens, 1972); Nikodimos, Metropolitan of Patras, 'O Arkhiepiskopos Athinon Khrysanthos', in Agathangelos Kharamantidis (ed.), *Mnimes kai Martyries apo to '40 kai tin Katokhi. I Prosphora tis Ekklisias to 1940–1944*, 2nd edn (Athens, 2001), pp. 64–75.
4. On this whole problem, see Ioannis Th. Panagopoulos, *To Arkhiepiskopikon Zitima* (Athens, 1946); Konstantinos N. Xenoyiannis, *I Eklogi ton Arkhiepiskopon Damaskinou kai Khrysanthou ex Apopseos Kanonikis* (Athens, 1959); Philippos C. Spyropoulos, *Die Beziehungen zwischen Staat und Kirche in Griechenland* (Athens, 1981), pp. 84–6; Andreas M. Wittig, *Die orthodoxe Kirche in Griechenland* (Würzburg, 1987), pp. 127–8; Giorgos Karayiannis, *Ekklisia kai Kratos 1833–1997*

(Athens, 1997), pp. 57–91; idem, *I Ekklisia apo tin Katokhi ston Emphylio* (Athens, 2001), pp. 17–104 and *passim*. See also the forthcoming book by Grigoris Psallidas on the politics of the Greek Church under Axis occupation (1941–44).

5. See Ioannis M. Khatziphotis, *I Ekklisia ston Agona tou Saranta* (Athens, 1982), pp. 121–46; Dorotheos Polykandriotis, 'To Thavma tis Pisteos', in *Mnimes kai Martyries apo to '40 kai tin Katokhi*, pp. 411–31.
6. See the speech by Professor Georgios Th. Sakellariou of the University of Thessaloniki given on 1 January 1941 in Korytsa entitled *I Elliniki Niki Thelima Theou* (Thessaloniki, 1941).
7. From the vast literature on this topic, see Demetrios J. Constantelos, *Byzantine Philanthropy and Social Welfare* (New Rochelle, NY, 1991); idem, *Poverty, Society and Philanthropy in the Late Mediaeval Greek World* (New Rochelle, NY, 1992). In general and regarding the present situation, see Effie Fokas and Lina Molokotos Liederman, 'Welfare, Church and Gender in Greece', in Ninna Edgardh Beckman (ed.), *Welfare, Church and Gender in Eight European Countries* (Uppsala, 2004), pp. 288–338.
8. For details, see Panayiotis Noutsos, *I Sosialistiki Skepsi stin Ellada apo to 1875 eos to 1974*, vol. 1 (1875–1907) and vol. 2 (1907–1925), parts 1–2 (Athens, 1990, 1991, 1992).
9. For details, see Agathangelos Kharamantidis, 'Stin Ethniki Antistasi', in *Mnimes kai Martyries apo to '40 kai tin Katokhi*, pp. 213–32.
10. See Karayiannis, *I Ekklisia apo tin Katokhi ston Emphylio, passim*.
11. For some of their responses, see Agathangelos Kharamantidis, 'Phoni Symparastaseos kai Diamartyrias apo Eterodoxous', in *Mnimes kai Martyries apo to '40 kai tin Katokhi*, pp. 433–7.
12. See Khatziphotis, *I Ekklisia*, pp. 39–47.
13. For details, see Ieronymos Kotsonis, 'I Pronoia ton Stratevomenon', *Aktines*, XIX (1956): 78–82; Nikodimos, Metropolitan of Attica and Megara, *Ieronymos Kotsonis. O Arkhiepiskopos ton Apostolikon Oramatismon* (Athens, 1990), pp. 80–95.
14. See Khatziphotis, *I Ekklisia*, pp. 58–62; idem, 'I Koinoniki Merimna tis Ekklisias to Saranta kai tin Katokhi', in *Mnimes kai Martyries apo to '40 kai tin Katokhi*, pp. 273–89, here pp. 273–80.
15. See Khatziphotis, *I Ekklisia*, pp. 63, 65–6.
16. For more details, see Evangelos Theodorou, *Ethnikos Organismos Khristianikis Allilengyis – EOXA. Epi ti Pentikontaetiridi* (Athens, 1991); Khatziphotis, 'I Koinoniki Merimna tis Ekklisias', pp. 281–9.
17. See Agathangelos Kharamantidis, 'I Antistasi mesa stis Phylakes', in *Mnimes kai Martyries apo to '40 kai tin Katokhi*, pp. 233–71.
18. For details, see Vlasios Pheidas, 'O Arkhiepiskopos Athinon Damaskinos', in *Mnimes kai Martyries apo to '40 kai tin Katokhi*, pp. 76–90.
19. See George Margaritis, 'The Greek Orthodox Church and the Holocaust', paper presented to the conference 'The Holocaust in Greece' (Haifa University, Israel, 12 December 2002), pp. 19, here pp. 11–14 http://hcc.haifa.ac.il/Departments/history-school/conferences/holocaust_greece/margaritis.pdf (accessed September 2006). See also idem, *Anepithymitoi Sympatriotes. Stoikheia gia tin Katastrophi ton Meionotiton tis Elladas. Evraioi, Tsamides* (Athens, 2005), pp. 91–132.

20. For more details, see Agathangelos Kharamantidis, 'I Merimna kai Synantilipsi tis Ekklisias pros tous Ellines Evraious', in *Mnimes kai Martyries apo to '40 kai tin Katokhi*, pp. 387–410.
21. See Khatziphotis, *I Ekklisia*, pp. 48–52.
22. For more details, see Khatziphotis, ibid., pp. 66–80; Nikos V. Nikolaou, *Periphronimena Rasa ston Antistasiako Agona tou Laou mas 1941–1944*, 3rd edn (Athens, 1997), pp. 28–82 and *passim* (regarding the activities of the Metropolitan of Karystias and Skyros Panteleimon); Agathangelos Kharamantidis et al., 'I Drasi tou Ierou Klirou', in *Mnimes kai Martyries apo to '40 kai tin Katokhi*, pp. 91–174.
23. For details, see Khatziphotis, *I Ekklisia*, pp. 111–18.
24. See Khatziphotis, ibid., pp. 63–4; idem, *Arkhiepiskopos Serapheim 1913–1998. Martyries kai Tekmiria* (Athens, 1999), pp. 28–34.
25. See Khatziphotis, *I Ekklisia*, pp. 83–97, 147–156; Agathangelos Kharamantidis, 'O Agonas sto Metopo', in *Mnimes kai Martyries apo to '40 kai tin Katokhi*, pp. 175–204.
26. See Agathangelos Kharamantidis and Dimitrios Papadakis, 'I Syndromi ton Ieron Monon tis Ekklisias tis Ellados', in *Mnimes kai Martyries apo to '40 kai tin Katokhi*, pp. 353–86.
27. See Khatziphotis, *I Ekklisia*, pp. 105–10; Agathangelos Kharamantidis, 'I Thysia', in *Mnimes kai Martyries apo to '40 kai tin Katokhi*, pp. 205–211; idem, 'Martyriko synaxari', ibid., pp. 479–559.
28. For more details, see Khristos Karayiannis, 'I Politistiki Katastrophi', in *Mnimes kai Martyries apo to '40 kai tin Katokhi*, pp. 439–78.
29. See Agathangelos Kharamantidis, 'I Voulgariki Katokhi stin Anatoliki Makedonia kai stin Thraki', in *Mnimes kai Martyries apo to '40 kai tin Katokhi*, pp. 49–57.
30. See Khatziphotis, *I Ekklisia*, pp. 53–4. For more details on the solidarity of other Orthodox churches with Greece during this period, see Agathangelos Kharamantidis and Grigorios Khatziouraniou, 'O Agonas kai i Synantilipsi ton Orthodoxon Ekklision', in *Mnimes kai Martyries apo to '40 kai tin Katokhi*, pp. 291–352.
31. From the extensive bibliography on *Zoi* and other related movements, see Angelos Giannakopoulos, *Die Theologen-Bruderschaften in Griechenland* (Frankfurt am Main, 1999).
32. See Ioannis Th. Kolitsaras, *Serapheim Papakostas (1892–1954). Viografia* (Athens, 1980), pp. 35–67, 72–9.
33. See ibid., pp. 67–71.
34. See Ioannis Th. Kolitsaras, *Apo tin Istorian tis Adelphotitos Theologon i 'Zoi' kata tin Periodon 1940–1944 (tou Ellinoitalikou Polemou kai tis Germanikis Katokhis)*, mimeo (Athens, n.d.), p. 2; idem, *Serapheim Papakostas*, p. 93.
35. See *Zoi*, XXXI (1452) (10 March 1941): 61–2.
36. See Kolitsaras, *Serapheim Papakostas*, p. 118.
37. See ibid., pp. 92–102.
38. A collection of such articles was reprinted in the book *Metapolemika. O Defteros Polemos kai ta Met'afton* (Athens, 1947), pp. 8–87.
39. See Kolitsaras, *Apo tin Istorian*, pp. 5–16.
40. For details about these activities, see Kolitsaras, ibid., pp. 16–22; idem, *Serapheim Papakostas*, pp. 102–12; Vasilios Stathakis, *I Khristianiki Prosphora sta Khronia tis Katokhis* (Athens, 1990), pp. 10–15.

41. For details, see Kolitsaras, *Serapheim Papakostas*, pp. 116–29; Nikos Logadis et al., *Ti prosephere o Khristianismos?* *Koinoniki Merimna ston synkhrono Orthodoxo Khoro* (Issue 4) (Athens, 1982), pp. 93–7; Stathakis, *I Khristianiki Prosphora*, pp. 16–22.
42. See Kolitsaras, *Apo tin istorian*, pp. 38–9.
43. See the editorial 'Khoris Anavolin', *Zoi*, XXXI (1461) (20 June 1941): 129–30.
44. See the editorial 'I idiaitera Apaitisis ton Kairon', *Zoi*, XXXI (1469) (1 December 1941): 193–4.
45. See, for example, *Zoi*, XXXII (1470) (1 January 1942): 7; XXXII (1471) (1 February 1942): 9–10, 13–14, 16; XXXII (1472) (1 March 1942): 17–18; XXXII (1473) (1 April 1942): 30, 32; XXXII (1475) (1 June 1942): 44, 46, 48; XXXII (1476) (1 July 1942): 52, 56; XXXII (1478) (1 September 1942): 65–6, 72. See further the collection of articles reprinted in *Metapolemika*, pp. 89–227.
46. See Kolitsaras, *Apo tin Istorian*, pp. 22–6.
47. See ibid., pp. 26–37.
48. See Kolitsaras, *Serapheim Papakostas*, p. 122.
49. See the editorial 'Syssitia – Agapai', *Zoi*, XXXII (1475) (1 June 1942): 41–2.
50. See Kolitsaras, *Apo tin Istorian*, pp. 39–45.
51. For many details. see Kolitsaras, ibid., pp. 46–89; Logadis et al., *Ti prosephere o Khristianismos?*, pp. 97–106; Stathakis, *I Khristianiki Prosphora*, pp. 26–38.
52. See Kolitsaras, *Apo tin Istorian*, pp. 45–6.
53. For details, see Kolitsaras, ibid., pp. 90–116; idem, *Serapheim Papakostas*, pp. 130–53; Stathakis, *I Khristianiki Prosphora*, pp. 39–48.
54. See Giorgos Ioannou, *To Katokhiko Imerologio khoris Perikopes. Eisagogi – Skholia – Epimetro: Antigoni Vlavianou* (Athens, 2000), pp. 27–72.
55. See Giorgos Ioannou, *I Protevousa ton Prosphygon*, 8th edn (Athens, 1984), pp. 113–81.
56. See Stathakis, *I Khristianiki Prosphora*, pp. 22–5.
57. For more details, see Aikaterini Leti, *Progevsi Paradeisou. Epilogos Diakonias Leonidou tou Thessalonikeon*, 3rd edn (Thessaloniki, 1998).
58. See Giorgos Kaftantzis, *To Nazistiko Stratopedo Pavlou Mela Thessalonikis 1941–1944 opos to ezise kai to perigraphei sto Imerologio tou enas Omiros o Leonidas Yiasimakopoulos (Arithmos Mitroou Phylakis 4436)* (Thessaloniki, 1999), pp. 78, 89, 112, 122, 142, 154, 255, 399–400, 403.
59. Ibid., p. 136.
60. See Dionysios Kharalambous, *Martyres. Diogmoi 1941–1945* (Athens, 1949), pp. 45–6, 55–6, 66, 69.
61. See Dinos Khristianopoulos, *Piso ap' tin Agia-Sofia* (Thessaloniki, 1997), pp. 48–9.
62. See, for example, Demetrios J. Constantelos, 'The Zoe Movement in Greece', *St Vladimir's Seminary Quarterly*, III (1959): 11–25.
63. See Kolitsaras, *Apo tin Istorian*, pp. 47, 48, 49.
64. See ibid., pp. 50, 74, 79, 80, 82.
65. Ibid., p. 75.
66. See ibid., pp. 49, 72–3, 76, 80–7.
67. See Solon G. Ninikas, *Prays kai Makhitis. O Mitropolitis Alexandroupoleos Konstantios (Khronis)* (Kavala, 1992), pp. 26–34.
68. See Kolitsaras, *Apo tin Istorian*, pp. 52–7.
69. See Kolitsaras, ibid., pp. 87–8; Ninikas, *Prays kai Makhitis*, pp. 35–63.

70. See Ninikas, ibid., *passim*.
71. See Kolitsaras, *Serapheim Papakostas*, pp. 169–72.
72. See Kolitsaras, *Apo tin Istorian*, p. 58.
73. See ibid., pp. 68–9.
74. See ibid., pp. 75–6, 81.
75. Ibid., pp. 94–5.
76. Ibid., p. 79.
77. See ibid., pp. 76, 118–22.
78. Ibid., p. 90.
79. Ibid., p. 119.
80. Demetrios J. Constantelos, *Understanding the Greek Orthodox Church*, 4th edn (Brookline, MA, 2005), pp. 163–4.
81. See Giorgos D. Karanikolas, *Rasophoroi. Symphora tou Ethnous*, 4th edn (Athens, 1985), pp. 196–212.
82. See Leonidas K. Diamantopoulos, *Ti prosepheren o Khristianismos*, 2nd edn (Athens, 1987), pp. 173–9.
83. For example, Ioannou, *I Protevousa ton Prosphygon*, p. 113.
84. See Vasilios N. Makrides, 'Ekklisiastiki kai Thriskeftiki Istoria tis Neoteris kai Synkhronis Elladas: Diaphores, Idiaiterotites kai Provlimata Anaptyxis', in Paschalis M. Kitromilides and Triantaphyllos E. Sklavenitis (eds), *Istoriographia tis Neoteris kai Synkhronis Elladas. IV Diethnes Synedrio Istorias. Praktika*, vol. 2 (Athens, 2004), pp. 587–620.

10
Quakers and Greeks in the 1940s

Mary Jo Clogg

Just two days before Great Britain's declaration of war in September 1939 two well-known British Quakers, who were veterans of ambulance work in the First World War, published a letter in *The Friend*, the Quaker weekly journal, suggesting the foundation of a new ambulance and relief organisation in which young Quakers and others might undertake non-military service during the new crisis. Just over a year later, British Quakers established an emergency committee, later to be known as the Friends' Relief Service, to deal with humanitarian problems arising out of the Second World War. Some time later, after the Allied blockade of occupied Europe was seen to be resulting in great food shortages and famine, especially in Greece and Belgium, a prominent British Quaker, Edith Pye, undertook a campaign of public awareness, government lobbying and fundraising in an attempt to alleviate the starvation being aggravated by the blockade. These three events were to impact upon humanitarian relief in wartime and post-war Greece in a small way, but one that was nevertheless significant.

The Oxford Committee for Famine Relief

The Religious Society of Friends, known popularly as Quakers, a radical Christian movement established in the mid-seventeenth century, has traditionally been pacifist. Thus Quakers attempted to ameliorate the suffering of war without engaging in conflict. An important manifestation of this effort during and after the Second World War was humanitarian relief work.

So it was on 24 May 1942 that Oxford Quakers responded to a letter from their co-religionist Edith Pye by asking her to speak at the Friends Meeting House in Oxford on the subject of famine in occupied Europe.

It was the plight of the civilian populations of those countries whose food supplies had been interrupted by the British blockade, especially Belgium and Greece, which was of concern. On 20 July, Pye addressed an audience consisting of Quakers and invited guests, among whom were a number of influential Oxford citizens.[1] On 5 October of the same year some of the prominent members of that audience, joined by a few others, held a meeting at which they established the Oxford Committee for Famine Relief. This committee was to play a significant role both in fundraising for the relief of famine in Greece and in lobbying the British government to ease the blockade that was preventing food from reaching the starving population. It was, after the war, to evolve into Oxfam, one of the largest and most influential charities engaged in humanitarian relief in the world.

At this time, however, the autumn of 1942, it was but one of over a hundred such groups which had sprung up around the country, due mainly to the efforts of Edith Pye. She was the driving force behind the national Famine Relief Committee, formed in May of 1942 and based in London. The committee's objectives were 'to obtain authentic information as to food conditions in German-controlled or invaded countries' and 'to promote schemes for the sending of food, vitamins and medical aid into such countries, wherever control is possible, in co-operation with existing organisations'.[2] Edith Pye was sixty-six, and was already well known for her relief efforts in Europe, which dated from December 1914 when she had established and run a maternity hospital in wartime France, efforts which she had continued in Austria, the Far East, Germany and in Spain during the Civil War.

Pye was not, of course, the only one to be concerned about the humanitarian plight of the civilian populations of Europe, especially those of Greece and Belgium. In September 1941 the International Red Cross in Geneva received a cable from Greece: 'Food situation in Greece extremely grave. Mortality increased sixfold in last two months. Catastrophe inevitable unless help arrives quickly.'[3] There had been articles and editorials about the famine in the British press. Vera Brittain had published a pamphlet, *One of these Little Ones*, which was one of a number of publications on the subject by the pacifist Peace Pledge Union, which had its own Food Relief Campaign. George Bell, the Anglican Bishop of Chichester, had spoken on 27 January 1942 in the House of Lords about the situation in Greece, and had been in contact with Gilbert Murray, the distinguished Oxford classicist and champion of the League of Nations, about the blockade. Murray himself had appealed to Dingle Foot, the Parliamentary Secretary to the Ministry of Economic Warfare, as early as

October 1941, arguing that the starvation was aiding the German cause, rendering the Greeks unable to resist the occupying forces. A Lord Mayor's [of London] Fund for Greek Relief was established in November 1940 and, in November 1942, the Archbishop of Canterbury and the Roman Catholic Cardinal Archbishop of Westminster visited the Foreign Secretary, Anthony Eden, on behalf of the Famine Relief Committee to request aid to Greek and Belgian children.[4]

But it was Edith Pye's vision of involving a large cross-section of people, her genius for strategic lobbying and her extraordinary energy that were instrumental in causing the issue to become a matter of nationwide concern, even in a Britain which was itself in the midst of wartime suffering and hardship, which included severe food rationing. The national Famine Relief Committee, which Pye founded, had its first premises in Drayton House, one of the Quaker-owned buildings in Euston Road. It published a regular newsletter, which was sent to over one hundred groups around the country, from Aberdeen in Scotland to Petts Wood in Kent, and included appeal flyers and current statistics of deaths from starvation. Pye published a number of articles, broadsheets and informative pamphlets: *Hunger in Europe, Controlled Food Relief . . . can it be done?* and *Famine Relief in Europe* among them. The first of these to be published by the Famine Relief Committee, *Food Conditions in Europe*, was a revised edition of a pamphlet issued earlier by the Quaker Friends Service Council. She distributed a prayer for famine relief to churches around the country. Small local groups engaged in a variety of fundraising projects and worked to raise public consciousness of the problem. They encouraged lobbying of MPs and letters to local newspapers.

Edith Pye was motivated as a Quaker by a 'concern'. The word 'concern' has a specific meaning in Quaker parlance, and refers to a divine leading which requires a response that cannot be denied; in Pye's words, 'I took up the concern because I could do no other.' She was, however, pragmatic, and realised that if she were to be successful in alleviating famine, she would have to involve a public much wider than that of Quakers alone, who at the time had a membership fewer than 20,000. In response to a letter in January 1943 from Roger Cowan Wilson, General Secretary of the Friends Relief Service, she said, 'when the concern took hold of me in 1941, it was obvious that if Friends alone took up the crusade we should not get far, as our right standing aside from the war effort made us unacceptable as councillors [counsellors].'[5] In other words, the Quakers' pacifism would hinder their lobbying efforts. So, if it were to be effective, the Famine Relief Committee and its attendant groups needed a wide membership. She attempted to calm Wilson's fears that the movement might be subsumed into wartime propaganda. 'It is the old dilemma – shall we stand aside and preach righteousness, or shall we go with others as far as we can in unity?'[6]

The issue was of sufficient interest to be the subject of a number of parliamentary questions, and important debates in the House of Commons on 8 July 1943, and then again in November of that year. On the former occasion Dingle Foot, Parliamentary Secretary in the Ministry for Economic Warfare, argued that there was no general famine in Europe, and that only a few places were affected, and these were, by international law, the responsibility of the occupying forces. Also, he said, relief supplies might be seized by German troops, and succour given to German food supply and transport problems. Besides, collaborators as well as others in the occupied countries would be recipients of the food. Similar governmental arguments in the House of Commons on 10 November 1943 were attacked at length by several MPs. 'We', said T. Edmund Harvey, 'are accomplices in this act of starving Europe.' Harold Nicolson was more moderate. 'The thing is too disproportionate to be mentioned. A little drop of benefit might accrue to them [the enemy], compared with the ocean of relief and encouragement which would thereby be given not merely to our allies, but to unborn generations in Greece and Belgium.'[7]

It was in Oxford, however, that the movement was to reap truly remarkable results. This was partly due to the number of eminent local citizens on the Oxford Committee for Famine Relief, including Gilbert Murray and Dr Henry Gillett, a Quaker and a future Mayor of Oxford, and greatly a result of the efforts of the wealthy businessman, Cecil Jackson-Cole (later to become a Quaker), who from the spring of 1943 devoted much of his energy to the cause. At the end of May 1943 £2100 had been handed to the Greek Red Cross, and in June a further £2378 was raised. In October of that year a 'Greek Week' was held in Oxford. Among the many activities in the city were concerts, lectures, folk-dance performances, a variety show, and the first-ever charity gift shop, now a common sight on Britain's high streets. At the end of the Greek Week an astounding £12,700, the present-day equivalent of a quarter of a million pounds, was handed to a grateful Dr A.P. Cawadias, the President of the Executive Committee of the Greek Red Cross in Foreign Countries.[8] The fundraising was to continue throughout the war and after, although Greece as a specific recipient gave way as a main focus of concern in the post-war period to 'former occupied countries and/or ex-enemy countries if permission be granted for the latter'.[9]

The wartime fundraising was accompanied by lobbying. A leading article in the *Oxford Times* in early 1944 was distributed widely, and a petition delivered to the Ministry of Economic Warfare in July had over 8000 signatures, including 75 per cent of the members of Oxford City Council. Earlier, on 3 January 1944, lobbying had reached a new level at a delegate conference of the national Famine Relief Committee in London. One hundred and twenty delegates from 82 groups, from right across the country, listened to speeches by Vera Brittain, Edith Pye, Dr Cawadias, and representatives from Greece and Belgium, while a small delegation met with Lord Selborne, the Minister of Economic Warfare. The conference group received reports of the current situation in the affected countries, including the statistic that Greeks were receiving only an estimated 29 per cent of the calories needed to sustain them. Cawadias expressed effusive thanks for what had already been sent; Greece was the only country to have received any food aid at all. 'If relief had not been sent in there would not have been one Greek alive today . . . I think there can be no exaggeration in saying . . . that marvellous Greek race . . . would have perished.'[10]

The delegation to the ministry reported back to the conference immediately upon their return. The reports of Hugh Lyon, the Headmaster of Rugby School, and the Anglican Bishop of Wakefield were more sympathetic to the government line than was that of Dr Henry Gillett. They had met with the usual governmental arguments that Dingle Foot had put forward in the Commons debate some six months earlier. Lord Selborne also stated that more was being done in secret, which the public was not allowed to know, and that 'the innocent must suffer in time of war'. This suggestion of secret information as to how Germany would benefit from relief activities, known only to the government, had been made previously by Quentin Hogg, the MP for Oxford, when lobbied. Hogg also advanced, as a unique argument for inaction, the suggestion that aid to one occupied country might cause others to be dissatisfied.

The delegation in reply pointed out that, in addition to ethical reasons for humanitarian aid, there was no history of Germans intercepting civilian relief supplies for themselves; that the Greek Red Cross was well established as a trustworthy distribution agent; and that a starving and weakened population could offer little resistance to occupation. The delegation had made its point, and had again brought the issue to the attention of the ministry and the public at large. It perhaps had some effect as the dispatch of an additional 900 tons per month of food was permitted.

Friends' Ambulance Unit

Paul Cadbury's and John Harvey's letter to *The Friend* of 1 September 1939 followed eighteen months of discussion among British Quakers on how they might best respond to the impending war. It stated that 'there are . . . an unknown number of our members of military age who wish to give positive proof that although they register as conscientious objectors they have no wish to be exempt from a period of constructive labour as a result of their convictions'. Within a few days, over 300 applications had been received, a provisional governing council had been set up, and a venue for training the recruits, Manor Farm in Birmingham, had been lent by Elizabeth Cadbury, a member of the prominent Quaker family. On 12 September a training course began with the first 60 men to be chosen for service. The second Friends' Ambulance Unit (FAU), which was to be involved in Greece as well as many other countries throughout much of the coming decade, had been born.

The first Friends' Ambulance Unit had been established during the First World War as a means by which those conscientious objectors – especially Quakers – who had a religious objection to war but who wished to engage in the relief of the human suffering occasioned by it could do so without compromising their anti-war stance. Like its successor in 1939 it was not an official body of the Religious Society of Friends (Quakers), but was very closely associated with it. It trained young men in first-aid and paramedical skills, obtained ambulances and sent relief teams, in cooperation with the military authorities, to areas of action as required.

Not all Quakers, or Quaker conscientious objectors, were in support of the scheme. There are varying degrees of objection to war, including the position which holds that any activity during wartime, be it working the land, fire-watching or manning an ambulance on the battlefield, constitutes support of military action. Hard-line conscientious objectors, including some Quakers, spent the war mainly in prison. Others felt justified in participating in civilian activities which were not directly involved in the conflict, and they were seconded to non-military civilian activities in lieu of military service. The minutes of the Meeting for Sufferings of London Yearly Meeting of the Religious Society of Friends, the 269-strong executive committee of British Quakers, as well as correspondence in the *The Friend*, reflect the diversity of opinion among Quakers at that time, and the unease which some felt over participation in any aspect of the war.

But many were drawn to service in the FAU, whose constitution specified that 'membership of the unit shall be limited to men and women who share Quaker views on peace and war'.[11] In all there were 65,000 registered conscientious objectors of all persuasions in Britain in the years between 1939 and 1945. Five thousand of these enquired about service in the FAU; over 1300 joined it, and were trained in 22 training camp sessions over the years. Quaker statistics for 1945 list only 219 male members of the Religious Society of Friends as serving in Quaker relief during the war; there may have been more, but they were certainly a minority.[12] At various times the units worked in both the Far and Near East, throughout Europe and North Africa, and in hospitals and centres on the home front in Britain. This chapter, however, will deal solely with their efforts in Greece and in Greek refugee camps in the Middle East.

Greece was one of the first fields of action for the newly formed FAU and involved men from the first training camp. This first foray into Greece, in the early months of 1941, was to be brief and dramatic, resulting in the capture of some of the volunteers by the Germans. The section involved, which was the first to be sent abroad, had gone first to Finland in January 1940. It then went briefly to Norway and then on to Cairo, via Russia. By the time this section left Egypt for Piraeus on 21 March 1941 it consisted of 22 men and ten ambulances packed with medical supplies and equipment. The possibilities of relief work in Greece had been discussed within the Friends Ambulance Unit since the time of the Italian attack, and the team was pleased at last to be on their way.

After a week in Athens, the ambulance convoy, under the auspices of the Greek Red Cross, headed off towards the Albanian border on 6 April 1941, which, as it happened, was the very day on which the Germans began their attack on Greece. The convoy had gone no further than Livadia, a hundred miles north-west of Athens, before receiving orders to report instead to Thessaloniki. Another change of orders sent them to help with patients from a hospital in Florina who had already been evacuated onto a train in Amintaion. They rescued about fifteen patients and half as many medical personnel, eventually depositing them in Larisa. Prevented from returning north by the destruction of the bridge over the Aliakmon River, they headed back towards Athens among the streams of people fleeing the oncoming German invasion, aiding individual casualties and evacuating another hospital en route.

At this stage the FAU section was split into two parts. One party, under Ronald Joynes, escaped by train, boat and foot, to the accompaniment of Stuka fire, to Nafplion, from where they were evacuated by merchant ship to Alexandria.[13] Their Greek adventure had been dramatic, but very brief indeed. The other part of the section, led by Oswald Dicks, stayed with the ambulances and joined with the Australian Field Ambulance

Unit, carrying the wounded and sick and the survivors of bombing raids, working the area between the constantly advancing front line back to Athens. Finally, on 23 April, they were forced to flee south to Kalamata, another hazardous journey. There they found the town hall crammed with battle casualties, some very severely wounded.

They established a temporary hospital in Kalamata town hall and continued their work without interference for some time after the Germans occupied the town, but finally, in mid-May, all sixteen of them were taken as prisoners of war to the German *Dulag* (transit camp) in Corinth. Within a month they were moved again, this time to the brutal *Dulag* in Thessaloniki. Here they found no shortage of work in the camp hospital, where the doctors were struggling to deal with rampant deadly diseases such as malaria, diphtheria, typhoid, dysentery and TB as well as caring for the wounded. The brutality of the camp regime and conditions of near-starvation also created patients for the camp hospital.[14]

Attempts by the men of the FAU to gain repatriation as Red Cross personnel under the Geneva Convention were unsuccessful, and beginning in September they were moved to various prison camps in Germany and Poland.[15] There they were to remain for much of the rest of the war, nine of them being released from late 1943 and 1944, but others not until the Allied capture of Germany, with one dying in captivity. The FAU was not to return to Greece until the autumn of 1944.

Friends' Relief Service

At about the same time that the FAU staff were being moved from Greece to the prison camps in northern Europe, back in London the Friends Service Committee (FSC), the permanent body dealing with Quaker international service, recognised the need for another group to address specifically the needs thrown up by the war. The Friends War Victims Relief Committee was established in November 1940, and was to change its name twice before settling on the title of Friends Relief Service (FRS) in September 1943. The overall number serving in the organisation, 1232, was similar to that of the FAU's 1314, but nearly half of the FRS staff were women, as opposed to only 7 per cent of the FAU's. The FRS was to work mainly in Europe, and with European refugees in Palestine as well as at home in Britain. They were unable to begin work in Greece until the Axis troops withdrew.

It would be wrong to view the Quaker effort as fitting neatly into the three separate compartments of FAU, FRS and famine relief. In fact, there was an overlapping of personnel as well as a concerted effort to complement each other's activities. Edith Pye, for example, was not only honorary secretary of the national Famine Relief Committee, but on the committee of FRS from its inception in September 1943, as was Tegla Davies of the FAU. The Oxford Committee for Famine Relief often used the FRS to distribute its relief. FRS, in November 1943, stated in their minutes that they wished to work with the FAU in a 'spirit of co-operation'. They hoped 'to keep in touch and establish a mutual respect and understanding', and expressed 'hope ... that a close personal connection may be maintained'.[16] The Lord Mayor's Greek Fund, which after the war so generously contributed to the FRS maternity hospital project in Thessaloniki, was originally formed in November 1940 to contribute to famine relief. Kanty Cooper, of the FRS team in Palestine, was 'lent' to the FAU project in Epirus. Norman Gilbertson (Illustration 10.1), who first went to Athens for the FRS in the summer of 1945, was asked by the FSC to return to help at the American Farm School in northern Greece in 1947. He also worked for UNRRA, and later led the programme of the Help to Greece Consultative Committee, an umbrella organisation of no fewer than fifteen British-based groups concerned with charitable work in Greece.[17] There were many such blurred boundaries in the different strands of Quaker work, as well as cooperation with a wide variety of non-Quaker bodies.

Illustration 10.1   Norman Gilbertson on the quayside at Thessaloniki, 1946

Both the FAU and the FRS worked closely with other agencies throughout the war and the post-war period. The way for both of the bodies was eased by the formation in January 1943 of an umbrella body for mutual consultation and coordination of voluntary societies, a body which could deal with government departments on their behalf. Along with a number of other groups the FAU and FRS became part of the Consultative Council of Voluntary Societies for Post-war Relief and Rehabilitation, which was subsequently to change its name to the Council of British Societies for Relief Abroad (COBSRA). This soon established itself as an essential link in planning and delivering overseas relief, and made arrangements so that the organisations were poised to act quickly as hostilities ended.

The FAU and the FRS were both to find themselves working with the military, with various branches of the International Red Cross, or with UNRRA (the United Nations Relief and Rehabilitation Administration, established in November 1943), according to their assignments. (On UNRRA's activities in Greece, see Chapter 11.) Problems did present themselves at times: the FAU was without the command structure and the ranking order in which the military functioned, and there were issues of uniform and lines of authority to be dealt with. The FRS team sent to Chios, for example, had been delayed leaving London because of difficulties in obtaining grey uniforms to distinguish them from the military's khaki. As luck would have it, the British military detachment stationed in Chios, known as Force 142, themselves wore an unusual grey outfit, forcing the Quaker volunteers back into the khaki they had eschewed. Some FAU members took exception to saluting officers, or to singing the national anthem. They refused some tasks which they considered to be military in nature, rather than humanitarian. The leaders, and sometimes the members, of the units were often accorded NCO status by the army, and on one occasion a group self-promoted themselves from corporal to sergeant in order to be taken more seriously. Such cavalier attitudes towards rank were not appreciated by the military, but, generally speaking, working with each other in war conditions seems to have bred mutual respect between the conscientious objectors and the military personnel.

On the whole, the British voluntary societies worked more easily with the British military than with UNRRA, which was dominated by Americans, who, it was felt, lacked the tradition of cooperating with autonomous voluntary societies, and were very wedded to their own structures. In the eastern Mediterranean there were difficulties especially after the spring of 1945 when UNRRA took over the aid activities previously organised by the British Military Liaison. UNRRA set up a field organisation with its own systems for supply and transport and expected all other agencies to work within this new framework, although in the case of the FRS it had been operating there long before UNRRA came on the scene. These problems were usually resolved eventually by compromise and common sense.

Quakers worked in the eastern Mediterranean from mid-1941 with the Free French in Syria, and in Egypt with the British army, Cairo being an important base for voluntary sector activity. A number of such societies with a presence in Cairo were brought together in cooperation with the Cairo Minister of State's refugee department, under the wing of the Middle East Relief and Refugee Administration (MERRA). This was to be absorbed into UNRRA's Balkans Mission in May 1944. As Cairo was also the base from which relief operations into post-war Europe were to be launched, the FAU increased their staff there at the beginning of 1944. In January of that year 32 FAU men and women, under Keith Linney and Arnold Curtis, left for Cairo, to be followed in March by 37 more under Lewis Waddilove. In all, in the spring of 1944 over 80 FAU personnel in Cairo awaited deployment in a Europe yet to be liberated. The FAU, together with other voluntary agencies, anticipating post-war needs, had transformed the wartime ambulance service into peacetime Mobile Hygiene and First Aid Units (MHFAU), consisting of doctors, nurses, sanitary inspectors, laboratory technicians and other staff of a practical nature. Relief and Refugee Units (RRU), Field Bacteriological Units (FBU) and Medical Supply and Transport Units (MSTU) were also formed.

Prior to the liberation of occupied Greece the work of Quakers with Greeks was to be in Greek refugee camps in Palestine, where both FAU and FRS members were sent while awaiting their post-war deployments. These camps were populated by those who had fled from the Greek islands and Thrace. A January 1943 newsletter from the Famine Relief Committee speaks of the Palestinian camps as places where financial donations could be received, and reports on the Quaker workers there. It quotes from a letter received from one such worker: 'Ten thousand [Greek] women and children escaped must be kept fit at all costs . . . the refugees in the Middle East . . . are one very thin hope of saving the Greek race.'[18]

A detailed report on four of the camps was produced by an FAU staff member, Michael Barratt-Brown, in August 1943.[19] It gives interesting detail and affords a sometimes colourful picture of the various camps, which were the responsibility of the British Ninth Army. The one in Aleppo was a transit camp for all refugees arriving in Syria through Turkey, including Greeks from the islands and Thrace, Bulgarians and Yugoslavs. Greek men of military age were transferred from there to the

Greek forces in the Middle East, and everyone else was sent on to other camps in Syria or Palestine. In Aleppo they lived in huts and barracks, with communal feeding arrangements and free access to the town. Morale was generally good, as it was in the Suk-el-Gharb camp in Aley near Beirut. This small group of about 950 Greek refugees were living in houses and hotels in the resort town, which in peacetime had been a desirable holiday destination. The Greeks themselves dealt with much of the day to day running: they catered for themselves, their housing was kept clean, and life was as normal as possible under the circumstances. There were few problems. 'In short, I was astonished', wrote Barratt-Brown.[20]

The camp at St Luke's, Haifa, was much smaller, with fewer than 400 Greeks, many from Thrace, there in August 1943. There was communal cooking but meals were taken in the individual family tents, except for the children who were fed together. It was in this camp that Sydney and Joice Loch provided a pint of milk a day to all of the children. FRS minutes of 1 December 1943[21] record a grant of £600 for work with Greek refugees in Palestine, made at the request of the Lochs. Sydney and Joice Loch, although not Quakers themselves, had spent their lives in Quaker relief work, had settled in Khalkidiki in the 1920s, and had close links with the American Farm School near Thessaloniki, which was to be a major focus of Quaker relief work after the war. At this time the Lochs were primarily involved with Polish refugees, many of them Jewish, whom they had accompanied from Poland to Palestine, via Cyprus. In September 1944 Sydney Loch was to accept the post of FRS representative in Cairo, and upon his return to Macedonia was to play a major role in developing relief projects there.

Barratt-Brown records that the refugees at St Luke's came 'from Thrace and are of a rather superior type to the usual fisherman peasant islander'. This was probably a reference to the inhabitants of the much larger and much less orderly camp at Moses' Wells, 27 miles east of Suez, where the Greek island refugees presented a constant challenge to the aid workers. 'They have very little conception of collective social responsibility. Appeals to them on grounds of common welfare have little effect', reads the report. There were discipline problems. Food was removed from the dining halls, unsanctioned cooking went on in the tents, tent walls would be cut up to make cleaning rags, and blankets and sheets would suffer the same fate in order to be made into garments, although there was no shortage of clothing. Various ploys were used to avoid medical inspection and treatment, although health seems not to have suffered as there were relatively few deaths recorded; those that there were, mainly of children from measles and pneumonia. There was also an aversion to personal hygiene. 'Compulsory baths are taken each week. These have to be taken before pocket money is drawn. Nurses . . . sometimes experience difficulty in persuading refugees to get themselves wet.'

Another large camp for Greek refugees, Nuseirat in the Gaza Strip, was established following a large exodus of Dodecanese islanders after the abortive Allied attempt to take the islands in the autumn of 1943. By July 1944 it contained 10,000 refugees from the islands of Kos, Rhodes, Karpathos, Simi and Kasos. The entire population of Kastellorizo, some 1000 people, were evacuated there by the British military in January 1944.[22] It was here that a newly formed Friends Ambulance Unit Mobile Hygiene and First Aid Unit found its first job, and here that 30 FAU members were working by June 1944. There were also a small number of Greeks in Jerusalem at the Monastery of the Cross, who were cared for by Emily Hughes and Jean Malcolmson after the departure of Joice and Sydney Loch. This group were, in mid-1945, regularly receiving a monthly grant of £100 from the Famine Relief Committee. Although the accommodation in the monastery was inadequate for families, they benefited from a more normal way of life than was possible in the camps.

Administration of these camps would usually be the responsibility of military liaison officers, with aid workers' duties being those of health and welfare, 'generally filling gaps in the official scheme'[23] and often working alongside, as well as with, the refugees. They worked as doctors, nurses and orderlies in the camp hospitals; distributed clothing; organised information services; instituted various workshops and activities; and organised labour rotas. At its peak, there were 1200 on the Nuseirat camp payroll, and the organisation of employment and pay was a large undertaking. Aid workers would meet refugees as they arrived, perform basic medical examinations, disinfect and inoculate them. After being assessed for need, clothing and basic living equipment would be issued and the refugees would be assigned to tents or huts. There, it seems, the tight pattern of Greek family life would quickly reassert itself.

A number of reports and memoirs record life in the camps. In Nuseirat, there was a camp newspaper in Greek, edited, curiously, by an Englishman, Michael Asquith, an FAU staff member. Donald Swann, the composer, one of a number of Quakers who ended up there, was intrigued by the Greek music in the camp, which became a great influence in his own work. He contributed a piano to the camp, buying it in Jerusalem for 100 Palestinian pounds. He treasured his time among the Greeks, but trenchantly commented that 'every man is a leader and they're all politicians'.[24] Keeping the refugees occupied was of primary importance, and in several instances dressmaking and sewing schemes were set up, with materials being supplied from nearby towns.

When liberation finally came, FAU teams filled a variety of roles. Some accompanied refugees home to their islands, helping them to resettle, and others went to areas of need on the Greek mainland. The first FAU members to enter Greece for post-war relief, Stephen Peet and Dennis Westbrook of the No. 12 Field Surgical Unit, did so prematurely when they landed on Kos with a medical team on 31 September 1943. When Kos and Leros were recaptured by the Germans in early October they were taken prisoner, although they continued medical work with the injured from both sides until December, when they were sent to a prisoner of war camp in Austria.

The next, more successful, attempt was made on 13 October 1944 when FAU members Lewis Waddilove and Jack Eglon arrived in Piraeus with the first British troops in the liberation of Greece. Because of the deteriorating political situation, however, only one small FAU group followed them at that time, joined by another on 24 November. They record marching to the train at Piraeus under banners reading 'Welcome Sons of Byron'.[25] Others arrived in mid-January 1944, and, being prevented by the December fighting in Athens between British troops and communist-led ELAS partisans from proceeding to their assignment in Epirus, settled to work in Athens. With the Medical Supplies and Transport Unit in Athens, composed of the Greek Red Cross and four other voluntary agencies, they used 23 vehicles to deliver large amounts of essential supplies to medical posts and hospitals to both sides in the conflict. They centralised scattered stores into large premises, and responded to the need for hospital repairs by transporting building materials as well as medical supplies.

On 13 February 1945 a Relief and Rehabilitation Unit (RRU) under Don Pitcher and a Mobile Health and First Aid Unit (MHFAU) led by Ray Bollam arrived in Corfu, where they found a ragged and hungry population as well as 2000 members of the non-communist EDES resistance group and 8000 civilian refugees who had fled from the ELAS forces on the mainland. The MHFAU started clinics in the villages and undertook surveys of malaria while the RRU established centres for information and clothing distribution. Beginning in mid-March the units began to move to Epirus, their original destination, and by mid-April there were some 20 unit members stationed in Preveza, to begin what was to be an extended period of work.

In Preveza they found 100 tons of gift clothing awaiting distribution, which they stored in one of the castles of Ali Pasha. The existing food distribution system being carried out in the local *nomoi* (prefectures) suffered as a consequence of corruption, nepotism and political favouritism. Some areas were receiving no aid at all. One of the workers, Kanty Cooper, could 'find almost no evidence of either honesty or public spirit'.[26] The team visited devastated villages as far north as Konitsa, determining need, and in six weeks had set up a fair, workable system. They found that in some villages total populations were suffering from malaria. There was also widespread scabies, and a typhoid outbreak in Konitsa. The FAU, which had sole responsibility for relief activities in Thesprotia, where there was no hospital, established two health clinics and a mobile service to the villages, and extracted from the Greek government a promise to provide 20 more clinics.

The FAU number 2 Field Bacteriological Unit undertook water-supply testing and decontamination duties, first in Athens with the International Voluntary Service for Peace in January 1945 and then in Patras with UNRRA. There the water supplies of 54 of the 61 towns and villages that were tested were found to be contaminated, and the unit cleansed them and made them potable. In Patras they were instrumental in setting up a Public Health Laboratory, which was named after one of them, Wilfred Dally. This unit then moved on to Edessa, where it worked with problems of venereal disease, until it returned to Britain in the summer of 1946.

At the same time Quaker relief work was proceeding in the islands. In January 1945 two FAU teams began work began in Simi, where about 600 refugees were living in unimaginable squalor. This work then extended to Kasos and Karpathos, and by mid-1945 28 FAU staff were employed in relief work in the Dodecanese. The usual relief work was undertaken jointly with UNRRA and the Military Liaison Relief Mission: clinics, hygiene arrangements, and distribution of scant clothing and food. There were the usual problems. 'You start', one worker wrote, 'by examining the personal effects of some hundreds of people who are doing their best to deceive you, and then draw an arbitrary line between what you choose to call "greater" and "lesser" need . . .'[27]

As these island camps emptied towards the summer of 1945 the FAU section moved to Rhodes. Until November its work there was mainly with health and accommodation, complicated by the mixed population. 'It proved impossible to billet Greeks in the houses of Italians', one report reads.[28] The work then extended to distribution of relief in the villages, agricultural regeneration and even construction. The FAU work in the Dodecanese, which ended soon after UNRRA took it over in 1946, was considered to be especially successful, and is commemorated by a plaque on the Terme Hospital.

The other Greek islands in which Quaker relief work took place were Chios, Samos and Ikaria, where FRS teams were, from March 1945, responsible for a two-way movement of displaced persons. Refugees were pouring into these newly liberated islands at an alarming rate, over 1000 onto Samos in March alone, although there was virtually no housing or food to maintain them. In addition to the refugees there were about 6500 islanders who were to return to damaged or purloined houses, fishing boats or businesses which no longer existed, and an inadequate food supply. In all an estimated 17,500 islanders were expected to return. Those of Italian origin had special problems upon their return; often unwelcome in their island homes, they had only questionable rights of residence elsewhere.

Quaker relief in Macedonia

The other main area of Quaker relief, in Macedonia, is inseparable from Sydney and Joice Loch,[29] who returned to Thessaloniki in December 1944 and February 1945 respectively. By that time Sydney was an FRS representative and also Acting Director of the Thessaloniki Agricultural and Industrial Institute, commonly known as the American Farm School (AFS),[30] which had been founded in 1904 by American Presbyterian missionaries. The school was established to train village boys in agricultural methods and good practice, and its alumni transformed farming in the villages and farms to which they returned. There is a long history of relief activities based at the school, dating from after the Balkan wars of 1912–13, and including a major American Quaker effort in 1923 on behalf of refugees from Asia Minor, Greeks who had been removed en bloc from their ancestral homes in Anatolia. After the German retreat of October 1944 the school became an obvious venue for relief and rehabilitation efforts. Although the retreating German army left a trail of destruction in their wake, the barracks built for their troops were spared, and they were also to prove useful for relief activities.

In March 1945 Sydney Loch proposed a policy to guide FRS work in the area. It should, he felt, concentrate on filling the gaps left by UNRRA, should work in areas in which it was already known, and should focus on just a few projects. One of the earliest of these projects was a fowl-breeding agricultural regeneration scheme based at the AFS. Pure-bred chickens were raised for sale at a reduced price throughout the surrounding villages, thus restoring the villages' poultry stocks and improving productivity and quality. FRS was asked for £250 in May 1945, but with the reassurance that with the sale of the 2400 fowl the cost would be unlikely to be that much. This was followed by similar schemes with Guernsey bull calves and pigs. A 'Preventorium' ran through the summer of 1945 in the now-vacated German barracks, in which groups of 150 'delicate children heading for TB' were brought to the farm school for several weeks of fresh air and strengthening. FRS was asked for £187.10s per month for milk, carefully costed to provide each child with a half kilo per day. The children's average weight gain during the three-week stay was about 4.5 kilos. The Lochs also supplied milk to the foundling home in Thessaloniki, which had scant resources to deal with the influx of orphans from the occupation and civil war. Throughout 1944 and early 1945 Loch's letters to FRS plead for the consignment of clothing which was supposed to be en route to him. Clothing, he said, was needed more than either food or seeds, but small sums of money for projects were also requested.

The effective use of small-scale aid is illustrated by Loch's appeal to FRS for 'the odd £10' to employ a destitute Russian to make tin cups for distribution to families, which by sharing one drinking vessel were spreading TB, a disease causing a major health crisis.[31] They appealed for funds to restore the boy scouts' camp on Mt Khortiatis, which had firstly been taken over by the Metaxas Youth Movement and later dismantled for building supplies. Theodore Litsas, of the American Farm School and a Quaker, was a strong proponent of the boy scout movement, and in the summer of 1945 about 1000 boy scouts and their leaders received training at the school before going on to the camp in the mountains. All of these projects thrived on cooperation with UNRRA and especially with the British Military Mission, which often provided transport.

Joice Loch appealed for Quaker support in revitalising crafts and small industries in the villages, such as silver-working in Gianitsa, and the 'Pontos Women's Weaving Centre'. The Lochs' concern for rehabilitating the villages began with the one in which they had settled, Prosphorion (Ouranoupolis), on the border with Mount Athos. In April 1945, £300 was sent by FRS to revive carpet weaving in Prosphorion, in the hope of creating jobs and bringing lucrative trade to the village. It was later to receive Oxfam project funding to bring water to the village.

A much more ambitious scheme, and one which was to leave a lasting legacy, was that of a midwifery training plan, intended to teach village girls the skills necessary to improve the often very primitive childbirth practices in the countryside. Planning began in the summer of 1945, and the scheme was officially inaugurated in April 1947, with 25 students. As a collaborative effort between the Greek government, which supplied housing for the maternity hospital and the students, and the

FRS, problems were encountered with bureaucracy in Athens, and with the prejudices of the very traditional Greek medical establishment, but these were eventually successfully overcome.[32]

The other lasting contribution that Quakers made to Greek life in Macedonia was the establishment of a domestic training school for village girls, commonly known as *Skholi Kuakeron*, or Quaker School. Situated in the American Farm School, this was financed initially by the FRS, and from June 1948 by the permanent British Quaker body, the FSC, which in turn handed it over to the AFS Trustees in 1966. It had also received a £200 grant from the Oxford Committee for Famine Relief, its first-ever funding of a specific project overseas. Its two-year programme opened with 40 students in November 1945. The girls were selected on grounds of need, both individual and of their villages, and came from both sides of the violent political divide. They were taught the rudiments of sanitation, animal husbandry, homemaking and childcare, the latter learned with the aid of an orphan baby borrowed from the foundling hospital.

The Friends Ambulance Unit handed over its remaining work in Greece to UNRRA and to local personnel at the end of June 1946, leaving behind equipment and vehicles provided by the unit. Some of the staff remained behind to continue work, but now directly for UNRRA. Although the Friends Relief Service was not formally disbanded until 1960 its general section was laid down in July 1945, and by mid-1948 it had handed over its projects, including the girls' school, and the majority of its funds to the FSC. The national Famine Relief Committee was wound down in late 1944, after handing on, in August, £4000 to the Greek Red Cross for Greek children.[33] In January 1945 the Oxford Committee for Famine Relief widened its financing, remit and scope to deal with the wider European post-war crisis, and in July of that year it closed its Greek Famine Fund, transferring the remaining money to the Greek Red Cross.[34] In 1965 it officially assumed the name, Oxfam, by which it was already widely known and is still known today.

The contribution made by Quakers to the humanitarian crisis in Greece in the 1940s was not, as we have seen, on a large scale. It did, however, leave behind some lasting monuments, especially in education and health welfare. For those individuals whose lives were improved, or in some cases saved, by Quaker action, the effort must have been worthwhile. And it was appreciated. 'We realise ourselves the human task accomplished by you, which you carried out successfully and profitlessly, for the assistance and welfare of the young Greek refugees, in continuation of the noble traditions of your Great Country', wrote E. Sophoulis, the representative of the Greek government in Egypt, to the Quakers in

Jerusalem in March 1945; 'we found noble supporters like you, who with their natural affection have given comfort to the souls of so many unfortunate creatures', he continued.[35] And as for the Quakers themselves, they had applied their energies and finances in an attempt to ameliorate human suffering caused by war, in many cases successfully.

Notes

1. Oxford Record Office (BOQM/1/vi/5).
2. Famine Relief Committee, *Controlled Food Relief – or Famine*, October 1942, 066 (Relief Pamphlets Box 2/13): Archives of Britain Yearly Meeting of the Religious Society of Friends, Friends House.
3. Maggie Black, *A Cause for Our Times* (Oxford, 1992), p. 5.
4. *The Friend*, 20 November 1942: 657.
5. Famine Relief Committee correspondence (FRS/1992/27): Archives of Britain Yearly Meeting of the Religious Society of Friends, Friends House.
6. Ibid.
7. Parliamentary Debates. House of Commons Hansard series 5, vol. 393, 10 November 1943.
8. Black, *A Cause for our Times*, p.16. Cawadias had been the director of the Evangelismos Hospital in Athens and doctor to the Greek royal family. He settled in England in 1924 on the abdication of King George II of Greece and took British citizenship, Mary Henderson, *Xenia – a Memoir: Greece 1919–1949* (London, 1988), pp. xv, xvii.
9. Oxford Committee for Famine Relief, *Minutes*, 26 November 1945.
10. Friends Relief Committee Newsletter, January 1944 (FRS/1992/27): Archives of Britain Yearly Meeting of the Religious Society of Friends, Friends House.
11. A. Tegla Davies, *Friends Ambulance Unit* (London, 1947), p. 484.
12. John Ormerod Greenwood, *Quaker Encounter*, vol. 1: *Friends and Relief* (York, 1975), p. 275.
13. Lyn Smith, *Pacifists in Action* (York, 1998).
14. Richard Early, *Weavers and War* (London, 1984).
15. Martin H. Lidbetter, *Friends Ambulance Unit 1939–1943* (York, 1993), pp. 80–100.
16. Friends Relief Service Committee, Minute no. 44, 18 November 1943, *Minutes 1943–1960*, p. 19: Archives of Britain Yearly Meeting of the Religious Society of Friends, Friends House.
17. Norman Gilbertson, *Greece 1945–53*, unpublished MS, n.d.
18. Friends Relief Committee Newsletter, January 1943 (FRS/1992/27): Archives of Britain Yearly Meeting of the Religious Society of Friends, Friends House.
19. FAU/1947/3/5 Dodecanese: Archives of Britain Yearly Meeting of the Religious Society of Friends, Friends House.
20. In a small pamphlet published in London at the end of 1943, Stelio L. Chourmouzios published a number of photographs of thriving Greek children in the various refugee camps in the Middle East, which he contrasted with harrowing photographs of child victims of the famine, *Starvation in Greece* (London, 1943).

21. Friends Relief Service Committee, minute no. 57, 1 December 1943, *Minutes 1943–1960*, p. 22: Archives of Britain Yearly Meeting of the Religious Society of Friends, Friends House.
22. Paul E. Boyatzis and Nicholas G. Pappas, *Embers on the Sea* (Rushcutters Bay, NSW, 1995), pp. 17–27.
23. *Friends Ambulance Unit Middle East Newsletter*, 47 (January 1944): p. 9 (FAU/1947/3/6/7): Archives of Britain Yearly Meeting of the Religious Society of Friends, Friends House.
24. Donald Swann, *Swann's Way* (London, 1991), p. 87.
25. Smith, *Pacifists in Action*, p. 284.
26. *The Friend*, 21 September 1945, p. 625.
27. Tegla Davies, *Friends Ambulance Unit*, p. 411.
28. FAU Report May 1946 (FAU/1947/3/5): Archives of Britain Yearly Meeting of the Religious Society of Friends, Friends House.
29. See the memoirs of Joice Nankivell Loch, *A Fringe of Blue: an Autobiography* (London, 1968).
30. Brenda L. Marder, *Stewards of the Land* (Macon, GA, 2004).
31. Sydney Loch: letters to Friends Relief Service, no.35 (FRS 1992/ Box 78 – Greece): Archives of Britain Yearly Meeting of the Religious Society of Friends, Friends House.
32. Roger C. Wilson, *Quaker Relief* (London, 1952), pp. 192–5.
33. *The Friend*, 18 August 1944, p. 539.
34. Oxford Committee for Famine Relief, *Minutes*, 2 July 1945.
35. Letter of E. Soufoulis to Emily Hughes and Jean Malcolmson, 20 March 1945. (FRS/1992/69 Palestine): Archives of Britain Yearly Meeting of the Religious Society of Friends, Friends House.

11
UNRRA's Relief Efforts in Late 1944 Greece: Political Impartiality versus Military Exigencies

Flora Tsilaga

As the fortunes of the Second World War changed decisively in 1943 so the preoccupation of the Allies with post-war issues began to emerge with increasing clarity. The establishment of the United Nations Relief and Rehabilitation Administration (UNRRA) in November 1943 as a humanitarian agency charged with providing relief supplies and services to war-devastated countries was designed to provide answers to one such issue: how to make the transition from war to peace as orderly and humane as possible, at least in material terms.

With regard to Greece, UNRRA became the sole agency responsible for the provision of relief in April 1945, following the conclusion of an agreement with the Greek government in March of that year. During the so-called 'military period' (autumn 1944–spring 1945), its personnel acted as agents of the military authorities and their organisation, the Anglo-American Military Liaison (ML). Not surprisingly, therefore, the first 'test' of UNRRA's operations in the country was conditioned by its subordination to military command. As the period of UNRRA's and ML's joint activities coincided with the extreme and convoluted circumstances of the first post-occupation months that culminated in the *Dekemvriana* of 1944, the insurgency of December 1944, when members of the communist-led resistance army, ELAS,[1] fought with the government of national unity, headed by Giorgos Papandreou, and its British backers, it is interesting to examine the course of their cooperation and examine the interplay between military and humanitarian considerations.

This chapter will seek to elucidate the ways in which UNRRA was integrated with the military and will examine the implications for its future operations in the country. After a brief account of the administration's formation, scope and main objectives, the chapter will concentrate on the following questions. What were UNRRA's relief activities during the first post-war months? Were these, in any way, obstructed by ML and, if so, to what extent? How did UNRRA react to the *Dekemvriana*? Finally, did cooperation with the ML create a precedent in jeopardising UNRRA's neutral status; or was the gradual descent into overt civil war in Greece from 1946 onwards enough to expose by itself the complexity of impartial relief provision and military exigency?

I

While the Allied invasion of Italy in the summer of 1943 has been widely perceived as the point of transition to the post-war era, a time when the problems of occupation and reconstruction were essentially realized,[2] the initiation of post-war relief measures had been practically, yet tentatively, prepared before the actual encounter with post-war diffi- culties. In June 1942, representatives of Argentina, Australia, Canada, Britain and the United States initiated the establishment of an International Wheat Council, which was to direct a wheat reserve for intergovern- mental relief in war-stricken countries.[3] An earlier, yet more decisive step, was initiated with the formation of the Allied Post-War Requirements Bureau. Established in late 1941 by fifteen states, based in London and dominated by British officials, the bureau in question (popularly known as the Leith-Ross Committee) was responsible for estimating post-war relief needs and directing the utilization of any spare supplies.[4] However, the limited scope of its function and membership (especially the non- participation of the US and the Soviet Union) led to its dissolution in March 1943. In turn, the way was paved for planning and negotiating the establishment of a more effective and appropriate organisation. This was epitomised by the formation of UNRRA, the first international relief and rehabilitation administration established before the end of the war, and designed to operate in its aftermath on a worldwide basis.

The agreement establishing UNRRA was based on a draft proposal pre- sented to the Allies by the US administration in June 1943,[5] and even- tually signed in Atlantic City, New Jersey in November of that year by representatives of 44 Allied and associated states. Membership of the administration increased with the inclusion of Denmark and two Soviet Republics (Belorussia and the Ukraine) in 1945, and of Turkey in 1946.[6] Thereupon, the signatory states resolved that immediately upon the lib- eration of any area that fell under their control:

> the population shall receive aid and relief from their sufferings, food, clothing and shelter . . . and that preparation and arrangements shall

be made . . . for assistance in the resumption of urgently needed agricultural and industrial production and the restoration of essential services.[7]

The funding meeting of November 1943 defined the framework of UNRRA's activities, delineated its principles and resolutions and established an administrative and operating system for the discharge of its relevant responsibilities. The key bodies of this machinery comprised a Council, a Central Committee – along with subordinate departments – and a Director General. The Council was the policymaking body of UNRRA. It consisted of one representative from each member state and was generally responsible for the determination and designation of relief and rehabilitation operations. The Central Committee was the Council's managerial agency. It initially comprised four members (representatives of Britain, China, the Soviet Union and the United States), which were increased to six in 1945 and to nine in 1946.[8] Last, but not least, the Director General was the executive authority of UNRRA. He was nominated by the Central Committee and appointed by the Council, and was responsible for the discharge of relief and rehabilitation operations. He assigned executive officials and had power and authority to decide the exact geographical areas in which the administration was to operate and, on the UNRRA side at least, the nature and content of operations it would undertake.[9] Finally, the technicalities of relief and rehabilitation operations were organized by several committees of an administrative, operational and technical character, which together with the other departments of the administration accounted for an elaborate, yet rather intricate and fairly bureaucratic organisation.[10]

UNRRA's 'resolutions on policy' formulated the scope of relief and rehabilitation operations, defined financial responsibilities and administrative arrangements and determined the administration's relationship with member-states, relief organisations and other intergovernmental agencies. Hence, UNRRA was to operate in the liberated countries of the United Nations,[11] contingent upon the signing of an agreement between the administration and the respective recipient state.[12] The gratis provision of assistance, however, was limited to those states that lacked foreign exchange resources and could demonstrate their inability to meet their own most urgent relief and rehabilitation needs. Conversely, countries that did not fulfil this prerequisite were to make their own financial arrangements for the purchase of supplies.[13]

This restriction in the administration's mandate was primarily based on differentiation between occupied and non-occupied member-states, a principle that determined the configuration of its financial plan. Although the funding agreement obliged every member-state to contribute towards relief and rehabilitation operations, it also provided for two types of expenses, which in turn classified the signatories according to their economic state and concomitant relief and rehabilitation requirements.[14] On the one hand, administrative expenses relating to clerical and policymaking functions were generally, yet unevenly, applied to all members.[15] Operational charges, on the other hand, pertaining to direct relief activities and involving the actual procurement and distribution of supplies, were preset and confined to non-occupied member-states.[16] Overall, the total contributions to UNRRA (both administrative and operational) amounted to about $3.9 billion, with approximately 93 per cent provided by 31 non-occupied member-states.[17] As for the operational costs themselves, 94 per cent was furnished by Britain, Canada and the United States, with the latter alone contributing 73 per cent of the total.[18]

UNRRA undertook two major activities, which were expressed in its title: relief operations, pertaining to the supply of essential consumer goods (such as food, clothing, fuel, shelter materials and medical stores) and the provision of health and welfare services, including the rendering of assistance for the care and repatriation of displaced persons; and rehabilitation operations involving the supply of materials and services needed to enable a recipient country to produce and transport relief supplies for its own and other liberated areas and the restoration of public utilities (such as power, water, sanitation, transport and communications).[19]

Along with relief and rehabilitation operations assumed and carried out totally by the administration, the administration was to cooperate with other organisations associated with relevant activities. Such liaison involved mainly military agencies, which would render assistance before the complete liberation of a member-state. Contingent upon their request, UNRRA would consult and cooperate with military authorities in the planning of relief and rehabilitation services as well as the procurement and distribution of supplies. In so doing, the smooth and orderly transition from the military to the civilian relief period should be given priority, while supplies and services should be offered and distributed fairly among the population.[20]

The above stipulation was closely related to the standard of impartiality, a concept that became UNRRA's fundamental principle, thoroughly defined in two pertinent resolutions. Accordingly, it was specified that when and wherever the administration was involved, either fully or partially, in relief and rehabilitation operations, such activities should be conducted fairly on the basis of the relative needs of the population and without favouritism on account of race, creed or political belief. By the same token, commodities and services should in no way be used as a political weapon, the distribution of supplies should be made without discrimination and all classes of the population, irrespective of their purchasing power, should receive an equitable share of essential supplies.[21]

The UNRRA mandate was carried out by field missions dispatched to member countries to discharge relief and rehabilitation responsibilities and act as the operational and organisational link between the recipient state and the administration. The field establishments assisted member governments in drawing up lists of requirements, offered advice on all matters relating to the distribution and usage of supplies[22] and observed every stage of assistance in order to ensure the effective and equitable treatment of all consumers.[23] Their administrative structure reflected the arrangements within the high levels of the administration, with much of the authority vested in the hands of the chief of mission. Acting as a director general in miniature, the chief was responsible for cooperation with the authorities of the recipient state, served as a liaison between the latter and the administration's headquarters and decided personnel appointments.[24] Missions were also structured into committees of an administrative, technical and operational character, generally organised in three major departments: finance and administration, relief services, and supply and distribution.[25] Finally, field activities throughout recipient countries were performed by a number of regional offices established in provincial centres. Manned and operated by UNRRA personnel, these offices were responsible for observing, reporting and advising governmental officials on the distribution and utilisation of supplies as well as informing the chief of mission on regional developments.[26]

II

In early October 1944 the Axis occupation was almost over as far as mainland Greece was concerned. Concurrently with the withdrawal of the Germans and the Bulgarians, guerrilla forces incorporated the liberated territories into 'free Greece', and ELAS had assumed control of almost all of continental Greece by early autumn.[27] In mid-October, the Greek government-in-exile, backed up by British troops, arrived in Athens. It was completely unprepared to face the twofold challenge of providing relief in the face of an acute shortage of supplies and massive inflation and of establishing its authority over a country threatened by internal strife.[28]

The government of national unity, headed by Giorgos Papandreou, inherited both a shattered economic system and a dysfunctional administrative structure. The sources of the country's revenues had been severely depleted and its permanent capital assets, such as roads, railways, ports and ships were seriously damaged.[29] In many areas, especially in villages of Thessaly, Epirus and Western Macedonia, the destruction amounted to devastation, with most of the communities completely ruined, the population homeless and destitute and the land uncultivated and infertile.[30] Overall, there was hardly a part of Greece that had escaped the war and the ravages of occupation, while the material destruction itself was enormous. The Paris Conference on Reparations in 1946 estimated the cost of destruction at approximately $8500 million,[31] while the Greek Ministry of Public Works appraised the damage to the public sector alone at 44,721 million prewar drachmas, and the total cost at one billion British gold sovereigns.[32]

As for the purely administrative and political aspect, the problems facing the Papandreou government were massive given the socio-political conditions in the country immediately after the occupation. As elsewhere in recently liberated Europe, socio-political discontinuity was an overwhelming characteristic of post-liberation Greece. The harshness of the occupation and the simple fact that fear and hunger spared none had brought a new sense of social cohesion and had radicalized public opinion.[33] This emancipation of the masses was in sharp contrast with traditional socio-political forces and the pre-war establishment. The inability of the latter to protect the population either in physical or symbolic terms had created a power vacuum which was manifestly being filled by newly emerging forces. These forces, emanating from the contradictory milieu of disorder and radicalism, expected to play a leading role in confronting the ruins, poverty, hunger and chaos caused by the war and the occupation. To this end, there would have to be either cooperation or confrontation with the traditional socio-political establishment.

The government of national unity was a coalition in name only. Comprising mainly the 'old guard' politicians, who had not played any active role in the resistance, it had little contact with the population and was rather mistrustful of developments in occupied Greece. In addition, the subordinate position of the left-wing representatives in the administration and the mutual suspicion that generally characterized relations between EAM, much the largest resistance organisation, and Papandreou made a real coalition elusive. Hence, for the 'Prime Minister of Liberation', the fact that EAM/ELAS controlled most of the country made an alleged communist insurgency a likely prospect.[34] As for EAM itself, it had been highly sceptical of the government's claim to embody national unity, given Papandreou's militant anti-communism, and his backing by the

British, who had been openly hostile to EAM/ELAS since mid-1943. However, despite such suspicion and distrust, in August 1944, EAM accepted the 'Lebanon Charter', and, in September it placed its military forces under the Papandreou government and agreed not to move any of its regular troops into the Athens-Piraeus area.

The first British forces to arrive in Greece in early October 1944 consisted of approximately 13,000 military personnel,[35] charged with the imposition and preservation of law and order so as to facilitate both the establishment of the Papandreou government in Athens and the introduction and distribution of relief.[36] In exercising those responsibilities, they were to act in a double role. In an exclusively British capacity, they were under the command of General Sir Ronald Scobie for military and political matters, and as an Allied organisation they had responsibility for operations related to the provision of relief. Indeed, both Scobie and Field-Marshal Henry Maitland Wilson (the British Supreme Commander in the Mediterranean) had been briefed by the War Office to be very careful to use the term 'Allied' only for operations related to relief and rehabilitation and not for any other military and/or administrative activities which were undertaken solely by British land forces.[37]

This complexity with regard to military, political and relief issues was further evident in the agreement between the British and the Greek governments which determined 'questions concerning civil administration, jurisdiction and relief arising out of the presence of the military force in Greece'.[38] Accordingly, and to facilitate the task of the British forces in the country, military areas, namely any regions that were either affected by military operations or were faced by a serious state of disorder, were automatically excluded from the authority of the Greek government and were placed under sole British jurisdiction and control. In spite of such concessions, it was maintained that these powers were 'extremely limited' compared with those possessed by a force in occupied enemy territory, and that the arrangements in question were intended to be 'essentially temporary and practical'.[39]

With regard to relief issues per se, British land forces had under their command Military Liaison (ML), an Anglo-American military relief organisation manned by army officers. This organisation assumed responsibility for the provisioning, planning and distribution of immediate relief to the distressed population.[40] In its task, it was assisted by the UNRRA mission that was established in Greece in the first half of October 1944 under the leadership of an American, Laird Archer.[41] The particulars of the relationship between UNRRA and the competent military authorities were established in the Cairo Agreement of 3 April 1944.[42] Accordingly, cooperation was confined to the so-called military period, after the end of which the relief organisation would assume full responsibility for the provision of assistance. For planning purposes, the military period was assumed to be of six months duration, which was defined as the transitional phase between the end of occupation and the final establishment of the government's authority in the country.[43]

While for UNRRA, cooperation with the ML at this stage was seen as a good option both in order to study conditions in the country and to do the preliminary planning for the work it was to assume,[44] ML held the view that no more than one Allied organisation should take on relief activities at the same time and that civilian relief must be harmonised with military operations.[45] Yet, UNRRA's firm belief that the transition to the civilian relief period should be as smooth and efficient as possible, reinforced by the practical issue of ML's shortage of relief personnel, made cooperation between the two organisations imperative.[46] Admittedly, the views of both entailed a somewhat superficial relation and the basis for a closer collaboration had not been agreed upon from the outset. Hence, there had not been any intensive joint planning in policy and operational issues such as the number, type and position of the UNRRA personnel required in the field.[47] Very soon, however, the complexity of the military and political situation led ML to seek a closer collaboration, in order to avert duplication and possible friction in relief work.[48]

The degree to which there was friction in their working relationship will be touched on later. Certainly, however, friction was not avoided in the negotiations to determine their relations. Hence, UNRRA officials maintained that all planning should be directed towards achieving the administration's earliest possible deployment as an organisation and that, in achieving this goal, its personnel should retain its own chain of command.[49] Conversely, while ML agreed with these aspirations, it maintained that the existence of a separate organisation with a pecking order parallel to that of the military was undesirable.[50] Furthermore, whereas for ML any independent liaison between local authorities and UNRRA was unacceptable, the latter deemed such cooperation imperative in order to facilitate the assessment of conditions in the country in relation to its future work and to smooth the transition from military to civilian relief.[51]

When it came to discussing the practical and specific issues of policy-making, this dispute gave rise to vigorous exchanges. Whereas the lack of joint planning in both operational and policy matters was mutually agreed, arguments differed. While ML attacked UNRRA's ignorance of the 'most elementary forms of general or technical military procedure', which prevented better policy arrangements and hindered the handing over of specific tasks to civilian personnel,[52] UNRRA laid the blame on the absence of definite instructions on the part of the military.[53] Nevertheless, for UNRRA personnel it was not so much such grievances over practical issues that prevented closer association with ML, but rather the political ramifications of a steady association with a military agency, an association which, in their view, would both jeopardise its international status, and 'compromise [the Administration] in that, instead of being the trustee of forty-four nations, it [would] make it a part of a military organisation which was under the direction of and governed by the policies of one nation only, possibly a second'.[54]

Whilst UNRRA's wish for cooperation on a functional basis diverged from the ML's desire for full integration and seemingly led to a deadlock, two senior officials of the administration arrived in Athens in late November 1944 to negotiate a compromise. In the event, an agreement on partial integration was endorsed the following day by both organisations. By this the military assumed full financial and policy responsibility for all relief activities during the military period, with the assistance of UNRRA, which was to act as its agent. ML and UNRRA personnel would be fully merged without regard to their respective status and both were to report through a single chain of command. UNRRA was to be the sole organisation assisting the military in relief issues and any other civilian bodies would be under its administrative authority, with the exception of the International Red Cross, and the Joint Relief Commission which would be under ML as 'voluntary societies' personnel.[55]

Relief operations were to be carried out through ML's Bureau of Requirements and Supply, which incorporated UNRRA's Divisions of Distribution and Transport, Food and Agriculture, Industrial Rehabilitation and Health.[56] UNRRA staff were to be consulted at all levels, acting both as advisers and as liaison links with local authorities. In order to discharge these responsibilities, UNRRA personnel would serve under the appropriate military commander or staff officer, attend pertinent meetings and participate in discussions on matters of policy organisation and operational procedure.[57] With regard to specific relief activities and operations, it was mutually agreed that these – whether carried out solely by ML or in conjunction with UNRRA personnel – were to be conducted in such a way as to ensure the equitable distribution of supplies on the basis of the population's relative needs and without discrimination on account of race, nationality, religion or political beliefs. To discharge this resolution, military directives were to ensure compliance with such a non-discriminatory policy.[58]

Full integration, however, was practically unattainable for two reasons. As the military period was by definition temporary and as the plan was for UNRRA to take over relief activities at a later stage, the administration reserved the right to contact the Greek government independently on policy issues concerning future operations. To do so, it retained its Office of the Chief of Mission, its Bureau of Finance and Administration, and its Divisions of Welfare and of Displaced Persons.[59] On the other hand, although it was mutually agreed that all possible efforts were to be made towards complete understanding of, and agreement on, operational procedures, it was clearly stated that in case of disagreement the view of the military would prevail,[60] and that, at ML's request, UNRRA would have to remove any of its personnel.[61]

Moreover, under the terms of two delicate and rather incompatible clauses, both organisations sought to secure their rather diverse priorities on the issue of relief provision. With regard to UNRRA, it was maintained that any cooperation with ML would be immediately subject to review and revision if the exigencies of the military situation required any contravention of the principle of non-discrimination.[62] As for ML, it reserved the right to refuse the provision of relief supplies in any area in which conditions of chaos and anarchy existed;[63] a clause that, if implemented, would not only annul UNRRA's stipulation with regard to impartial relief provision, but it could also suggest a controversial reading of the agreement between the British and Greek governments. Under the latter, although the British committed themselves to relief provision in line with the principle of non-discrimination, they also retained the right to exercise complete authority in the so-called military areas of the country and consequently the 'privilege' either to permit or prohibit the distribution of relief to those areas.[64]

Disputes and friction in cooperation between UNRRA and ML occurred both in field operations and on issues of high policy. While some UNRRA members admitted that they were 'receiving the most cordial treatment and best evidence of respect and confidence by [their ML] superiors', the majority felt that they were being kept in the dark on general plans[65] and that 'the military said one thing on paper and d[id] exactly the opposite'.[66] Hence, the recommendations of UNRRA officials were not even considered by their military superiors, much less acted upon, and UNRRA representatives were excluded from several committees and policy conferences of ML, although they were supposed to participate under the agreements.[67] As for the field work itself, there was a general feeling among UNRRA personnel that they were being used by the military as they deemed convenient. Thus, they were appointed to whatever assignment ML officials wanted, even if the particular individual was not trained for the specific job.[68] The fact that, at this stage, ML was the agency possessing both the supplies and the means to do the actual relief work, along with its tendency to use its military status in designating plans as highly confidential and thus keeping UNRRA in the dark, seems to have made the exclusion and marginalisation of UNRRA personnel easier.[69] Should such grievances, however, simply be seen as the exaggerated views of oversensitive or overzealous United Nations officials? Or was it the case that integration between a military and an international humanitarian agency on relief issues was inherently doomed from the outset?

When the clash over the demobilisation of ELAS and the resulting resignation of EAM's representatives from the Papandreou government culminated in the *Dekemvriana* insurgency in December 1944, UNRRA personnel found themselves in a peculiar position. The 'acute restlessness and impatience over inactivity' that they had initially felt gave way to a 'growing criticism of high political policy and insistence upon withdrawal from close integration with ML'.[70] The fact that UNRRA's headquarters in Greece were located in the Hotel Grande Bretagne and the majority of its personnel witnessed the shooting of EAM demonstrators on 3 December by the police,[71] and the dead bodies lying in Constitution Square, seems to have been the *coup de grâce* for relations between the two organisations.[72]

On 10 December 1944, a week after the outbreak of the December events, Laird Archer, chief of the UNRRA Mission in Greece informed both ML and senior officials of the administration that:

> We recognize that there is an armed insurrection against the Greek Government by a political group; AFHQ [Allied Forces Headquarters] for whom we are acting as an agent is taking steps to quell this insurrection by force. We therefore as UNRRA are unavoidably associated with a regime of force and discrimination. We therefore feel our position as UNRRA is being prejudiced and we feel ourselves compelled to disassociate ourselves from the present activities of 3 Corps until the position has been clarified.

He maintained, however, that in order to meet the emergency situation, in which people were forced to go without food and medical attention, UNRRA personnel would not only welcome but, indeed, request any opportunity to carry out as a mission such relief functions as were in conformity with the principles of UNRRA as defined by the United Nations Council.[73]

Archer's superiors, however, appeared to take a different view. The chief of the Balkan mission, Major General Hughes, to whom the Greek mission reported, tried to mitigate the stance of the UNRRA personnel in a letter of the next day. Pointing out that ML was a separate organisation from the British military forces and insisting upon the fact that there had been no instance of discrimination by the ML in the distribution of relief, he requested specific information as to whether the withdrawal was permanent or temporary and tried to draw Archer's attention to the fact that the issue of withdrawal was a question of high policy that would inevitably affect UNRRA's future operations in the country.[74]

It was probably this reference to high policy that moderated the tenor of Archer's reply the following day. Although the reasoning behind disassociation with ML was repeated, he also stated that no discrimination on the part of the military in the distribution of relief had ever been suggested and he further claimed that relations with ML had been both cordial and constructive. Finally, he insisted that since it was due to present local conditions the proposed withdrawal was temporary.[75]

Nevertheless, while exchanges within UNRRA as to the nature and character of the mission's withdrawal persisted, things took a totally different turn. Under the emergency conditions prevailing in the capital, General Scobie ordered the temporary evacuation of all unnecessary personnel from Athens.[76] Since the military had had full responsibility for relief provision, this decision was within its purview. However, one could question both the reasoning behind such an order as well as the behind-the-scenes consultations that led to it. How could the presence of redundant personnel be justified in December, when, only a month earlier, integration with UNRRA had been keenly pursued by ML on account of its lack of adequate staff?[77] Off the record, it was frankly admitted that ML not only disagreed with UNRRA's withdrawal, but it also questioned the authority of its personnel in Greece to take such a decision.[78] What is more important, ML clearly stated that UNRRA's insistence on adhering to the principle of equal distribution under conditions of civil war and its consequent withdrawal had inevitably caused 'a little embarrassment' both to the military[79] and the Greek government.[80] Thus, it could reasonably be argued that the term 'unnecessary' referred to the civilian personnel and, notwithstanding the pretext of redundancy, ML ordered the evacuation of the UNRRA staff, making use of the pertinent clause in the integration contract according to which, in case of disagreement between the two organisations, the view of the military would prevail and UNRRA would have to withdraw any of its personnel at the military's request.[81]

One can speculate whether it was the so-called 'little embarrassment' or demonstrable military considerations that prompted Scobie's order.[82] Yet, there was a financial issue that further complicated the situation. In line with the agreement between ML and UNRRA, and on the grounds that the latter functioned as an agent of former, the military was to provide funds for all UNRRA administrative expenditures in the country.[83] However, from December 1944 onwards, the British Treasury was not in a position to continue such an arrangement due to the demands of the military situation in Greece that had absorbed the necessary funds and consequently necessitated the evacuation of the UNRRA personnel.[84]

The decision on evacuation was certainly a great blow to UNRRA.[85] The mission's activities and stance in the complex circumstances of December 1944 were admittedly peculiar, as the conflict not only complicated its relations with ML, but also resulted in the cessation of relief provision to the population. As early as 7 December, UNRRA's Director of Welfare in Greece had insisted that the mission should restore essential relief services.[86] The fact that the division in question was not integrated with ML[87] facilitated the establishment of a welfare office in Athens. Under its direction UNRRA staff allocated provisions to the Greek Red Cross hospital that had been without any food and water for days, and to children's hostels in the Kifisia area north of Athens. Moreover, they volunteered to drive to regions where fighting occurred and act as emergency personnel, distributing food and medical supplies to hospitals and soup-kitchens.[88] In carrying out such tasks, there was a general feeling among UNRRA personnel that they were respected by Greeks on both sides of the political divide.[89] EAM/ELAS in particular had openly stated that it would prefer to see UNRRA taking over distribution of relief, as they were sceptical of Red Cross activities, on the grounds that the Red Cross was unable to carry out distribution due to British pressure; and they had no faith in ML's operations.[90]

In the event, on 18 December, and in line with Scobie's order, the UNRRA mission as a whole was withdrawn to Cairo, where the headquarters of the Balkan mission were situated, leaving only observers behind. The following day, in an attempt to explain the situation, UNRRA's Director General released a press communiqué. After expressing his deep disappointment at the tragic situation in Greece that had caused the evacuation of UNRRA personnel, he maintained that the military authorities were solely responsible for this decision and that the evacuation order had only been issued after several employees of the administration had been wounded in the course of their duties.[91] Therefore, without any reference either to his personnel's resolution to withdraw from integration with ML, or to the reasons behind such a decision, he left his staff in the country defenceless.

The stance of the Director General notwithstanding, the Greek mission personnel continued in the same tenor. At its meeting in Cairo, ten days later, conditions were again studied and two resolutions determining UNRRA's future status in the country were adopted. By admitting that integration with ML had gravely jeopardised UNRRA's status as an international relief organisation and that any sustained identification with the military forces would put its international integrity at further risk, it was resolved that UNRRA should return to Greece as an international civilian organisation and not under military authority. It was further determined that its return should be preceded by an internal reorganisation of the Greek mission, in order to ensure the establishment and maintenance of high standards of administrative and operating efficiency.[92]

Indeed, UNRRA did in the event return to Greece with a completely different status. Following agreement with the Greek authorities in March 1945, the administration became the sole responsible agency for relief and rehabilitation services in the country. However, the events of December 1944 and UNRRA's stance tested the adaptability of its first operational mission, its impartiality, the morale of its personnel and its capacity for emergency service. Furthermore, they revealed important differences in ideology and thinking between the senior officials of UNRRA and its rank and file. In this instance, UNRRA personnel in Greece firmly refused to yield to military considerations that jeopardised the administration's principle of neutrality. The issue remains, however, whether in UNRRA's subsequent activities in Greece such principles were pursued with the same determination or whether they were engulfed by the political divisions and civil war conditions prevalent in the country.

III

The agreement between UNRRA and the Greek government defined relief and rehabilitation operations and provided the framework of mutual responsibilities and obligations. Thus the Greek state assumed full responsibility for the distribution and use of supplies provided free of charge by the administration, with two restrictions. Firstly, compliance with conditions as to impartiality made by the provider should be observed and, secondly, the proceeds from the sale, lease or transfer of UNRRA supplies should be used for further relief and rehabilitation ventures.[93] In order to observe these rules, as well as to facilitate cooperation between the administration and the Greek state, the UNRRA mission to Greece would supervise the movement, distribution and use of supplies, concurrently providing technical advice and assistance.[94]

The specifics of the cooperation between the mission and the Greek government were officially established in May 1945, with the formation of the Joint Policy Committee (JPC), a purely advisory body that constituted the liaison channel between the two sides.[95] In this context, with the limitation of the administration's responsibilities to a purely advisory role, administrative and operational duties after the import of supplies remained, at least on paper, an entirely Greek responsibility. For this purpose, the country was divided into eleven regions[96] codified by Latin characters, with an administrative centre serving as the region's headquarters and a major port used for the clearance and movement of supplies.[97] On the UNRRA side, officials of the mission supervised the management and distribution of relief, and served as the link between the provinces and the Athens headquarters.[98]

The relief and rehabilitation system was vertically formulated in geographical and administrative levels, with the formation of two interdependent mechanisms, those of welfare and distribution. Under the direction and supervision of the respective ministries (welfare and supply), the system was activated by Athens, spread into regions and prefectures and ended in towns and villages. At each level, welfare and distribution committees were responsible for the determination of 'resourceless' people and the final allocation of supplies. Membership of the committees was decided by prefects in line with ministerial directives. The provision of relief aimed at ensuring a minimum level of essential consumption of food and clothing to all classes of the population, with supplies either sold to those who could pay, or offered free of charge to the destitute.[99]

The above allocation procedure was confined to food, clothing and medical supplies, namely commodities allocated for personal use and related to the immediate relief of the population. Industrial and agricultural rehabilitation supplies were distributed under a different system, and were, in any case, sold at prices specified by the ministries of agriculture, public works and finance. Agricultural supplies (seeds, fertilisers, pesticides, animals and machinery) were allocated by a distribution machinery similar to the one for welfare, with local needs forwarded from villages to regional committees, which in turn decided on specific allocations to peasants.[100] Industrial supplies, which also comprised construction materials (for the restoration of the transportation system and the housing of the population), were either directly allocated to the relevant ministries, or assigned to industries after the submission of the relevant applications to industrial committees controlled by the state.[101]

The total sum of UNRRA's assistance to Greece amounted to roughly $347 million over a period of approximately two and half years (April 1945–June 1947). The peak in the flow of imports covered the sixteen-month period from June 1945 to September 1946, during which more than 90 per cent of the administration's programme was realized. As for the allocation of the assistance between specific commodities, food-related imports (agricultural supplies and foodstuffs) amounted to almost 75 per cent of the total (14.2 and 59.5 per cent respectively), industrial rehabilitation supplies amounted to 12.7 per cent, clothing to 11 per cent, while medical and sanitation supplies came to a mere 2.6 per cent of the programme.[102]

In January 1947, five months before the formal completion of UNRRA's operations in Greece and four months after the actual termination of the programme, a distribution control unit was sent to the country in order to examine the allocation and use of supplies. It consisted of three UNRRA members of American, British and Soviet nationality, who travelled around the country for a month consulting with Greek and UNRRA officials and investigating relief developments. Their report, communicated in secret to the chief of the Greek mission as well as to the administration's headquarters, was extremely critical. They found 'mass political discrimination against the Left Wing element of the population', and additional 'maldistribution of essential supplies that resulted in discrimination against the indigent and the lower income groups'. They further reported that, although UNRRA was aware that its principles were not being adhered to, 'no strong and effective action was taken to remedy the situation'. On these grounds, they recommended two courses of action. Firstly, that the Greek government should explicitly assure UNRRA that political discrimination would cease at once and that any relief assistance withheld from politically sensitive areas of the country should be immediately dispatched there. Secondly, they advised that no further relief deliveries would be made to Greece, unless the government demonstrated its willingness and ability to comply with the administration's resolutions.[103]

The response from UNRRA officials in Greece was prompt and disgruntled. Convinced that the distribution control unit was unfavourably disposed towards the Greek government, the chief of mission asserted that discrimination in the distribution of relief was bound to exist in Greece, as it did in every other country in the world. In addition, he argued that although the allocation of supplies had not been ideal, the situation had not 'increased his blood pressure'.[104] The reaction of the administration's headquarters was rather similar. The deputy director general claimed that the report in question was the work of an independent group that did not necessarily represent the views of UNRRA, whose 'attitude towards the Greek government and its present difficulties had been one of sympathetic understanding'.[105]

While such a mollifying reaction by UNRRA officials in Greece may be understandable, since their concern to downplay both the importance of the report and the existence of adverse relief conditions in the country was certainly prompted by the fact that they were largely to be held responsible for the defiance of UNRRA resolutions, the apathetic stance of the headquarters, which actually sent the distribution control unit, is more surprising. For one thing, the classification of an official UNRRA division as an 'independent group' questions the administration's coherence and unity as an organisation. More importantly, the statement on 'sympathetic understanding of present difficulties', which directly relates to the civil war conditions that existed in Greece at the time, certainly raises doubts about UNRRA's impartiality.

Indeed, the recommendations of the distribution control unit were not implemented. Relief deliveries to Greece did not stop, although supplies to sensitive areas of the country were constantly withheld. In fact, although the government assured the administration that political discrimination would cease at once, information to the contrary continued to reach all levels of the mission. Yet, again no action was taken to remedy the situation. In any case, UNRRA was to withdraw formally from Greece in less than three months and its actual contribution to the relief of the population had, by and large, come to an end.

Admittedly, this contribution was not an impartial one. Although there is no strong evidence of UNRRA's direct involvement in irregularities, in reality, political discrimination in relief provision was actually effected with their own supplies. What is more, their responsibility to supervise and enforce the impartial distribution of supplies was by and large abandoned. In this context, one should reconsider UNRRA's reaction two years earlier to indications that relief activities by ML were not impartial. At that time, the fact that they were 'associated with a regime of force and discrimination' had prompted UNRRA personnel in Greece to disassociate themselves from such a policy. In January 1947, however, strong evidence of political discrimination in relief provision was played down by the very same people. Hence, it seems that values advocated before the end of the war, when feelings of common suffering were strong, and the aspiration for a bright collective future enticing, were gradually abandoned as a result of the emergence of a bipolar world system. As far as the UNRRA mission to Greece is concerned, the vigorous endorsement of the administration's neutrality was confined to the ML period. The fact that they were not in charge of relief operations may have played a role in preserving impartial standards. However, when they assumed responsibility for relief, this firmness was replaced by feelings of 'sympathetic understanding' towards those who actually contravened UNRRA's fundamental principle of impartiality and used its supplies as a political weapon.

Notes

1. The Greek People's Liberation Army, founded in February 1942, was the military wing of EAM.
2. Mark Mazower, *Dark Continent: Europe's Twentieth Century* (London, 1998), p. 216.
3. George Woodbridge, *The History of the United Nations Relief and Rehabilitation Administration*, 3 vols (New York, 1950), I, p. 8.
4. Ibid., I, p. 11. See also UNRRA, *A Compilation of the Resolutions on Policy: First and Second Sessions of the UNRRA Council* (Washington, DC, 1944), p. 4 (Article III); UNRRA, *Organization, Aims, Progress* (Washington, DC, 1944), p. 4; George Politakis, *Greek Policies of Recovery and Reconstruction, 1944–1952*, unpublished PhD thesis, University of Oxford (1990), p. 70.
5. UNRRA, *A Compilation of the Resolutions on Policy: First and Second Sessions of the UNRRA Council* (Washington, DC, 1944), p. 5.
6. Associated states were affiliated with the Allied forces in the war effort against the Axis. The signatories were Australia, Belgium, Bolivia, Brazil, Canada, Chile, China, Colombia, Costa Rica, Cuba, Czechoslovakia, the Dominican Republic, Ecuador, Egypt, El Salvador, Ethiopia, France, Greece, Guatemala, Haiti, the Honduras, Iceland, India, Iran, Iraq, Liberia, Luxembourg, Mexico, the Netherlands, New Zealand, Nicaragua, Norway, Panama, Paraguay, Peru, the Philippines, Poland, the Union of South Africa, the Soviet Union, the United Kingdom, the United States, Uruguay, Venezuela, and Yugoslavia; ibid., pp. 83–7 (Appendix 1); UNRRA, *A Compilation on the Resolutions on Policy: Third and Fourth Sessions of the UNRRA Council* (Washington, DC, 1946), p. 9 (Resolutions 62 & 63); p. 27 (Resolution 84).
7. UNRRA, *A Compilation of the Resolutions on Policy: First and Second Sessions of the UNRRA Council* (Washington, DC, 1944), p. 1 (Agreement, Article I).
8. Canada and France were included in 1945, and Australia, Brazil and Yugoslavia in 1946; UNRRA, *A Compilation on the Resolutions on Policy: Third and Fourth Sessions of the UNRRA Council* (Washington, DC, 1946), pp. 21, 26–7 (Resolutions 77 & 83).
9. Ibid., pp. 2–6 (Agreement, Articles III, IV and VI); p. 9 (Resolution 1).
10. These included the Central Committee, two advisory committees on supplies and on financial control, two regional-advisory committees on Europe and on the Far East, and five technical-advisory committees on agriculture, displaced persons, health, industrial rehabilitation, and welfare; UNRRA, *A Compilation of the Resolutions on Policy: First and Second Sessions of the UNRRA Council* (Washington, DC, 1944), pp. 46–51.

11. Originally the term United Nations was used to denote the countries participating in the struggle against the Axis which in January 1942 pledged not to make a separate peace with the enemy.

12. UNRRA, *A Compilation of the Resolutions on Policy: First and Second Sessions of the UNRRA Council* (Washington, DC, 1944), p. 9 (Resolution 1).

13. UNRRA, *UNRRA: Structure and Operations* (London, 1946), p. 8; UNRRA, *A Compilation of the Resolutions on Policy: First and Second Sessions of the UNRRA Council* (Washington, DC, 1944), p. 32 (Resolution 14); France, Belgium, Holland and Norway fell under the second group; UNRRA, *Fifty Facts about UNRRA* (Washington, DC, 1946), p. 8.

14. UNRRA, *A Compilation of the Resolutions on Policy: First and Second Sessions of the UNRRA Council* (Washington, DC, 1944), p. 7 (Agreement, Article V).

15. These contributions did not cover the administrative cost of the field missions and of the camps for displaced persons; ibid., p. 7 (Agreement, Article V). See also George Woodbridge, *The History of the United Nations Relief and Rehabilitation Administration*, I, pp. 133–4.

16. UNRRA, *A Compilation of the Resolutions on Policy: First and Second Sessions of the UNRRA Council* (Washington, DC, 1944), p. 32 (Resolution 14). Resolution 80 of the Third Council Session (London, August 1945) amended Resolution 14 and increased the contribution of non-occupied states by another 1 per cent of their national income for the year ending 30 June 1943; UNRRA, *A Compilation on the Resolutions on Policy: Third and Fourth Sessions of the UNRRA Council* (Washington, DC, 1946), pp. 23–4.

17. Australia, Britain, Bolivia, Brazil, Canada, Chile, Colombia, Costa Rica, Cuba, the Dominican Republic, Ecuador, Egypt, El Salvador, Guatemala, Haiti, the Honduras, Iceland, India, Iran, Iraq, Liberia, Mexico, New Zealand, Nicaragua, Panama, Paraguay, Peru, the Union of South Africa, the United States, Uruguay and Venezuela; UNRRA, *Report of the Director General to the Council for the Period 1 January 1945 to 31 March 1945* (London, 1945), p. 49.

18. UNRRA, *Report of the Director General to the Council for the Period 1 April 1945 to 30 June 1945* (London, 1945), pp. 49, 108.

19. UNRRA, *A Compilation of the Resolutions on Policy: First and Second Sessions of the UNRRA Council* (Washington, DC, 1944), pp. 11, 21–3 (Resolutions 1 & 10).

20. Ibid., pp. 12–14 (Resolution 1).

21. Ibid., pp. 14–15, 17–18 (Resolutions 1 & 7).

22. George Woodbridge, *The History of the United Nations Relief and Rehabilitation Administration*, I, pp. 189–90.

23. In accordance with Resolution 2 on impartiality; UNRRA, *A Compilation of the Resolutions on Policy: First and Second Sessions of the UNRRA Council* (Washington, DC, 1944), p. 14.

24. UNRRA, *Report of the Director General to the Council for the Period 1 January 1945 to 31 March 1945* (London, 1945), p. 45.

25. United Nations Relief and Rehabilitation Administration Archive (hereafter UNRRA-A) S-0527-0711: Chart 1, chief and senior deputy chief of mission (15 December 1945).

26. UNRRA-A/S-0525-0061: GP-7, field organization and operation (3 April 1945); UNRRA-A/S-0527-0720: Chief of field liaison officer, regional operations (6 November 1945).

27. Angeliki Laiou-Thomadakis 'The Politics of Hunger: Economic Aid to Greece, 1943–1945', *Journal of the Hellenic Diaspora*, VII (1980): 27–42.
28. Public Record Office, Foreign Office Files (hereafter FO) 371/41170/UR1281/296: UNRRA, notes on economic and financial policy (10 October 1944).
29. UNRRA, *Operational Analysis Papers No 25, Post-War Public Finance in Greece* (London, 1947), pp. 141–2.
30. UNRRA-A/S-0527-0532: Report on destroyed villages in occupied Greece (n.d.); UNRRA-A/S-0527-0733: Economic information report, B no 44&45, March–April 1944 (n.d.).
31. The total cost is calculated as the amount of occupation expenses, together with government expenditures and total material losses; UNRRA, *Operational Analysis Papers No 20, Industrial Rehabilitation in Greece* (London, 1947), p. 9. See also Bickham Sweet-Escott, *Greece: a Political and Economic Survey, 1939–1953* (London, 1954), p. 94.
32. Jon Kofas, *Intervention and Underdevelopment: Greece during the Cold War* (University Park, 1989), p. 8.
33. Gabriel Kolko, *The Politics of War. Allied Diplomacy and the World Crisis of 1943–1945* (London, 1969), pp. 3–5.
34. As E.D. Smith has put it: 'Papandreou was deeply concerned that the wrong people in Greece had arms while his Government would have nothing' (*Victory of a Sort. The British in Greece, 1941–1946* (London, 1988), p. 145).
35. Public Record Office, War Office Files (hereafter WO) 204/8577/HS-AFHQ/232/2: AML HQ (Greece), S&T Appreciation and Plan (March 1944); WO 216/183/E1627: C. in C. Middle East to War Office (17 October 1944). By the end of October 1944 their number had increased to approximately 26,500, Smith, *Victory of a Sort*, p. 155.
36. WO 204/3089/AFHQ 2100: Wilson to AGWAR for Combined Chiefs of Staff, FX 92210 (4 September 1944).
37. WO 204/3089/AFHQ 2100: AGWAR to Wilson, WX81353 (16 August 1944); AGWAR to Wilson, WX27481 (8 September 1944).
38. The agreement between the British and Greek governments, which was drafted in anticipation of the arrival of British troops in the country, was effected by an exchange of communications between the two governments and came into force on 24 November 1944; UNRRA-A/S-0527-0793: ML Agreement with Greek Government (25 November 1944).
39. UNRRA-A/S-0527-0793: ML Agreement with Greek Government (25 November 1944).
40. Although its official name was Allied Military Liaison (AML), it was commonly referred as ML. The omission of the term 'Allied' is not, probably, fortuitous.
41. WO 204/3089/AFHQ 2100: Wilson to AGWAR for Combined Chiefs of Staff, FX 92210 (4 September 1944); UNRRA-A/S-0527-0793: ML Agreement with Greek Government (25 November 1944).
42. FO 371/41211/UR391/391: War Cabinet, Relief Policy Committee, R.C. (44) 129 (2 August 1944). Apart from Greece, ML operated in Albania and Yugoslavia; for its work in those countries see: George Woodbridge, *The History of the United Nations Relief and Rehabilitation Administration*, II, pp. 140–3, 171–3.
43. UNRRA, *Report of the Director General to the Second Session of the Council* (Washington, DC, 1944), p. 18; FO 371/41211/UR391/391: War Cabinet, Relief Policy Committee, R.C. (44) 129 (2 August 1944).

44. UNRRA-A/S-0527-0531: Minutes of the meeting of Greece Mission personnel (6 January 1945).
45. UNRRA-A/S-0524-0019: Participation of UNRRA in Balkans (Greece, Yugoslavia and Albania) during the period of military responsibility (28 March 1944); (3 April 1944); UNRRA-A/S-0527-0722: UNRRA Greece Mission 'Bible', structure, orders and administration, July–November 1944 (n.d.).
46. UNRRA-A/S-0527-0531: Minutes of meeting of Greece Mission personnel (28 December 1944); (6 January 1945).
47. FO 371/41170/UR700/296/: Relief-General, UNRRA Balkan Mission 1944 (2 September 1944).
48. UNRRA-A/S-0527-0531: The Greek Situation (n.d); FO 371/41170/UR1615: Athens to Foreign Office (26 November 1944).
49. WO 204/8625/HS-AFHQ-L22815: AGWAR to ASME (13 July 1944).
50. WO 204/8625HS-AFHQ/22815: Directive Concerning Employment of UNRRA by the Military during the Period of Military Responsibility (16 September 1944); UNRRA-A/S-0527-0722: UNRRA Greece Mission 'Bible', structure, orders and administration, July–November 1944 (n.d.). WO 204/3089/UR2100: Allied Force HQ to Chief Administrative Officer (24 August 1944).
51. WO 204/8678/HS-AFHQ-L2019: Joint Staff Mission to War Cabinet Offices (4 July 1944).
52. FO 371/41170/UR700: Cairo to Foreign Office (9 September 1944); FO 371/41170/UR700/296/: Cairo to Foreign Office, no 2127 (9 September 1944).
53. FO 371/41170/UR700/296: Relief-General, UNRRA Balkan Mission 1944 (2 September 1944).
54. UNRRA-A/S-0527-0531: Minutes of Meeting of Greece Mission Personnel (28 December 1944).
55. UNRRA-A/S-0527-0533: Basic Principles Agreed at a Meeting (24 November 1944); UNRRA-A/S-0527-0722: Lehman to Matthews (7 November 1944); UNRRA-A/S-0527-0722: Leet to Creagh (8 January 1945); Creagh to Leet (9 January 1945).
56. UNRRA-A/S-0527-0533: GP 4, integration of UNRRA and ML (2 December 1944); for the specific functions of those divisions see: UNRRA-A/S-0527-0722: UNRRA Greece Mission 'Bible', structure, orders and administration, August 1944–July 1946 (n.d.); Organizational Chart (20 September 1944); UNRRA-A/S-0524-0011: Balkan mission budget (n.d.).
57. UNRRA-A/S-0527-0722: Directive Concerning Employment of UNRRA by the Military during the Period of Military Responsibility (16 September 1944).
58. UNRRA-A/S-0527-0722: Lehman to Matthews (7 November 1944).
59. For the specific functions of those divisions – save that of Welfare – see: UNRRA-A/S-0527-0722: UNRRA Greece Mission 'Bible', structure, orders and administration, August 1944–July 1946 (n.d.); Organizational Chart (20 September 1944) of the functions of the Welfare Division see UNRRA-A/S-0527-0531: UNRRA Greece Mission Appreciation and Plan (n.d.).
60. UNRRA-A/S-0527-0722: Directive Concerning Employment of UNRRA by the Military during the Period of Military Responsibility (16 September 1944); this clause had been discussed and approved within the administration since April 1944; WO 204/8678/HS-AFHQ/201/9/B/2017/L: Matthews to Gerstenzang (25 April 1944).

61. UNRRA-A/S-0527-0722: Participation of the United Nations Relief and Rehabilitation in the Balkans (Greece, Albania, Yugoslavia) during the Period of Military Responsibility (3 April 1944).
62. UNRRA-A/S-0527-0533: Basic Principles Agreed at a Meeting (24 November 1944); see also UNRRA-A/S-0527-0531: Organizational Chart, Bureau of Finance and Administration (2 December 1944); UNRRA-A/S-0524-0025: An Abbreviated Account of the Integration between UNRRA and ML (18 December 1944).
63. UNRRA-A/S-0527-0722: Lehman to Matthews (7 November 1944).
64. See pp. 198ff.
65. UNRRA-A/S-0527-0531: Archer to Matthews (3 December 1944).
66. UNRRA-A/S-0527-0531: Minutes of Meeting of Greece Mission Personnel (28 December 1944).
67. See pp. 195ff.
68. UNRRA-A/S-0527-0531: Subject files 1944-49 (3 December 1944).
69. UNRRA-A/S-0527-0531: Minutes of Meeting of Greece Mission Personnel (28 December 1944).
70. UNRRA-A/S-0527-0531: Archer to Matthews (8 December 1944).
71. Lars Baerentzen, 'The Demonstration in Syntagma Square on Sunday the 3rd of December 1944', *Scandinavian Studies in Modern Greek*, 2 (1978): 3–52.
72. The previous day UNRRA personnel had been warned by the Chief of Mission to remain indoors; UNRRA-A/S-0527-0531: Archer to Matthews (3 December 1944).
73. UNRRA-A/S-0524-0025: Archer to General Hughes and General Sadler (10 December 1944).
74. UNRRA-A/S-0527-0531: Hughes to Archer (11 December 1944).
75. UNRRA-A/S-0527-0531: Archer to Hughes and Sadler (12 December 1944).
76. UNRRA-A/S-0527-0531: Message from 3 Corps (12 December 1944). 632 UNRRA employees participated in relief activities during the military period, but there is no precise information as to the exact number of those considered 'unnecessary'; UNRRA-A/S-0524-0019: Participation of UNRRA in Balkans (28 March 1944).
77. See pp. 196ff.
78. UNRRA-A/S-0524-0025: Greek aid to Mideast (n.d.).
79. UNRRA-A/S-0527-0531: Message from 3rd Corps (12 December 1944).
80. FO 371/48297/R2892/52/19: AFHQ to AMSSO (7 February 1945).
81. See pp. 196ff.
82. FO 371/41170/UR1891/296: Athens to Foreign Office (17 December 1944).
83. WO 204/8625/B/2213/FIN/HS-AFHQ 228: Matthews to Hughes (14 October 1944).
84. UNRRA-A/S-0527-0531: Archer to Lehman (17 December 1944); UNRRA-A/S-0527-0533: Archer to Miller (23 December 1944).
85. UNRRA-A/S-0527-0531: Archer to Hughes and Sadler (12 December 1944); Hughes to Archer (13 December 1944).
86. UNRRA-A/S-0527-0531: Leet to Creagh (7 December 1945).
87. See pp. 196ff.
88. UNRRA-A/S-0527-0531: Welfare Division, December Monthly Report (12 January 1945); Public Relations Division (16 December 1944); Archer to Matthews (8 December 1945).
89. UNRRA-A/S-0527-0531: Welfare Division, December Monthly Report (12 January 1945).

90. UNRRA-A/S-0527-0533: Archer to Lehman (21 December 1944).
91. FO 371/41170/UR1891/296: Foreign Office to Athens (19 December 1944).
92. UNRRA-A/S-0527-0531: Minutes of Meeting of Greece Mission Personnel (28 December 1944).
93. Such projects could pertain to industrial and agricultural rehabilitation, welfare services, and the care and movement of displaced persons (these quite broad categories could be construed liberally), with proposals initiated both by UNRRA and the government; UNRRA-A/S-0517-0035: Administrative Order GA-37 (17 April 1945).
94. UNRRA-A/S-0527-0722: Agreement between UNRRA and the Greek Government (1 March 1945).
95. Its membership included nine Greek ministers, five UNRRA representatives, five British advisers and an official from the Joint Relief Commission; UNRRA-A/S-0517-0065: GP-11, institution of JPC (11 May 1945).
96. Photini Konstantopoulou wrongly refers to a thirteen-region division, *I Ellada sto Metaikhmio enos Neou Kosmou: Psikhros Polemos, Dogma Trouman, Skhedio Marshall, mesa apo Diplomatika kai Istorika Engrapha*, 3 vols (Athens, 2002), II, pp. 43–5.
97. Region A included Attica, Boeotia, Euboea, Fthiotida and Kythira; region B, Lakonia, Messenia, Arkadia and Argolida; region C, Akhaia, Elia, Zakynthos, Kephallonia, Ithaki, Phokida, Aitoloakarnania and Evrytania; region D, Levkada, Kerkyra, Paxoi, Antipaxoi, Thesprotia, Ioannina, Preveza and Arta; region E, Kozani, Kastoria, Thessaloniki, Pella, Khalkidiki, Kilkis and part of Serres; region F, Larisa, Karditsa, Magnesia and Trikala; region G, Drama, Kavalla, part of Serres, Xanthi, Rodopi and Evros; region H, Lemnos and Lesvos; region I, Chios, Ikaria and Samos; Region J, the Cyclades and region K, Crete; UNRRA-A/S-0525-0061: GP-7, Field Organization and Operation (3 April 1945).
98. UNRRA-A/S-0525-0061: GP-7, Field Organization and Operation (3 April 1945); UNRRA-A/S-0527-0720: Chief of Field Liaison Office, Regional Operations (6 November 1945); UNRRA-A/S-0525-0019: GA-24, Duties and Responsibilities of the Regional Director (3 April 1945); UNRRA-A/S-0527-0725: Chart V, Regional Office (15 December 1945).
99. UNRRA, *A Compilation of the Resolutions on Policy: First and Second Sessions of the UNRRA Council* (Washington, DC, 1944), p. 17; UNRRA-A/S-0518-0941: Background Material for Welfare Planning (n.d.); UNRRA-A/S-0520-0226: Breakdown of Law 312 (n.d.); UNRRA-A/S-0518-0807: Public Assistance Plan (16 April 1945); UNRRA-A/S-0524-0058: Circular Determining Need for Food (23 May 1945); Compulsory Law 388 (9 June 1945); Decree Regarding Meaning of and Procedure for Establishing Indigence (24 August 1945).
100. UNRRA-A/S-0527-0533: Ministry of Agriculture, Distribution of Agricultural Supplies (13 February 1945); UNRRA-A/S-0527-0723: Bureau of Distribution and Transport, Distribution of Agricultural Supplies (16 September 1944).
101. UNRRA-A/S-0527-0541: Pricing and Distribution (25 February 1946); UNRRA-A/S-0527-0531: Maben to Archer (10 December 1944).
102. UNRRA, Bureau of Supply, Final Operational Report (Washington, DC, 1948).
103. UNRRA-A/S-0524-0019: Report of the Distribution Control Unit (n.d.).
104. UNRRA-A/S-0517-0065: Athens to London (21 March 1947).
105. UNRRA-A/S-0518-0543: Brown to Photias (22 April 1947).

12
'Helping the Good Greeks': Yugoslav Humanitarian Aid to the Greek Leftist Movement 1945–49

Milan Ristović

During the dramatic years of the Greek civil war, Yugoslav-Greek relations were extremely complex and subject to different internal and external influences. The position of the Yugoslav leadership and (controlled) public opinion toward events in Greece were anything but neutral and simple. While it provided the communists in Greece with considerable assistance of various kinds (which made a very important contribution to the combat readiness of the Communist Democratic Army of Greece (*Dimokratikos Stratos Elladas* – DSE)), the Yugoslav leadership also clashed with the Communist Party of Greece (*Kommounistiko Komma Elladas* – KKE) over the Macedonian issue, which proved to be a major stumbling block in overall relations between the two parties.

From the beginning of the civil war, Democratic Army forces had to rely on outside sources to meet their needs. Apart from some hidden or captured provisions and weaponry, all weapons, ammunition, means of communication and other military materiel for the insurgents originated from foreign sources. The leadership of the Democratic Army requested aid from the recently established 'People's Democracies' in Eastern Europe, which were considered as 'natural allies', with Yugoslavia playing the central role in providing this external assistance. As the available sources demonstrate, the systematic supply of the Democratic Army from Yugoslav sources began in the second half of 1946. It was particularly intense until the second half of 1948 and continued on a considerably reduced scale until the complete breakdown of all ties between the Communist Party of Yugoslavia (CPY) and the Communist Party of Greece, after the Greek communists obediently sided with Moscow in the split with Belgrade which led to Yugoslavia's expulsion from the Cominform.

In addition to military materials of various kinds, this aid included medical equipment, medicines, food, clothing and footwear, as well as accepting the wounded and refugees in Yugoslav territory and providing them with medical treatment and convalescence. Radio Station Free Greece broadcast from Yugoslavia and KKE presses were supplied with paper and equipment. Yugoslavia also provided financial aid and services, gave 'cover' for trips abroad to KKE cadres, contributed to the propaganda-driven promotion of the Democratic Army struggle and offered moral and political support. Yugoslav territory provided a logistics base, as well as training for Democratic Army combatants and officers.[1] In addition, military advisers travelled from Yugoslavia to Greece, providing professional assistance at Democratic Army headquarters in training and the handling of particular weapons.[2] Belgrade was also the main channel of communication between the KKE in Greece and Moscow.

All these forms of open and concealed support were justified, explained and defended to domestic and foreign public opinion by reference to 'proletarian internationalism', 'aid to the brotherly Greek people in their justified struggle against the monarcho-fascists', 'international imperialism', 'aid in building a people's democracy' and so on. Before international bodies, including the United Nations (UN), allegations that aid included military material were resolutely denied as unfounded, with assertions that the aid had a 'moral', 'internationalist' and exclusively 'humanitarian' motivation. This gave rise to counter-accusations, as occurred for example in February[3] and June 1947, when a British diplomat pointed out to Yugoslav officials that the British government was well aware that armaments, money and manpower were being sent from Yugoslavia to Markos Vaphiadis, the commander of the Democratic Army; that their units were given the opportunity to retreat across the border; and that hospitals were organised for them. The Yugoslav answer was 'that everything he is saying about our aid is not true; what is true and what the whole world knows is that America is sending dollars, armament, experts, military advisors, etc. to Greece and that England, not Yugoslavia, has its army there'.[4]

Upon his return from Moscow at the beginning of April 1946, the KKE General Secretary, Nikos Zakhariadis, met in Belgrade with Tito, who promised material as well as political aid. An agreement was reached that part of the Central Committee of the KKE would relocate to Belgrade, from where it would coordinate the organisation, collection and sending of aid, recruit soldiers among those who had recently entered Yugoslavia and maintain ties with foreign countries.[5] A group of KKE officials, led by Ioannis Ioannidis and Petros Rousos, arrived in Belgrade in August and immediately began to work with the Minister of the Interior, General Aleksandar Ranković, who had been authorised on behalf of the

Communist Party of Yugoslavia to manage 'the Greek affair' and coordinate the organisation of aid.[6] At the end of August, the Yugoslav ambassador, Dr Izidor Cankar, was forced to leave Athens as a result of the anti-Yugoslav policy of the Greek government and of attacks in the Greek press.[7]

Pleas sent by the Greek communists to the Yugoslav leadership and the leaderships of the other Balkan 'People's Democracies' from the late summer of 1946 met with a different reception than those made during the Athens uprising in December 1944, which had provoked little response. An organised, and to some extent coordinated, campaign to help the Greek communists was launched in neighbouring Balkan countries. Assistance on smaller scale also arrived via Yugoslavia from the 'People's Democracies' outside the Balkans.[8]

Dominique Eudes has claimed that, as early as December 1945, a meeting was organised in the Bulgarian border town of Petritch between KKE and Communist Party of Yugoslavia delegations and that the Yugoslav representatives promised 'substantial aid in the event of an insurrection in Greece', and that Tito then appointed Ranković to engage in organising and finding ways to deliver aid.[9]

On 12 September 1946, the KKE representatives in Belgrade requested assistance 'to prepare 15–20,000 partisans'. In addition to the lack of military equipment, there was also a great shortage of clothing and food. Financial and organisational aid was requested for the KKE and EAM, the communist-controlled National Liberation Front, as well as for the parties and organisations that cooperated with them.[10] In a cablegram of 17 September 1946 from the Democratic Army headquarters, the assessment was made that insurgent units would grow to 20,000 soldiers by the spring of 1947 and that the communist leadership was counting on Yugoslav assistance to equip these forces. With this objective in mind, a list of emergency needs was supplied. Besides armaments, 5000 pairs of shoes, 5000 heavy military overcoats, 2500 pairs of trousers, 2500 jackets, 3000 sets of underwear, food for 3000 people for two months, medical supplies, radio sets, batteries and engines for battery charging, were requested.[11]

The main storehouse for material to be sent to Greece was located in Pančevo near Belgrade.[12] In the autumn of 1946 four bases were set up in the Yugoslav People's Republic of Macedonia for the secret transfer of material and people across the border, under the supervision of senior officers of the UDB (Yugoslav State Security) administration.[13] The complex organisation and deep secrecy surrounding this activity as long as it lasted were confirmed in a UDB report, which mentions that after several months 'neither the people in the villages through which transports passed . . . nor our border guard units have noticed the transfer of material'.[14]

This chapter will only focus on forms of aid that can be considered as not being solely military in character and that can therefore be deemed as humanitarian aid. Such assistance primarily refers to the treatment of wounded and ill Democratic Army combatants and civilians from war-afflicted zones, deliveries of medical material and equipment, and campaigns in Yugoslavia for collecting food and clothing from the general population for Greek 'democrats' and refugees.

Medical aid and secret hospitals

The wide-ranging provision of medical aid to the wounded and ill Democratic Army soldiers and civilians from war zones was of great importance. In addition to sending shipments of medicines and medical material to Greece, Yugoslavia played a crucial role in the organisation of the medical corps of the Democratic Army. With this objective, instructors from the Yugoslav Army Medical Corps were sent to Greece, and the training of Greek medical personnel was organised in Yugoslavia. Special hospitals and convalescent centres were established on Yugoslav territory to provide medical treatment and recuperation to the wounded and ill. It should be noted that at this time, the situation regarding health care and medical treatment of the population in Yugoslavia, exhausted by war and the spread of infectious diseases, was anything but good due to the lack of professional medical staff, equipment and medicines. Yugoslavia's health care system in the first few years after the end of the Second World War was highly dependent on external aid from the International Red Cross and the United Nations Relief and Rehabilitation Administration. Consequently, deliveries of medicines, medical material and equipment to the Democratic Army constituted a major sacrifice on the part of the Yugoslav authorities.

Contaminated wounds, gangrene, infectious diseases, poor diet, exhaustion caused by physical and psychological strain, the lack of professional medical staff and a shortage of medicines and medical equipment resulted in high death rates for wounded and ill members of the Democratic Army, as well as for civilians in the war-afflicted zones. Almost all deliveries of military equipment from Yugoslavia that can be traced were accompanied by a quantity of medical material, which was very valuable considering the almost complete absence of facilities for care and treatment of the wounded and ill combatants in the guerrilla-controlled areas of Greece. Thus, in early June 1948, a large shipment from Yugoslavia included 140,000,000 penicillin tablets and 150,000 anti-tetanus doses.[15] Despite such shipments, transferring large numbers of the wounded and sick to Yugoslavia to receive treatment proved the most effective way of saving lives.

Reception centres for the wounded were built in the border area, while the first secret, improvised hospital was built in 1947 in the Osogovo Mountains in the Yugoslav Republic of Macedonia.[16] Due to overcrowding, the situation in this hospital had already begun to deteriorate in the early summer of 1947. Although designed for a maximum of 110 severely wounded patients, in June 1947 there were over 250 patients. In the building for the less severely wounded, planned for 80 patients, there were 200 patients. Serious concerns were raised regarding the possible outbreak of epidemics.[17] Requests for efforts to alleviate the situation sent to the UDB representatives in charge of the hospital were fruitless and the only response received was that 'nothing can be done because this issue can only be resolved in Belgrade'. The lack of transport for the rapid transfer of the wounded to the hospital was a major problem. One report stated that 'many wounded . . . wait from five to ten days at the border . . . to be received (by Yugoslav staff)'.[18]

Because the high influx of wounded continued, the hospital moved from the Osogovo mountains to Katlanovska Banja near Skoplje. In November 1947 there were 200 wounded Democratic Army soldiers and some civilians in four wards under the care of 75 members of the hospital and auxiliary staff. From the first half of June until 20 November, about 800 ill and wounded patients passed through the hospital, with only six deaths being recorded.[19] The assessment of Lieutenant-Colonel Dr Jovan Bijelić in a report to Ranković about the hospital in Katlanovska Banja and the centre for convalescents in Kumanovska Banja in 1947 was that 'the situation . . . is nevertheless satisfactory, both in terms of accommodation and food and in terms of medical care'. The greatest problem was providing clothing and footwear for patients when they had recovered and were released from hospital to return to their units. Dr Bijelić compared this with 'the situation of our partisan units in 1941 and the first half of 1942'. He complained of problems in transporting the wounded and of the long delay between the initial wound and the first surgical intervention (five–six days on average, sometimes as long as ten–fifteen days). This resulted in the worsening of the condition of the wounded, the occurrence of blood poisoning and exhaustion caused by blood loss, which in a number of cases caused fatalities. Until their arrival in Yugoslavia, the wounded were kept in poor, unsanitary conditions, were meagrely fed and left with virtually no medical care. Bijelić proposed that a solution be found for accommodation outside the hospital for 'definite invalids, children and pregnant women', who were also provided refuge in Katlanovo in the absence of other suitable places. He asked that two specially equipped trucks be provided for the purpose of transporting the wounded, with an escort of experienced paramedics and provided with medicines, food and equipment for the treatment of the severely wounded. He proposed that the presidency of the Yugoslav government approve a special loan to the Yugoslav Red Cross for this purpose.[20]

The costs of maintaining the hospital and its necessary services were extremely high given Yugoslavia's current circumstances, and covering these costs created problems. According to Dr Bijelić's estimate, the cost of ten trucks assigned to the Red Cross of Macedonia for transport of the wounded (also used by UDB in Macedonia) was about 10 million dinars; huts for accommodation were estimated at 1,600,000 dinars; with another 1,100,000 dinars for setting up the hospital. All the while the money received from the UDB was entered in the Red Cross accounts. Food for 500 patients receiving military hospital rations cost the Yugoslav army 600,000 dinars per month. These costs did not include heating, lighting and other expenditures. Salaries for medical staff, furniture, linen, instruments, medicines and other needs were listed as separate items in the budget.[21]

Bijelić also gave his assessment of the situation of the Democratic Army medical service, based on the observation of the wounded and sick who came from Greece. He thought that the sanitary and epidemiological service of the Democratic Army units was '. . . either . . . very poorly organized or non-existent'. The wounded were often not given adequate first aid. They were 'dirty, infested with lice, unkempt, needing a haircut, unshaved, etc.' In such a situation any infection, 'typhus fever, dysentery, abdominal typhus and cholera could cost the army severely and in a short time put whole battalions, brigades or a division out of action'. He proposed that the Democratic Army be assisted by training 30–50 Greek paramedics and nurses on special courses (basic knowledge of combat surgery, epidemiology, first-aid on the battleground, treatment of fractures and wounds, precautions against frostbite, transport of the wounded) lasting six–eight weeks, which would enable them to become medical officers or to run hospitals.[22] To alleviate the pressure on hospitals in Yugoslavia, at the end of January 1948 the 'comrades' were advised not to send lightly wounded soldiers to Yugoslavia, as they could be treated in mobile hospitals in Greece.[23]

During the fighting on Vitsi in September 1948, over 1000 wounded were transferred across the border in a single day. Due to overcrowding and the inability to receive and adequately treat the increasing number of wounded, construction of a new, bigger and better equipped surgical hospital on Mt Babuna was started in conditions of the utmost secrecy.

After fourteen months of construction it was ready in April 1949 and could receive about 800 wounded.[24] It had two operating rooms, an X-ray machine, a gym, a theatre, a pharmacy, warehouses, accommodation for the staff, its own generating station, and water and sewage systems. The renowned military surgeon, Dr Velimir Majstorović, was appointed as hospital director, while all the hospital's needs were met by the resources of the Yugoslav army. Apart from a number of Yugoslav doctors and a section of the medical staff, the political leadership and remaining medical staff were Greek.[25]

According to Yugoslav data, a total of 890 people (110 severely wounded, 360 moderately seriously and 130 lightly wounded, together with 290 sick patients) were admitted for treatment during 1947. On these 180 operations were performed. During 1948, a total of 3947 persons were admitted for treatment (591 seriously wounded, 1252 moderately seriously and 1422 lightly wounded, together with 682 sick patients) with 1701 operations performed. In 1949, the numbers were 1479 of whom 355 were severely wounded, 154 moderately severely and 395 lightly wounded, and 595 were otherwise sick, and 479 operations were performed. There were 146 fatalities, 46 of whom were either already dead on arrival or dying when they reached Yugoslav hospitals. After treatment, 2917 persons were returned to Greece, 1132 were transferred to the Greek camp in Buljkes for recovery, 1882 were sent to Bulgaria and 226 to Czechoslovakia. Only 13 former patients remained in Yugoslavia.[26] Formerly wounded and disabled persons who were provided with accommodation in Buljkes were transferred to Czechoslovakia in September 1949, together with other villagers. From early June 1947 to August 1949, 6317 wounded and ill Democratic Army members and civilians were treated in Yugoslavia, and 2333 major operations were performed at a cost of over 80 million dinars.[27]

The political upheaval caused by Yugoslavia's expulsion from the Cominform affected the situation in the hospitals. Tensions between the Yugoslav and Greek staff in Katlanovska Banja developed in the summer of 1948 following the visit of Leonidas Stringos, who, when the Yugoslav administration and staff were not present, criticised their work at the hospital, prompting bitterness on the Yugoslav side.[28] Ideological cleavage at the hospital in Katlanovska Banja was fomented by a political commissar, Bangos, who represented Zakhariadis's 'hard', pro-Moscow, line, and who exerted pressure on 'politically vacillating' wounded. He accused wounded Slav Macedonians of 'treason' and 'espionage' and demanded that the hospital administration evacuate the patients to other Eastern European countries. The complete breakdown in relations between the Greek and Yugoslav communist parties led to the Yugoslav leadership's decision in the summer of 1949 to transfer the Greek staff and most of the wounded (or at least those willing to go) from the new hospital on Mt Babuna to Czechoslovakia, via a special ambulance train.[29]

Aid collection campaigns among the Yugoslav population

In January 1948, while heavy fighting between the government and Democratic Army units was under way in areas close to the Yugoslav border, causing heavy casualties among the civilian population, a simultaneously organised, broad campaign among the people of all the Yugoslav republics began, under the slogan of collecting 'aid for the Greek people', by which was understood Democratic Army combatants, their sympathisers in war-torn areas and refugees in Yugoslavia. Committees for Aid to the Greek People were founded in each republic and they coordinated the collection of aid.[30] The initiative came from the mass organisations (People's Front, Antifascist Women's Front, Trade Unions, People's Youth), all under the control of the Communist Party of Yugoslavia. Dušan Petrović-Šane, a senior Serbian Communist Party official, was appointed as president of the committee in Serbia, while the secretary was Jovan Popović, an author and an experienced propagandist. It is not possible to establish with certainty how much food, clothing and footwear were collected in the Yugoslav campaign, or how much of the collected aid was delivered to Democratic Army units and how much to the civilian population.

The existence of similar campaigns in other 'People's Democracies' is demonstrated by a cablegram of early February 1948, in which the Central Committee of the Communist Party of Greece asked the Central Committee of the Communist Party of Yugoslavia to ensure that 'serious steps to aid us are undertaken in friendly countries' and that 'all food sent to us from different friendly countries' be collected in Yugoslav territory and forwarded to Greece. The Yugoslav party leadership was to inform Stalin himself of what was being done.[31]

Reserves under the command of the Democratic Army Headquarters – as reported to Belgrade – reached 6000 in early February 1948 and it was hoped that they would increase to 10,000. Providing food was a major problem and the basic daily ration required 5000 kilograms of flour and appropriate quantities of fat and vegetables. The Democratic Army dealt with shortages by the simple expedient of cutting rations.

Within a short time twenty-nine local Aid Committees had been set up in all the major cities in Serbia, with an additional 60 in county centres, where money and food were collected. Money and personal voluntary donations were raised in Slovenia by organizing concerts, theatrical performances and through propaganda campaigns. Four hundred and ninety-seven tons of corn and 527 tons of wheat, 12.5 tons of lard, oil and bacon (including donations from Slovenia) and 2600 items of clothing and 899 pairs of footwear were collected in Serbia, Croatia and the People's Republic of Macedonia during the first month of the appeal.[32] By mid-May, aid collected in all republics totalled 1107 tons of corn, 23,383 tons of corn on the cob, 37,532 tons of wheat, 85 tons of beans, 7 tons of lard and 8 tons of bacon, in addition to quantities of other foodstuffs.[33]

On 18 April, a large shipment arrived in Yugoslavia from Hungary. This contained 20,000 kg of flour, 20,000 kg of corn, 3000 kg of soap and 10,000 tins of food, 20 cases of medical material, 9 cases of shoes and clothing and 2 duplicating machines. On 23 April, Belgrade announced new shipments from Hungary and Yugoslavia, containing food, medical material, clothing and footwear, duplicating equipment, soap, engines for charging batteries and similar goods (in addition to 250 'bazookas', three 20 mm anti-aircraft guns and 5000 grenades).[34]

The quantity and variety of aid collected in Yugoslavia through voluntary donations from the population is a reflection of the modest living standards and poverty of the Yugoslav population. The small quantities of fat, meat, clothing and footwear dispatched show that these were products which the average Yugoslav could not easily procure. In addition, the campaign was organised at a time when the forced collection of agricultural produce from the peasants was under way, a process that involved harshly oppressive measures.

In late spring and throughout the summer of 1948 new requests for more weapons and food came from Greece to Yugoslavia with increased frequency, and were fulfilled only in part. Aid campaigns could obviously not meet all these needs. However, the worsening of relations in connection with the Cominform dispute influenced the volume of further deliveries of these and other forms of material aid. Very soon, the satisfaction of the Democratic Army representatives in Yugoslavia and the words of gratitude to Yugoslav 'comrades' were replaced with accusations of an 'unfounded reduction' of aid, 'sabotage' and the confiscation or concealment of consignments that were sent via Yugoslav territory. At meetings between Petros Rousos, Leonidas Stringos and other KKE and Democratic Army representatives with Ranković, during 1948 and the first half of 1949, these allegations were rejected, with emphasis on the fact that despite the new circumstances, assistance would be continued 'within possibilities'. However, further aggravation of the conflict within the family of communist parties caused serious disruption to these campaigns. Finally, the last remaining channel for sending aid from Bulgaria via Yugoslavia was closed on 13 April 1949 on the orders of Moscow.[35] Bulgaria and Albania closed their borders with Greece on 13 May and Yugoslavia did the same on 21 May. On behalf of the Yugoslav Communist Party, General Jovo Kapičić, Ranković's deputy, told Stratis, the KKE representative in Belgrade, that the party leadership had decided to cease further cooperation and prohibit the transit of persons and material across the border.[36]

Emigrants and refugees

Thousands of Greek citizens, of both ethnic Greek and Slavo-Macedonian origin, members of different leftist political and military organisations, as well as civilians, mainly villagers from the areas along the border, arrived in smaller or larger groups (sometimes even whole villages) between the end of 1944 and the autumn of 1949, driven by political instability, hunger, military operations, political terror and ideological and political dissent. If we exclude the first groups of emigrants, who, due to their connections with the Bulgarian occupation regime, came from the areas around Florina, Kastoria and Edessa to the neighbourhood of Bitolj (Monastir) during 1944, events in connection with the 'second round' of the Greek civil war resulted in the emigration to Yugoslavia of a larger number, consisting primarily of members of ELAS and of its Slav-Macedonian counterpart SNOF (Slav-Macedonian National Liberation Front), often accompanied by their families. The next, and larger, wave, at the end of 1946 and the beginning of 1947, consisted of villagers and members of migrant worker families from villages in the vicinity of Serres and Drama, partly colonized by the Bulgarians in 1941–43 during the occupation. The next large groups, consisting of inhabitants of Slav-Macedonian villages around Florina, Edessa and Kastoria, moved northwards during 1947 and 1948 as a result of military operations in the region. The last refugee wave came to Yugoslavia via Albania, following the defeat and break-up of the Democratic Army in the summer of 1949.

Most of the refugees and migrants of Slav-Macedonian origin were temporarily or permanently housed in the territory of the People's Republic of Macedonia, where they were placed in the care of the Yugoslav central and local authorities, the Yugoslav Red Cross and other organisations. According to official data, the government of the People's Republic of Macedonia in 1945 spent some 24.4 million dinars (about 450,000 US dollars) for their needs. Due to the lack of accommodation, the government of the People's Republic of Macedonia built new settlements for refugees, such as the villages of Ergjelija, Kadrifakovo and Nova Mezra, but most them lived in poor conditions, often in houses confiscated from the Church. In 1945–46 there were about 13,000 refugees in the People's Republic of Macedonia. Circumstances in the southernmost and poorest Yugoslav republic were not favourable for the care of the refugees, and it was necessary to mobilise different, sometimes newly-founded organisations and institutions of the new Yugoslav regime (federal and republican ministries of social care, finance, health, the Yugoslav Red Cross and the Yugoslav Communist Party). The Yugoslav army and security services (KNOJ, UDB) were charged with control of the border region and played the major role in the reception, transport and, frequently, the provision of supplies for refugees. In May and June 1945, the UDB transferred 2700 persons, mostly ELAS combatants, including a small number of family members, from reception camps in the People's Republic of Macedonia to the village of Buljkes near Novi Sad. These were the first members of the Buljkes Greek community. By the end of the summer of 1949 when the community was dismantled by the Yugoslav authorities, the number of inhabitants fluctuated around an average of three to four thousand as people returned to Democratic Army units in Greece or were transferred to other localities in Yugoslavia. From the beginning of the civil war, this village, with its 'autonomous status' and with its own local administration, but above all on account of the military and ideological training afforded to Democratic Army units, came to be regarded as the epitome of the 'communist evil' by the Greek government and its allies. When the majority of the leadership of the commune in Buljkes and most of its inhabitants sided with the Cominform, it was disbanded on Tito's orders and transferred to Czechoslovakia.[37]

The other two refugee communities in Vojvodina, Gakovo and Kruševlje (near Sombor) consisted of 1500 families. Some 8000 Slavo-Macedonian refugees were moved against their will in 1948 from the People's Republic of Macedonia to alleviate humanitarian pressure. Like the members of the community in Buljkes, they were allocated land, essential farming implements and cattle, in the hope that they would at least be able to produce some of their own food. Schooling for children was provided in their mother tongue and infirmaries were opened as well. These two villages were not involved in the activities that earned Buljkes its radical reputation.

As of 1952, the Yugoslav government had spent over 14,600,000 US dollars in support of refugees from Greece. According to official data, there were about 23,000 refugees in Yugoslavia at the beginning of 1953, 6500 of whom accepted Yugoslav citizenship. This number fluctuated, however, because part of this population left for other Eastern European countries, while others came from these countries to Yugoslavia.[38] Some decided to emigrate to Western countries (primarily Canada, the USA and Australia.)

Children who were transferred from war-afflicted areas to neighbouring countries in the areas controlled by the 'Provisional Democratic Government' were a special category of the refugee population, and at the same time a phenomenon that symbolised the tragic experience of the Greek civil war. Some of the larger groups of child refugees arrived across the border on foot, after an exhausting journey usually led by women from the villages in the war zone. The first groups started to arrive at the Yugoslav border at the end of February 1948. They came in larger numbers in the subsequent months in an effort that had been coordinated with the Yugoslav authorities. Some groups of children used Yugoslav territory only as a transit station en route to other countries (Romania, Czechoslovakia or Hungary). According to some assessments, between 30 March 1948 and the end of September 1949, a total of 14,028 children passed through Yugoslavia en route to other destinations.

The sudden influx of a large number of children of all ages, most of them in poor health, prompted the Yugoslav authorities to authorise the Central Board of the Yugoslav Red Cross to establish a separate Commission for the Protection of Greek Children in May 1948. This commission was charged with dealing with the problems of reception, accommodation, treatment and recuperation, while the federal Ministry of Health organized separate medical services for the treatment of the Greek children.

A report dated 9 April 1948, from the Yugoslav Red Cross addressed to the League of the Red Cross Societies (Ligue des Sociétés de la Croix-Rouge) in Geneva, gave the number of Greek children who had arrived in Yugoslavia as 7000, but by mid-1949 this number had risen to over 11,000. Special homes were established for their accommodation in the People's Republics of Macedonia, Serbia, Croatia and Slovenia. The biggest home for children was founded in Bela Crkva, a town near the border with Romania, which accepted 672 children of all ages in 1948. This home was in operation until 1958.[39]

The fate of these children was from the outset the focus of harsh accusations by representatives of the Greek royal government. They accused the leadership of the Democratic Army and the 'Provisional Government of Greece', the Yugoslav government and the governments of the other 'People's Democracies' of organising and collaborating in the 'abduction of children', the so-called second *paidomazoma*, a term which recalled the child tribute of Christian children in the Balkans in the early centuries of the Ottoman Empire. Accusations and counter-accusations were made by the royalists and communists. The United Nations General Assembly, on 19 November 1948, recommended the return of children to Greece in cases where the parents, or, in their absence, their closest relatives, sought it.[40]

Repatriation of some of the child refugees began as a result of the political upheaval caused by the breakdown of relations between Yugoslavia and the other communist parties of Eastern Europe, with the KKE siding with Yugoslavia's critics. The Greek Committee for the Help of Children (EVOP), which had its headquarters in Budapest, pressed the government in Belgrade to transfer the children to the countries of Eastern Europe. The subsequent normalisation of relations between Belgrade and Athens resulted in the repatriation of a number of child refugees. The first small transport of children to Greece was dispatched in November 1950, and 580 children had been repatriated to Greece by the end of July 1953, while about 100 others were sent to join their parents in Australia, Canada and France.[41] The reuniting of Greek refugee parents in the countries of Eastern Europe with children from Yugoslavia started in 1954, following the restoration of relations between Belgrade and Moscow.[42] Repatriation lasted until the early 1960s, with the mediation of the League of the Red Cross Societies and the Swedish Red Cross. The debate as to whether the children were 'abducted' behind the Iron Curtain or 'saved' from monarcho-fascism and the controversies prompted by this tragic question are indicative of the profound political and ideological cleavages that existed during the civil war in Greece, and which, in different ways, continued long after the war was over.[43]

Ideological solidarity, political motives, active interest in the fate of the Slav-Macedonian minority, humanitarian reasons and many other factors influenced Yugoslavia's involvement from the beginning of the civil war in providing aid to the KKE and the Democratic Army. Furthermore, the involvement of the new Yugoslav regime in the Greek crisis was the result of the aspirations of the newly-established authorities in Yugoslavia to assume the role of regional power. Aid – material, moral, and military and humanitarian – was understood, and was presented as such to domestic and international public opinion, as support for the 'just struggle' of 'democratic Greece' against the 'monarcho-facist regime' and 'international imperialism'.

While political and ideological motives led to the Yugoslav engagement on the side of Greek communists, after the breakdown of relations between Moscow and Belgrade in 1948, when the vast majority of Greek communists followed the pro-Moscow 'line', the same motives brought cooperation to an end and led to the gradual withdrawal of Yugoslav aid. The volume, diversity and intensity of Yugoslav aid, including the kinds discussed in this chapter, were, as we have seen, of exceptional importance for the survival and operation of the Democratic Army during the period of the 1946–49 civil war.

Notes

1. See Milan Ristović, 'Eksperiment Buljkes. "Grčka republika" u Jugoslaviji 1945–1949', *Godišnjak za društvenu istoriju*, II–III (Belgrade, 1997), pp. 179–202, and the same author's *To Peirama Mpoulkes. 'I Elliniki Dimokratia' stin Giougkoslavia 1945/1949* (Thessaloniki, 2006).
2. Dragan Kljakić, *Izgubljena pobeda Generala Markosa. Gradanski rat u Grčkoj 1946–1949. i KPJ* (Belgrade, 1987), pp. 280–1; Arhiv Jugoslavije, Arhiv Centralnog Komiteta Saveza Komunista Jugoslavije, KMOV, Greece, IX, 33/VI 1–48, 1942–1947, k 17. V. Biljanović to General A. Ranković, 18 XI 1946; ibid., k-6, Nr. 4, Vasilis (Central Committee Communist Party of Yugoslavia) to Vasilis (Central Committee of Communist Party of Greece, 31 January 1948; ibid., Nr. 11, 18 February 1948.
3. Archive of Josip Broz Tito (AJBT), I-3-b/933. Memorandum of the conversation between M. Nešić, Secretary of the Ministry of Foreign Affairs, with W. Steward of the UK Embassy, 17 February 1947.
4. AJBT, I-3-b/940, Memorandum of the conversation between A. Bebler, Deputy Foreign Minister, with Watson, Assistant Head of the Southern Department, Foreign Office, 14 July 1947.
5. R. Kirjazovski, *Makedoncite i odnoste na KPJ i CPG (1945–1949). Oficijalni dokumenti so komentari* (Skopje, 1995), p. 11.
6. Kirjazovski, *Makedoncite*, p. 27.
7. Jadranka Jovanović, *Jugoslavija u Ujedinjenim nacijama 1945–1953*, Institut za Savremenu Istoriju (Belgrade, 1985), p. 67. Relations were reduced to the level of chargé d'affaires.
8. AJBT, I-3-b/940, Memo of the conversation between A. Bebler, Deputy Foreign Minister, with Watson, Assistant Head of the Southern Department Foreign Office, 14 July 1947.
9. Dominique Eudes, *The Kapetanios: Partisans and Civil War in Greece, 1943–1949* (New York, 1972), p. 258. No one from the Soviet side attended the meeting and there was no alternative but to be satisfied 'with "hoping" that Stalin would supply material aid'. There is no confirmation (available) in Yugoslav archive sources.
10. AJ, A CK SKJ, KMOV, Greece, IX, 33/I -1-100, 1942–1957, k 1, Neki aktuelni zadaci našeg pokreta, unsigned, 12 November 1946.
11. AJ, A CK SKJ, KMOV, Greece, 1944–1975, IX 29-III/3, k 11,17. IX1946.
12. 20 km north-east of Belgrade.
13. Dragan Kljakić, *Izgubljena pobeda*, p. 282; AJ, A CK SKJ, KMOV, Greece, IX,33/IV-1-48, k 15, 1942–1947, Ministry of the Interior of the FPRY, report of Lieutenant Colonel V. Biljanović: Transfer of material for Greece, 18 November 1946.

14. Ibid.
15. Arhiv Vojnoistorijskog Instituta (AVII), Nr. Reg.3, f-1,191–194, k-4.General J. Kapičić's report to A. Ranković concerning aid to the Democratic Army, 1 June 1948.
16. Kljakić, *Izgubljena pobeda*, p. 191.
17. AJ, A CK SKJ, KMOV, Greece, k 15, Unsigned report on the situation in the hospital for Greek wounded in the Osogovo Mountains, 29 July 1947.
18. Kljakić, *Izgubljena pobeda*, Supplement 22, pp. 331–4.
19. Ibid.
20. Ibid.
21. Ibid.
22. Ibid.
23. AJ, ACK SKJ, KMOV, k-6, br.4, Vasilis to Vasilis, 31 January 1948.
24. Kljakić, *Izgubljena pobeda*, p. 191.
25. Ibid., p. 193, names the Greek physicians, members of the DA medical corps, according to the recollections of Dr Majstorović: Dr Lukos, Dr Zoras, Dr Kolovos and Dr Filaktos.
26. Ibid., p. 335, Review of the number of those admitted by categories: operated, cured and died.
27. Ibid.
28. Ibid., p. 193.
29. AJ, A CK SKJ, KMOV, Greece, IX-33/I-1-100, 1942–1957, k-1, J. Broz-Tito to Marko (A. Ranković), 8 July 1949.
30. AJ, A CK SKJ, KMOV, Greece, IX-33/VI-49-89, 1948–1951, Archive of the Committee for Aid to the Greek People (17 February–10 May 1948).
31. Ibid., No. 6, Vasilis to Vasilis, 4 Febuary 1948. A similar aid committee was founded in Bulgaria, which gave rise to considerable – and for Bulgaria, unpleasant – attention, particularly in the USA; ASMIP, Pa Greece, 1948, f 58, d 4221, Ambassador Sava Kosanović (Washington) to Stanoje Simic (Ministry of Foreign Affairs), 30 December 1947.
32. V. 95, ibid.
33. AJ, A CK SKJ, KMOV, Greece, k 16. Table of the total amount of foodstuffs collected by 10 May 1948.
34. AJ, A CK SKJ, KMOV, Greece, k 4, No. 10, Ilijas to Markos, 23 April 1948. 10,000 kg of flour were sent to Central Macedonia (Laikos); 3750 kg of lard, 3750 kg of sugar, 70 sacks of beans, 90 sacks of peas, 140 sacks of soap, 6000 tins of food, 10,000 kg of flour, 10,000 kg of corn, 50 pack saddles, 5 engines for recharging batteries were sent to Phereos (Western Macedonia), ibid. A new shipment arrived on 11 May; ibid., No. 18, Ilias to Markos, 13 May 1948. Other shipments had similar contents.
35. AJ, ACK SKJ, KMOV, Greece, k 6, CK KPJ-CK KPG, 30. V 1949.
36. Kirjazovski, *Makedoncite*, p. 173; AJ, ACK SKJ, KMOV, Greece, k 6, 102, Stratis to Vasilis Bartziotis, 21 May 1949.
37. A JBT, I-3-b/279, Report: The Situation in Buljkes, July 1949.
38. Ministry for Foreign Affairs, Political Archive (AMIP PA), Greece, 1965, f 43, d 3, 442729, 3.XII 1965, Report on Greek political emigration by the General Director of National Security, Greece, Aristides Vlakhos. According to the data from this report, there were 22,498 refugees from Greece living in Yugoslavia in the mid-1960s.

39. A-JCK, f-480, 1948–1958, 18 November 1948, Report on the situation in the homes of Bela Crkva and Plandište. In Serbia homes were organised in Vršac, Šid, Novi Sad and Bogovada; in Slovenia in Šent Vid, Borl, Stara Gora, Okroglo and Dutovlje; in Croatia in Rovinj, Crikvenica, Samobor and Osjek; in PR Macedonia in Skoplje, Bitolj, Kumanovo and Ohrid.
40. This resolution was passed at the plenary session on 27 November.
41. Arhiv Jugoslovenskog Crvenog Krsta (A-JCK), 1948–1958, f 480, Review of child transports to Greece as of 1 August 1953.
42. A-JCK, 1950–1960, f-483. Report on the situation of Greek children in 1957, 26 December 1957.
43. On this problem see Milan Ristović, *Long Journey Home. Greek Refugee Children in Yugoslavia 1948–1960* (Thessaloniki, 2000) and Eirini Lagani, *To 'paidoma-zoma' kai oi Ellinoyougoslavikes skheseis, 1949–1953* (Athens 1996).

Index

Page numbers in *italics* refer to illustrations.

labour movement, repression of 125
Laiki Voithia (People's Aid) 125
land ownership 30–1, 38n84
Langer, William 147n74
Larisa concentration camp 133–4, 136
Lazoros, Aristides 78n16
League of Nations 170
Leith-Ross Committee *see* Allied Post-War Requirements Committee
Lesbos 83n68
Lesvos 19, 20
Liakos, Gen. Demetrios 142, 146n73
Lieberg, Jean 102, *6.6*, 108–9
Linnér, Sture 109, 110
Linney, Keith 179
Litsas, Theodore 185
Loch, John 2
Loch, Sydney and Joice 180, 181, 184–5
Logothetopoulos, Konstantinos 43, 93, 129, 155
Long, Breckinridge 80n38
Lord Mayor's Fund for Greek Relief 171, 177
Lykourezos, Amalia 100
Lyon, Hugh, Bishop of Wakefield 173
Lyttleton, Oliver 48, 70–1

Macedonia 188, 194, 212
  agricultural projects 177, 184–5
  FRS in 180, 184–6
  Greek refugees/emigrants in 221–2
  as Yugoslav people's Republic of 214, 221
Macedonian Red Cross 217
Mackenzie, Compton 9
  Wind of Freedom ... 5
MacVeagh, Lincoln and Margaret 12n12, 19, 40, 64, 66
Majstorović, Velimir 218
Makris, Orestis 139, 146n59
Makronisos concentration camp 143
malaria 29–30, 38n75, 182, 183
Malcolmson, Jean 181
Mallet, Victor 72
Mandilaras, Nikiforos 140
Maniadakis, Konstantinos 125

marriages, number of 32, 38n87
Matthopoulos, Archimandrite Evsevios 156
Mavromikhalis, P. 11n7, 88
Mavrou, Athina 136
medical aid 135, 136, 129, 158, 159, 179, 182
  midwives 185–6
  Yugoslavian, to Leftists in civil war 213, 215–19
  see also Friends' Ambulance Unit
Medical Supplies and Transport Unit, Athens 182
Medical Surgical Relief Committee of America 71
Metaxas, Ioannis 125, 132
  Greek Orthodox Church and 142, 148, 149, 152–3, 155
  Zoi and 157
Middle East Relief and Refugee Administration (MERRA), Cairo 179
Mikhalopoulos, André (Andreas) 5
  Greek Fire 9
Military Liaison (ML) (Anglo-American) 189, 195
  purpose 195
  UNRRA personnel and 189, 190, 192, 195–202, 205–6
Mohn, Paul 107
  Inter Arma Caritas ... 57n30
mortality rates
  in Communist Democratic Army 215, 218
  famine related 15–16, 26–31, 32, 39–40, 69, 82n50, 84n75, 85, 90, 99, *7.10*
  fertility rates and 32
  infant 26–7, 37n70
  life expectancy 26, 32, 33, 37n70
  sex ratio 32, 38n87
  see also death/burial
Murray, Gilbert 170, 172
Murray, Wallace 81n47
Mykonos 15–17
  famine in 29–31
  mortality rates 26, 27, 28, 29, 31
Mytilini 104, 108